Traditional Wing Chun

The branch of great master Yip Man

by *Igor Dudukchan*

Wing Chun Kuen - is the most famous and dynamic style of Wushu in the world. Its distinguishing features are simplicity and economy of movements, softness and flexibility, as well as the effectiveness of protection and power of attacks. The main purpose of this direction of Chinese martial arts is the fastest achievement of victory in battle with the minimum efforts and energy.

Over the long history of Wing Chun, the original style was divided into several large branches. It should be noted that at the similarity of the principles that were put to the basis of the style, technique and forms of different versions of Wing Chun Kuen, there are very big differences.
This book, proposed to the attention of the readers is devoted to the overview of Wing Chun Kuen technique, transmitted to us by the great master **Yip Man**.

© 2017, Dudukchan I.M.
All Rights reserved.
Author: Igor Dudukchan
Translator: Marina Kondratenko
ISBN: 9781520739144

This Book, together with all its parts, is protected by copyright and should not be copied, sold or transmitted without the expressed consent of the author.

Contents:

Introduction..4
Chapter 1. **Origin and Development of Wing Chun Kuen**..............5
Chapter 2. **The theory of Wing Chun**..11
Chapter 3. **Stances and movements**...14
Chapter 4. **Strikes technique**...21
Chapter 5. **Defense technique**...40
Chapter 6. **Throws and grabs**..51
Chapter 7. **Training combinations**...56
Chapter 8. **Methods of attack**..66
Chapter 9. **Methods of defense and counterattack**....................75
Chapter 10. **Sticky hands - Chi Sau**..90
Chapter 11. **Special exercises**..96
Lop Sau..96
Fon Sau..99
Chapter 12. **Forms**..101
Siu Lim Tao...102
Martial combinations..115
Chum Kiu..133
Martial combinations..145
Biu Jee..153
Martial combinations..171
Chapter 13. **Training at the wooden dummy**...........................176
Conclusion..193

Introduction

Wing Chun Kuen - is the most famous and dynamic style of Wushu in the world. Its distinguishing features are simplicity and economy of movements, softness and flexibility, as well as the effectiveness of protection and power of attacks. The main purpose of this direction of Chinese martial arts is the fastest achievement of victory in battle with the minimum efforts and energy.

Over the long history of Wing Chun, the original style was divided into several large branches. It should be noted that at the similarity of the principles that were put to the basis of the style, technique and forms of different versions of Wing Chun Kuen, there are very big differences. Originally the writer studied the Vietnam branch of Wing Chun. Because of the desire to expand his horizons, he it began to gather and organize the information about other areas of this great martial art. Then there was a desire to share knowledge with all who were interested in the martial arts. As it turned out, the collected information was sufficient to prepare for the publication several books with a review of the technique of several directions of Wing Chun: **Yip Man**, **Chan Wah-Shun** (Chan Yiu Min), Vietnamese Wing Chun - **Vinhxuan** and others.

The book, proposed to the attention of the readers is devoted to the overview of Wing Chun Kuen technique, transmitted to us by the great master *Yip Man*.

The book contains many pictures detailing the features of the technique of the style and will be useful to all the students of the martial arts.

Chapter 1
Origin and Development of Wing Chun Kuen

The Wing Chun - it is a traditional style of the Chinese Kung Fu. The Wing Chun is very popular in the whole world thanks to its high efficiency application techniques.

There are several theories about the origin of the style.

Theory 1
The Wing Chun was developed by a South-Shaolin monk whose name was **Zhi Shan** (Jee Shim). First, he taught monks the technique of the style Zhi Shan, after that, he began teaching all the willing residents of villages situated nearby .

Theory 2
The Martial Arts School of Wing Chun was created by five masters of the **Southern Shaolin**. They reformed the technique of the old monastic style of the unarmed combat. This work was carried out in the "Praise of Spring Hall" (**Wing Chun Tan**), in the honor of this hall the new style of kung fu had been named.

Theory 3
Wing Chun was developed by a woman whose name was **Yim Wing Chun**, the daughter of the south-shaolin novice Yan Si. It's system is based on the teachings of her father, who was a great master of the martial arts, and the teachings of nun Ng Mai, who taught the style of a crane and a snake.

Theory 4
The modern Wing Chun Kung Fu – is a simplified style of Fujan **Yung Chun Bai he quan** (White Crane of the Yung Chun Village). It has become popular thanks to the efforts of actors of the Cantonese Opera "The Red junk."

According to one of the legends **Yim Wing Chun** married **Leun Bok Chou**, was the resident of Canton and moved to his place to live. **Leun Bok Chou** was proficient in Kung Fu and praised the martial techniques, which his wife was good at. **Yim Wing Chun** and **Leun Bok Chou** began to practice and to develop their family martial art.

One of the few students Leun Bok Chou was **Leung Lan Kwai**. Leung Lan Kwai had six students: **Leung Yee Tai**, **Wong Wabo**, **Dai Famin**, **Lo Wanguan**, **Siu Fook** and **Gao Laochzhun**. Most of them were actors of the Cantonese Opera.

The advantage of the tour of the actor group in the South of China was that the Wing Chun style became popular in **Foshan**, **Guangzhou**, **Shunde**, **Gaohe** and in many other cities. During this period the Wing Chun style divided to the Foshan and the Canton schools.

Wong Wabo and **Leung Yee Tai** left the Chinese Opera and moved to the Foshan city. They taught the Wing Chun style to the resident of the Foshan city, whose name was **Leung Jan**. Leung Jan was a famous doctor and chemist. Having mastered the Wing Chun Kung Fu technique, Leung Jan became famous as a great fighter. He became known as a **Wing Chun King**. Leung Jan taught his sons, **Leung Bik** and **Leung Chun**. One more student was **Chan Wah Shun**. Chan Wah Shun was a very strong man and was famous as a very dangerous fighter.

After Leung Jan and his sons moved out of town, **Chan Wah Shun** became the most authoritative expert of the Wing Chun in Foshan. Among the students of this master were **Ng Jung So** and **Yip Man**.

Thus, the direction of Foshan Wing Chun Kung Fu started its beginning from Leung Jan and his students. This direction is represented by such schools:
- *The School of Yip Man*
- *The School of Yu Choi (Yu Choi initially trained with Yuen Chai Wan, then with Ng Jung So)*
- *The School of Pan Nam (this school was powerfully influenced by the Hungar Kung Fu style)*
- *The School Gulao (this school was founded by Leung Zan, when he returned to his native village Gulao).*

The *second* and the *third* large directions of the Wing Chun come from the Cantonese opera actors **Dai Famin** and **Lo Wanguan**, who trained **Feng Shaoching** and **Ho Baoquan**. Feng and Ho trained two brothers **Yuen Kay San** and **Yuen Chai Wan**.

Yuen Kay San, founded a large school in Canton together with his students.

Great Master Yuen Kay San

Yuen Chai Wan moved to Vietnam and founded the Vietnamese Wing Chun direction. And he called himself the name Nguyen Te Cong.

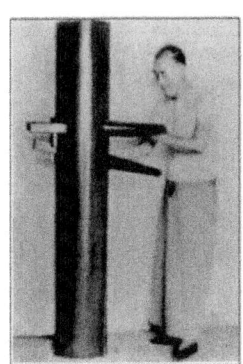

Great Master Yuen Chai Wan (Nguyen Te Cong)

Yuen Chai Wan was born in 1877 in Canton and started training Wing Chun Kung Fu with his brother from his childhood with the master Fan Shaching and the master Ho Baoquan.

Many Wing Chun researchers believe that Ho Baoquan had a great influence on the technique of Yuen Chai Wan. His style was very soft and was called "snakes form Wing Chun". The style consisted of such technical sections:
- Siu Nim Tao - the form of the initial idea;
- Chisao - sticky hands
Muk Yan Jong Fa - training on the wooden dummy;
- a long pole technique;
- a butterfly - swords technique ;
- Qi gong - the art of the internal energy Qi control .

Master Yuen Chai Wan had three very capable students in China. One of them Yu Choi, who also studied with Ng Jung So, and after that he founded his own school. In 1930 Yuen Chai Wan moved to Vietnam and there he took the name Nguen Te Cong after a famous Buddist saint.

He opened a martial arts school in Hanoi, and began training Wing Chun (Vinhxuan in Vietnamese language) to all willing people. The technique of the style has changed a little bit. The animal styles had been added and Chisao exercises changed a little .

Te Cong participated in the resistance movement and became a general during the Second World War (1939 - 1945).

In 1954, he and his family moved to South Vietnam, where he lived until his death in 1961.

Nguyen Te Cong had trained many talented students who extended Wing Chun worldwide : Ngo Si Quy (1922-1997), Chan Wan Fung (Tran Van Phong) (1900-1987), Chan Tuc Tien (Tran Thuc Tien) (1911-1980), Ho Hai Long (1917-1988), Li Ba Fa.

Nguyen Te Cong trained his students in individual and different ways. So today the schools of Vietnamese Wing Chun differ from each other a little bit.

The *fourth* largest branch of Wing Chun Kuen is an interesting version of this type of martial arts, leading its tradition from the famous **Chan Wah-Shun** and his son **Chan Yiu Min**. Its main feature is the harmonious combination of methods of traditional Wing Chun Kuen with a tight and powerful technique of the Southern Shaolin Wushu. In this style, in addition to the well-known forms such as Siu Nim Tao, Chum Kiu, Biu Jee, there are many new less-known forms such as: Four Gates - Siu Men, Subdue the tiger - Fufu, Hung Sa Shou and others.

There are also many less well-known directions of the Wing Chun Kuen style such as: Fujian Weng Chun Kuen («Fist of the eternal spring of Fujian province), Futsao Wing Chun Kuen (Fist of praise of spring of Buddha's arms), Nanyang Wing Chun Kuen (Fist of praise of spring of Southeast Asia), etc.

Currently there are many organizations involved in the proliferation of the style throughout the world . Most of them were based by the students of Yip Man and the students of his students. There are also federations involved in the popularization of other directions of Wing Chun Kuen, such as: Association of Yuen Kay San Wing Chun Kuen, Gulao Wing Chun Kuen, Society for the Study of Foshan Wing Chun Kuen, Association of Wing Chun Nguyen Te Cong, Malaysian Association of martial arts of Chingwu Wing Chun etc.

Despite this diversity of Wing Chun schools, traditional and standard version of this martial art is the direction developed and passed on to the subsequent generations by the famous master **Yip Man**.

Yip Man
(1898-1973)

Great Master Yip Man

Yip Man was born in 1898 in Foshan, the city famous for its martial arts. He lived and was brought up in a wealthy family, engaged in trade. At the age of nine, the boy began to study Wing Chun Kuen with the master **Chan Wah-Shun**. Chan taught his youngest student without much enthusiasm, as Yip Man was very young and very fragile for the martial arts. Nevertheless, thanks to his perseverance and help of "elder brothers" of Wushu, he earned respect of his teacher, who began to teach a talented student seriously.

When Yip Man was 13 years old, the teacher Chan Wah-Shun died. Before his death, the master asked his senior student **Ng Jung-So** to remain his teaching in the school and to pay special attention to Yip Man.

Having studied two years with **Ng Jung-So**, Yip Man moved to Hong Kong to continue his education. There he met **Leung Bik**, son of **Leung Jan**, with whom he continued his studies. Yip Man himself said: "... The master Chan Wah-Shun taught me the basics of Wing Chun, and I got the difficult technique from Leung Bik ...».

Back in Foshan, Yip Man continued to practice Wing Chun Kuen with Ng Jung-So and his disciples. The study with Leung Bik raised his skills at a very high level, making it easy to win his "brothers" in the school.

During the war, Yip Man was drafted into the army, after that he returned home and took over as captain of police patrols. Participating in clashes with dangerous criminal elements, he further strengthened his power and skills.

In 1949, after the Chinese mainland passed to the communist power, the master and his family moved to Hong Kong. Settling in a new place, after a long hesitation, he accepted the invitation of his friend and master of Wushu Lee Man, to open a martial arts school at the Union of restaurant owners of Hong Kong.

Since that time, the Wing Chun Kuen style has become increasingly popular.

In May 1970, when his school stood firmly on its feet, Yip Man decided to stop teaching and go into retirement. He transferred his duties to **Leung Ting**.

In 1973, the great master died.

During his life, Yip Man trained a large number of students the most famous of which are: **Bruce Lee**, **Leung Ting**, **Yip Chun**, **William Cheung**, who continued the work of their teacher and spread Wing Chun around the world. This book is devoted to the review of this particular technique of Wing Chun direction.

Chapter 2
The theory of Wing Chun

The whole technique of Wing Chun is based on the traditional Chinese philosophy concepts of **Yin-Yang**.

According to the ancient Chinese philosophy, there existed **Wuji** (unlimited) - boundless emptiness (Fig.1).

Taiji (the Great Limit) was born from wuji (Fig. 2) it is also called the two origins **Yin** and **Yang**. **Yang** – is an active origin. **Yin** – is a passive origin.

It is expressed in the tactics of Wing Chun in the principle of simultaneous defense and counterattack. One hand meets the opponent's attack and diverts it towards the side (**Yin**). The second hand counter-attacks the opponent at the same time (**Yang**).

The theory of the Central Line

The Central Line - is a conditional line that runs along the central axis of the body. The attackable points are situated on the central axis they are: the eyes, the throat, the solar plexus, the bladder, the groin. The central line divides the body into two parts: the left and the right parts (Fig. 3). Each of these sides is supposed to be **Yin** (taking an opponent's attack) and **Yang** (counter-attack).

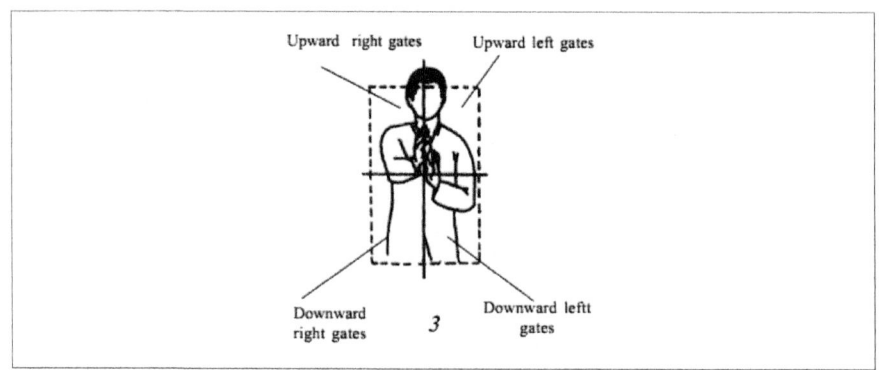

3

If you draw a conditional line across the body, you can divide it into upper and lower sectors. There are four areas in the theory of Wing Chun these four areas are called Four gates (*Siu Men*). There are upward left gates, the downward left gates, the upward right gates and the downward right gates.

There are one hand in the front and the second hand is behind in the fighting stance. This way, there are the external upward gates and the external downward gates from the front hand. There are the internal upward gates and internal downward gates from the hand behind.

Yin and Yang begin to move and give birth to five elements in the Chinese philosophy (*Wu xing*) (Fig. 4). They are: the **wood**, the *fire*, the **earth**, the **metal** and the **water**. In the technique of the Wing Chun this five elements correspond to the five basic punches, five basic blows by an elbow and five basic blocks (protections).

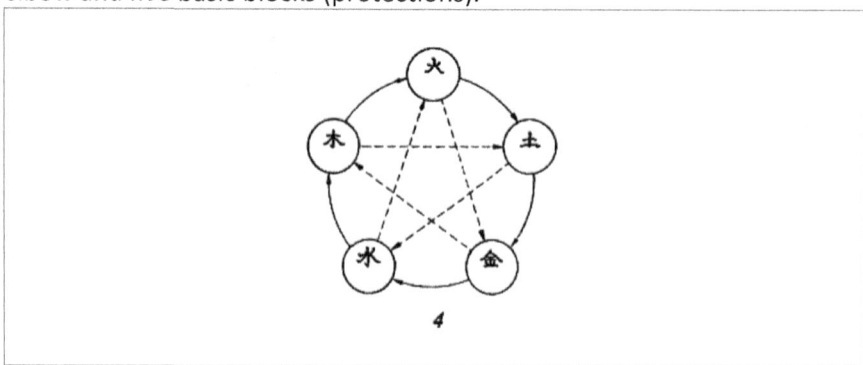

4

The Wing Chun emblem is a flower with five petals, which represent the five primary elements (Fig. 5).

5

Compliance with all the principles of the Wing Chun forms a perfect martial art.

Chapter 3

Stances and movements

The first and very important step in the development of the basic technique of any style of Wushu is the study of stances, positions and methods of movements.

Under the term "stance" it should be understood by position of the legs and body. The position involves taking a certain position of the legs, body and arms.

The main stances in the Wing Chun style are **Yee Gee Kim Yuen Ma** - basic training stance means "to clamp the wild animal (basic training stance, sometimes this stance is called the Frontal stance) and **Cheun Ma** - Turning stance (Another name for the stance is - **Pien San Ma**, which means that the side fighting stance, or simply the Side stance).

Yee Gee Kim Yuen Ma Stance is very easy to perform and does not require great physical efforts, but, nevertheless, it protects the groin, and allows you to save a stable equilibrium, uniting the body into one (Fig. 1).

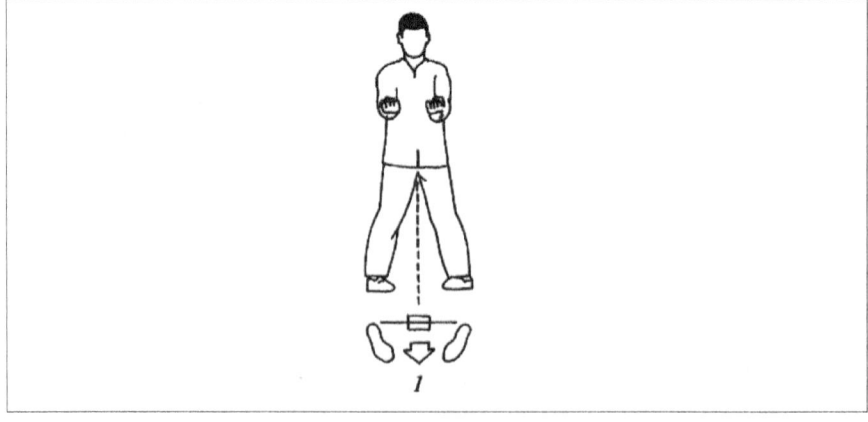

This stance is the training one and is used during the training of the forms (Tao-Lu) and some paired exercises. It is characteristic for it a equal distribution of the body weight on both feet. The knees should be slightly bent and directed inwards. The feet position corresponds to the shape of a triangle – the toes are directed inside, heels apart. The distance between the centers of the feet are about 35 - 40 centimeters. The pelvis is slightly leaning forwards. The torso is straight. The head is aligned with the torso. Arms are bent at the elbows. Hands are clenched into fists and are located on the sides at the chest level.

In order to take the Yee Gee Kim Yuen Ma stance properly, it is necessary from the natural stance (legs straight, feet together, body straight, hands lowered down on the sides) to clench the hands into the fists and lift them to the sides at the chest level. Bend your knees. Next, expand the feet the toes apart about 45 degrees from the central line of the body. Then dilute the heels apart about 45 degrees from their original position.

After you learn to take the Yee Gee Kim Yuen Ma stance, you must start the static work in it. To do this, after the taking of the stance you need five - seven minutes to remain in it. You can not straighten your knees, bend your back and lower the hands. The purpose of this exercise - to strengthen the muscles of the legs and to achieve stability state (Rooting).

Then you can get back to the natural stance again. To do this, first the heels approach each other, then the toes get together. Straighten the knees and lower the arms down.

Turning the body 45 degrees to the right or to the left, shifting the center of gravity on one leg, you can take a right-hand or left-hand **Cheun Ma** side stance (Fig. 2). This rotation of the body allows evading effectively the direct attacks with a minimum expenditure of force. In addition, the turn of the body reduces the distance to the opponent, which makes it possible to perform both defense and counterattack.

If you move your body weight on one leg and make a step along the arc with the other foot, you will find yourself in the frontal combat **Ching San Ma** stance (Fig. 3). Body weight is shifted to the backward leg. The feet are located almost parallel to each other. The legs are slightly bent at the knees. Knees are directed inward, as if drawn to each other. The body is turned in the direction by about 30 degrees. Hands are in the main combat position. The body is straight. The head is slightly tilted down, eyes are directed forward.

Hands combat position in the style of Wingchun is such a position of the limbs, which allows to make equally effective both attacks and defense, as well as easily to move from one movement to another. Besides the position of the hands should cover the most vulnerable areas of the body. At the right- hand stance the right hand stretches forward (Fig. 4), at the left – hand stance - the left one (Fig. 5).

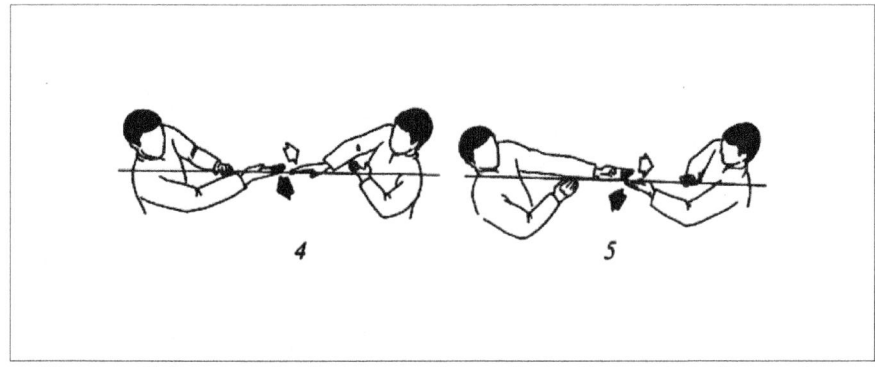

Fingers of the stretched arm are directed up - forward and are oriented to the center line of your opponent. Elbow of the arm is located at a distance of about 15 centimeters from the body. Hand of the backward arm is opened, fingers are pointing upwards. This hand protects your central line. This hand position is the best for defense and counterattack.

Every match is a dynamic process, followed by the movement in space of participants. This movement is carried out through a combination of different types of steps. A properly produced movement allows quickly and the shortest distance, depending on the task, to move closer to the opponent or to break distance. A reliable defense and effective attack depends on it. In addition, the movements are the basis for building of the combinatorial technique.

Consider the basic exercises of this section.

Side step forward

Starting position is the right-hand fighting Ching San Ma stance (Fig. 6). Make a sliding step forward with the right foot, lowering the foot from heel to toe (Fig. 7). As soon as the right foot touches the surface of the ground, make a step with the left foot (Fig. 8).

Side step back

During the side step back from the right-hand Ching San Ma stance (Fig. 9), the first step back is made by the backward left leg (Fig. 10). Then pull back the right leg (Fig. 11).

Full step

Starting position is the left-hand Ching San Ma stance (Fig. 12). Make a small step with the left leg forward and to the left (Fig. 13). With the right foot make a big step forward to the right (Fig.14). With the left foot make a step forward (Fig. 15).

The rotation in the frontal stance

Starting position is the frontal Yee Gee Kim Yuen Ma stance (Fig.16). Move most of the body weight on the left leg and turn about 45 degrees to the right (Fig. 17). Change the stance on the opposite (Fig. 18).

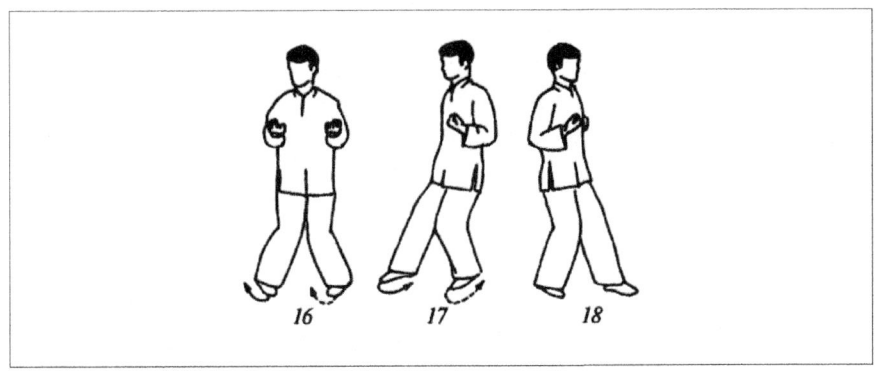

This exercise is very important in the system of Wing Chun, so such a rotation should be repeated many times at each training.

Change of the stances

Starting position is the right-hand Ching San Ma stance (Fig. 19). With the right foot step back and take the Yee Gee Kim Yuen Ma stance (Fig. 20). Bring along the arc the left leg forward, change the position of the hands and take a left-hand Ching San Ma stance (Fig. 21).

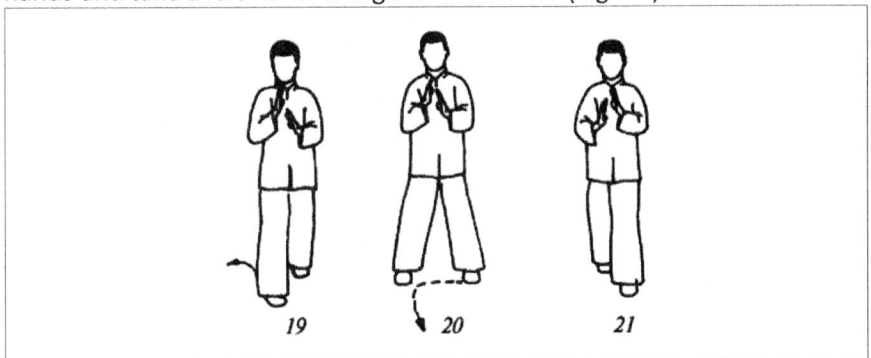

This exercise should also be repeated many times.

Movement to the left

Starting position is the right - hand Ching San Ma stance (Fig. 22). With the left foot make a step to the left (Fig. 23). After that, pull the right foot to the right and take the right-hand Ching San Ma stance (Fig. 24).

Movement to the right

Starting position is the right-hand Ching San Ma (Fig. 25). With the right foot make a step to the right (Fig. 26). After that, pull the left foot to the left and take the right-hand Ching San Ma stance (Fig.27).

Chapter 4
Strikes technique

As in most styles of Chinese Wushu, the basic techniques of Wing Chun Kuen are a variety of strikes made with different parts of the body of the fighter. This is the more important as the basic concept of the style is a fast, lightning, and devastating attack.

The strike is the foundation on which almost any attack is built. Without a well-trained, strong and precise strike it is almost impossible to win the fighting. Therefore, a lot of attention should be given to the training of strikes.

Punches

Work of the hands is the "hallmark" of Wing Chun Kuen. The density of the strikes in the fight reaches such a level that it is often impossible to capture them visually, and the strength of one of them is enough to knock down a person of an average build. Besides this, attacking movements are often used in the protection too in the style. For example, a straight vertical fist punch, made at a certain angle, can play a role of a divertive block and counterattack simultaneously.

Straight punch - Chung Chui

The attacking fist moves from the solar plexus, the thumb is directed upward. The punch is made directly without rotation. The striking surface are knuckles of the ring finger and little finger.

The hand of the other arm is in front of chest, covering the body from possible counterattack of the opponent (Fig. 1-3).

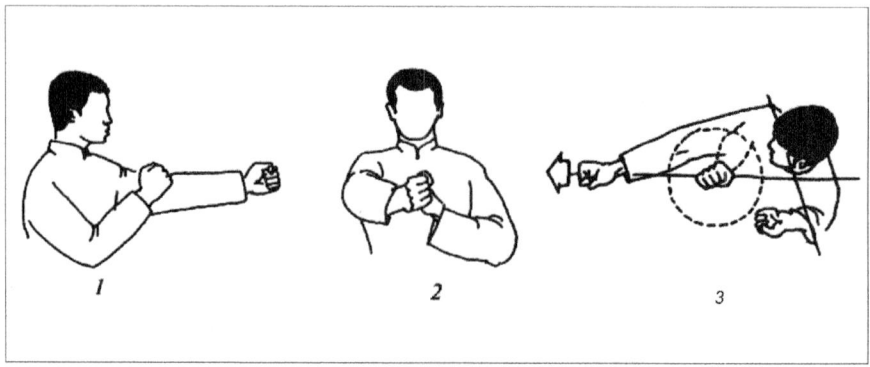

Most often, this punch is used by the front hand for the start of the attack (Fig. 4), or during the counterattack (Fig. 5). It should be noted that in the latter case Wing Chun Kuen fighter at the same time makes a blocking of the opponent's attack with one hand and the counterattack with the other one.

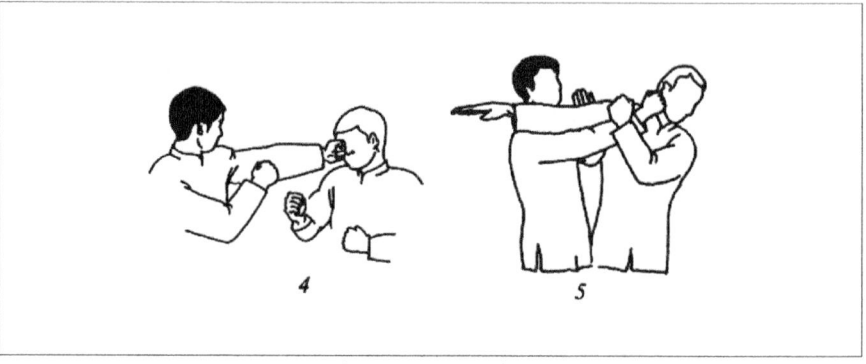

Important points:
- *Fist moves strictly along the center line,*
- *In the final phase the elbow joint of the attacking arm is fully straightened,*
- *On the whole trajectory of the strike the arm moves in a relaxed state, and only at the end, the muscles tense the most.*

Training of the direct punch
1. Striking the air

Starting position is the Yee Gee Kim Yuen Ma stance (Fig. 6). Squeeze the hand into a fist, then with the left hand, make a direct Chung Chui punch. At the same time move the right hand to the chest. The punch is accompanied by a rotation of the body 45 degrees to the right. You are at the left-hand side Cheun Ma stance (Fig. 7). Make the same punch with the right fist, making a90 degrees turn of the body and taking the right-hand side Cheun Ma stance (Fig. 8).

Continue to make punches alternately with right and left hands. Do not forget about the turnings on the spot. Start from 30-40 punches per cycle. Gradually bring the number up to 150 punches.

Important points:
- It is important to watch the synchronicity of movements,
- Turn of the body and a punch should start and end at the same time.

2. Exercise with a partner

Both partners are located opposite each other in the Yee Gee Kim Yuen Ma stances. The distance between the partners should be a little more arm's length (Fig. 9).

At the same time turn 45 degrees to the left and taking the right-hand side frontal Pien San Ma stances, make direct punches to the head with right hands. During the punch the forearms are touching each other, and moving forward, with rubbing movements divert the punches to the sides (Fig. 10).

At the same time turn 90 degrees to the right and make the straight punches with the left fists (Fig. 11).

Continue the exercise, making punches with right and left hands.

This exercise teaches how to use the punch as blocking means. You neutralize the opponent's attack and do attack him at the same time.

3. Making punches at the wall-mounted bag

In Wing Chun Kuen for training the direct punches the three-section wall-mounted bag is used (Fig. 12). Each section is filled with sand. The bag is attached to the wall so that the top edge was located at the level of the chin.

Starting position is the Front Yee Gee Kim Yuen Ma stance. Stay at a distance of not fully straightened hand from the bag. Make a direct Chung Chui punch with the left hand (Fig. 13). Then make a punch with the right hand, left hand is moved to the chest (Fig. 14). Again, make a punch with the left hand (Fig. 15).

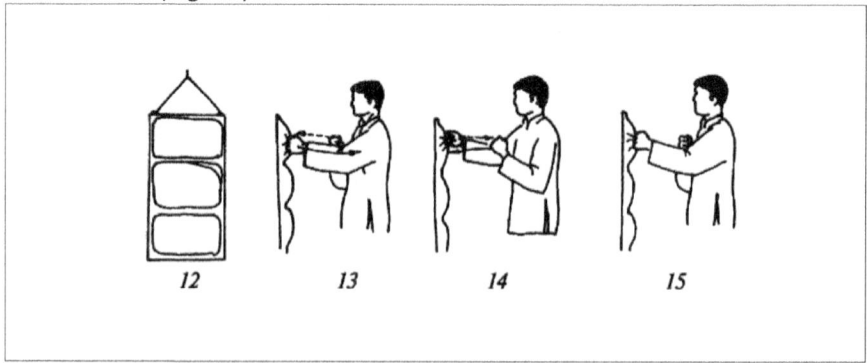

Continue to make punches alternately to the bag. During one cycle you must make 30-50 punches.

This exercise can be performed in conjunction with the turn on the spot.

On the next stage of training, punches at different levels are made.

There are several ways of attacking the wall-mounted bag:
- *Slow, alternate punches,*

- Series of punches of two or three punches,
- Punches with both hands simultaneously at different levels.
   Important points:
- In the final phase of the punch do not fully straighten the arm at the elbow joint,
- The punch must be made as if in the depths of the bag with the concentration of the whole power a few centimeters behind it,
- After each cycle of exercises, make 10 punches with each hand to take the stress off the joints of the limbs.

Upward punch

The punch is made forward-up in the direction of the center line of the body. Palm is directed upwards. The striking surface are knuckles. From boxing uppercut this attack differs in that the attack is made deeper. The elbow passes near the torso and is directed downward (Fig. 16, 17).

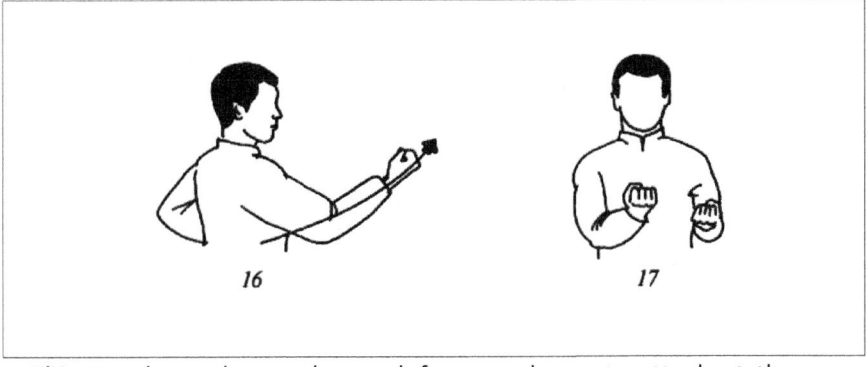

16   17

This punch can be used as a defense and counterattack at the same time (Fig. 18) or after the tacking and fixing the head of the opponent on the spot (Fig.19-21).

18

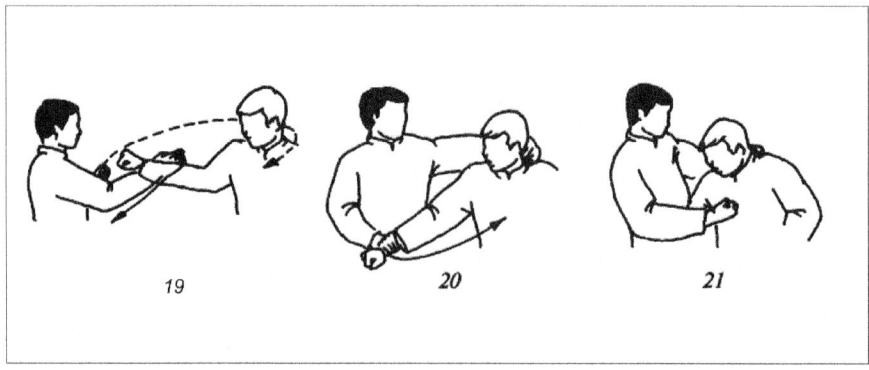

The aims of the attack, as a rule, are: chin, throat, solar plexus, liver and groin area.

The punch is initially trained at the air on the spot, then with the turn of the torso is combined with various kinds of movements and then start to work out the punch on the wall-mounted bag.

Side punch

The punch is made in a circular path outside-in. The attacking limb is moved away from the body. The fist makes a rotational movement along a predetermined path and in the moment of the punch turns palm down (Fig. 22-23).

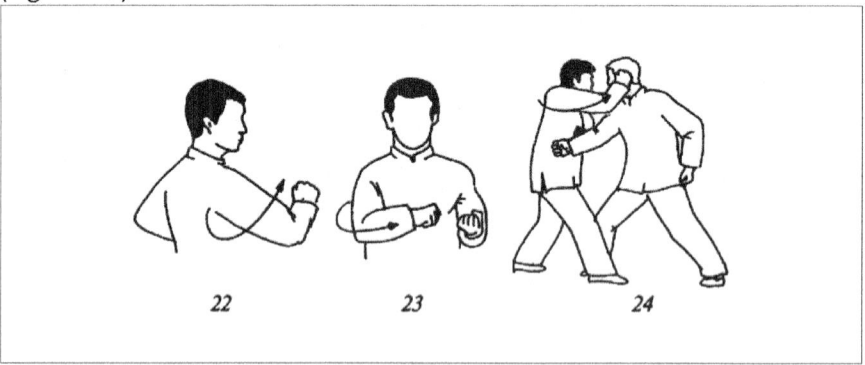

The aims of the attack are: jaw side, the temple (Fig. 24) and the area of the liver.

The punch is initially trained at the air on the spot, then with the turn of the torso is combined with various kinds of movements and then start to work out the punch on the wall-mounted bag.

Chopping punch
(Back Fist)

During the punch the fist moves in a fairly wide circular path from you forward and down. The impact surface are the knuckles on the back side of the fist. The movement is made not by force, but due to sharp movements of the elbow, which acts as an axis of rotation (Fig. 25).

The aims of the attack are: face (Fig.26-27), shoulder, elbow joint of the opponent.

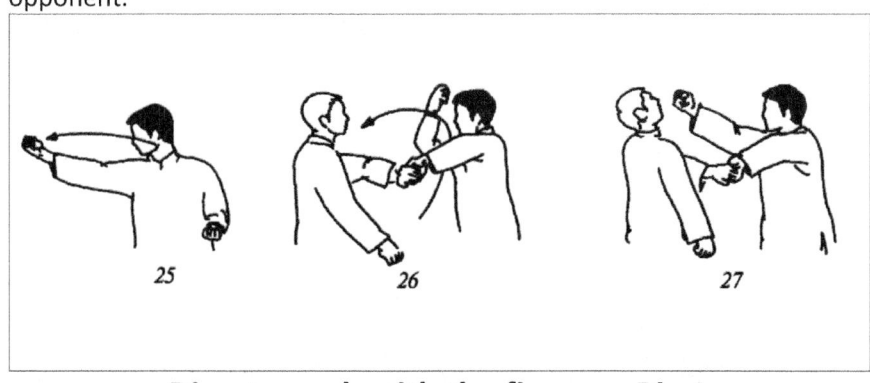

Direct punch with the fingers - Biu Jee

The punch is made with the fingertips, put together. The technique of the punch is similar to the direct punch, but with the rotation of the hand inwards (Fig.28-29).

In the long distance the punch is made with the palm down, in the close distance the hand can be placed vertically.

Effective use of Biu Jee, requires a fairly good knowledge of the vulnerable points on the human body. The punch is not strong but with the right performance it can permanently bring the opponent out of action (Fig. 30-31).

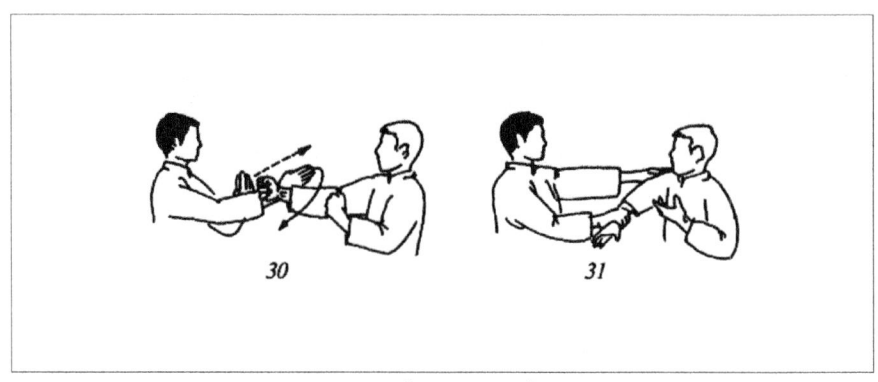

Palm punch

The technique is similar to the direct punch with the fist, but the impact surface is the base of the palm. The fingers may be directed upwards (Fig.32, 33) or to the side (Fig.34, 35).

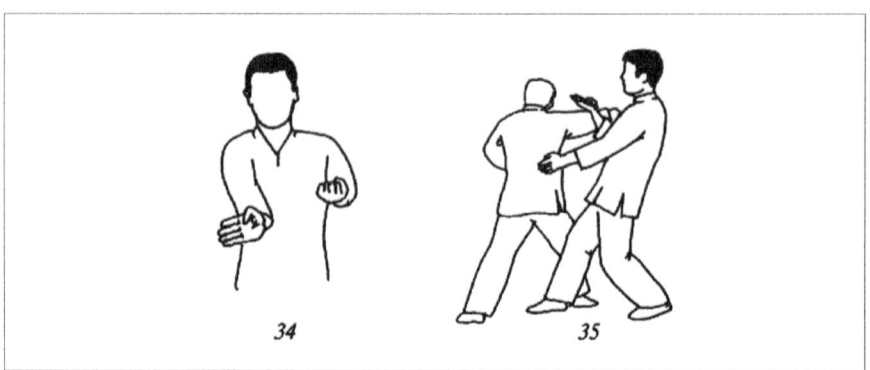

The aims of the attack are: face, chest, solar plexus, abdomen, liver area, etc.

Punch with the edge of the palm

The punch is made in an arcuate path and in virtually any plane. The impact surface is the edge of the palm (Fig. 36). This attack is very powerful and has a huge damaging effect. Its purpose can be any part of the human body, especially dangerous are punches to the neck, throat (Fig.37), as well as the breaking punches to the limbs.

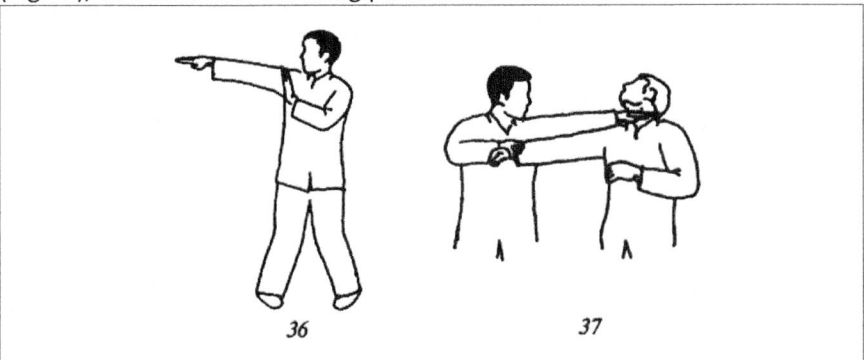

36   37

Quite an important section in the arm training is strengthening (hardening) of the impact surfaces. The frontal side of the fist is strengthened during the work on the wall-mounted bag, the other parts of the hand straighten on the lying bag filled with sand. The bag looks like a pillow that is placed on the stand at the level of the abdomen.

Exercise #1

Stand a meter away from the stand with a bag and start the exercise with the right hand.

Make a punch with the open palm downwards (Fig. 38, 39), then with the back of the hand (Fig. 40), then with the edge of the palm (Fig. 41), with the base of the palm (Fig.42), with the fingers (tiger claw) (Fig.43), the second phalanges of the fingers (Fig.44), with the fist (Fig.45), and finally with the fist edge (Fig. 46).

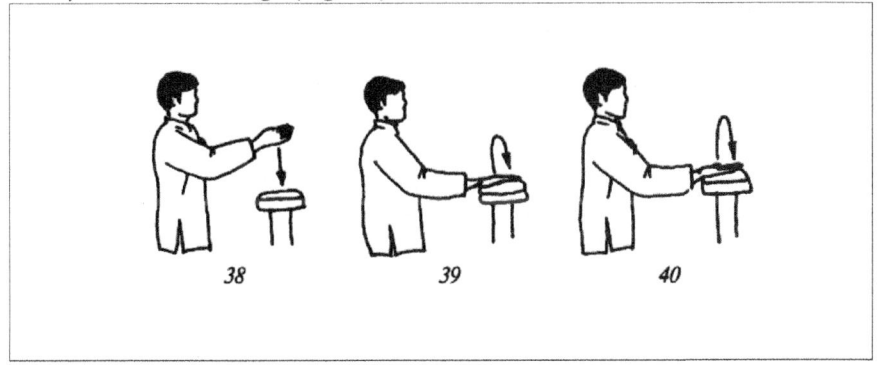

38   39   40

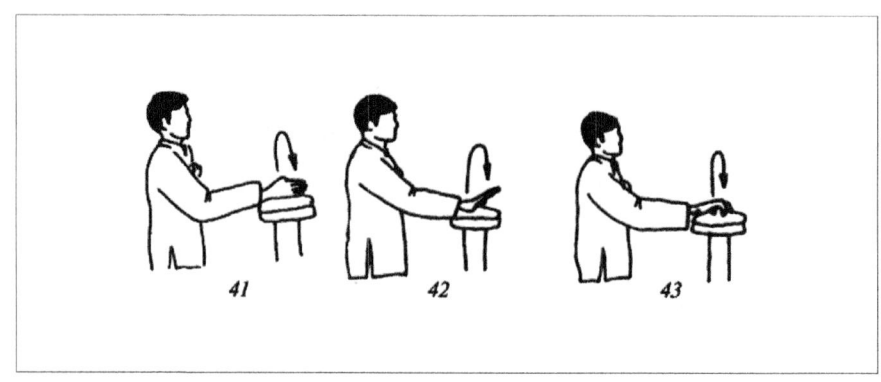

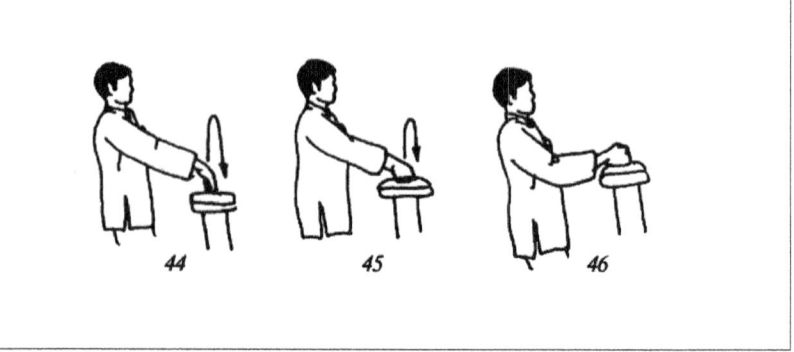

Repeat the exercise with the left hand.

It is necessary to make at least ten cycles for each hand. Before and after the exercise it is necessary to rub the hands thoroughly. After the training, be sure to keep the hands in the warm salted water.

Exercise #2

In this exercise lying and wall bags are used.

Stand at a distance of one meter from the wall - mounted bag. The stand with the lying bag should be 20-30 cm from the wall. Make a punch with the edge of the palm of the right hand to the bag on the stand (Fig.47, 48). Then quickly make a straight punch the wall-mounted bag (Fig.49). Repeat 20 times, then make the exercise with the other hand.

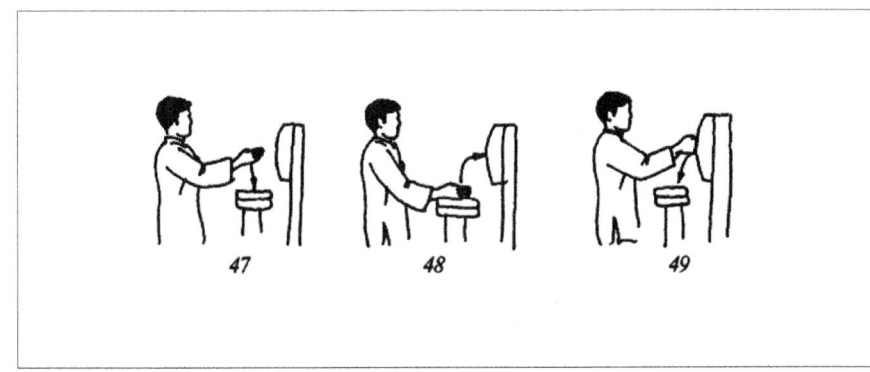

47   48   49

Elbow strikes

It is believed that the technique of Wing Chun Kuen is most effective in the close combat. The fight on a short distance involves the active use of elbows as a powerful weapon. Basic technique of style includes 5 elbow strikes in all possible directions. Knowledge and skills to use this technique give the fighter a huge advantage in the combat.

Each of the main strikes can be practiced alone or in a small "Five elbows" form.

Starting position is the Front Yee Gee Kim Yuen Ma stance. Hands are clenched into fists and are located on the sides at the chest level (Fig.50).

With the right elbow make a downward strike (Fig. 51). Then return the arm to its original position (Fig.52). Without stopping the move the elbow back and up - to the side (Fig.53), then make a downward strike with the elbow (Fig.54). Then make a strike with the elbow to the side (Fig.55). Turning to the left, make the circular strike with the elbow in a horizontal plane (Fig.56). Returning to the original Yee Gee Kim Yuen Ma stance, make a strike with the right elbow backwards (Fig.57, 58). Return to the starting position.

50   51   52   53   54

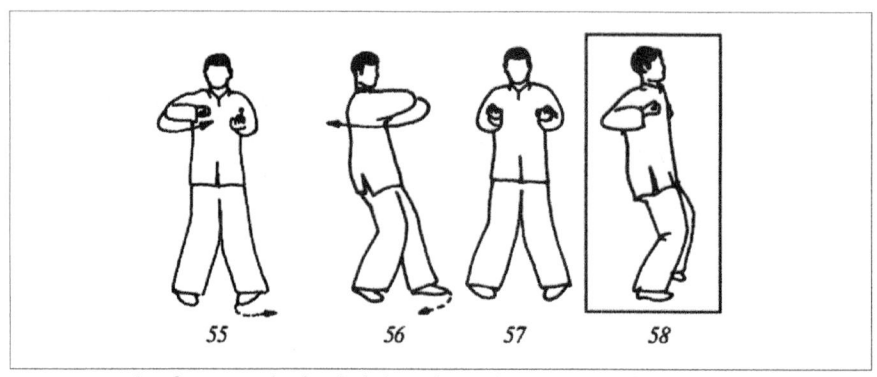

Repeat the form with the left hand. Make to 10 cycles with each hand. Consider the application of the described elbow strikes.

1. Elbow strike from upwards-downwards

The opponent makes a direct punch to the chest with the right fist. With the left hand, make the Pak Sau block. With the adjacent step move to the opponent and with the right elbow make an upward strike from the bottom up to the chin (Fig.59, 60).

2. Elbow strike from downwards-upwards

The enemy makes a punch with the right fist to the head. With the left hand, make the Pak Sau block. Quickly step up to him and make a strike with the downward diagonal right elbow downwards (Fig.61, 62).

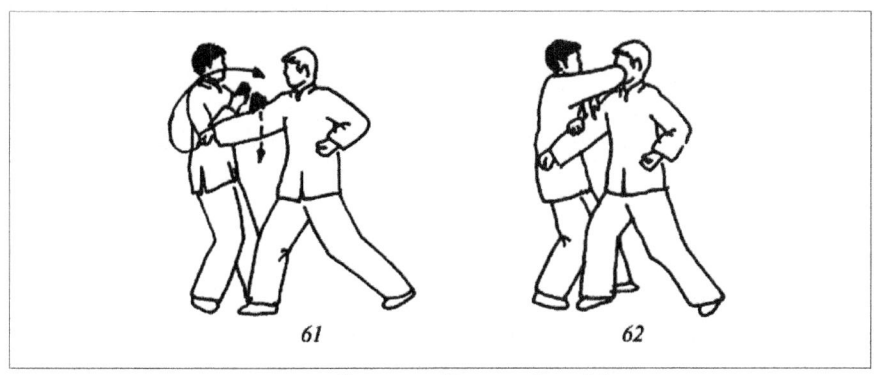

61 *62*

3. Elbow strike to the side

The opponent makes a direct punch to the head with the left fist. With the right forearm make a block of his attack outside-in. With the left hand grab his attacking limb. Then step up forward and make a strike with the right elbow from you to the side to his ribs (Fig.63, 64).

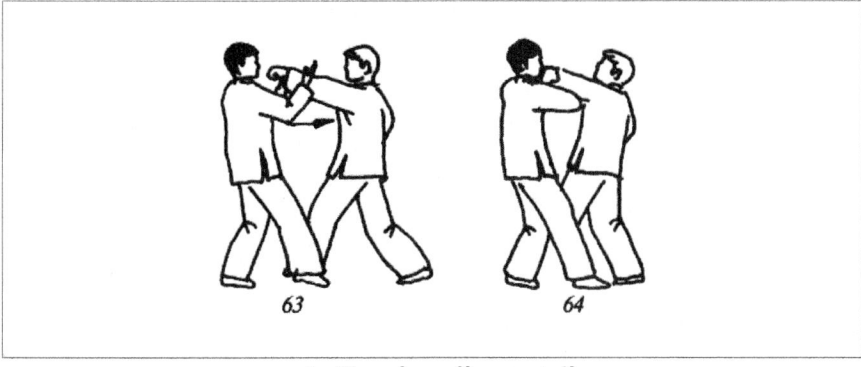

63 *64*

4. Circular elbow strike

The opponent makes a direct punch to the head with the right fist. Block the attack with the left palm. Make an adjacent step forward and with the right elbow make a circular strike from outside to inside in a horizontal plane to the chest or solar plexus area (Fig.65, 66).

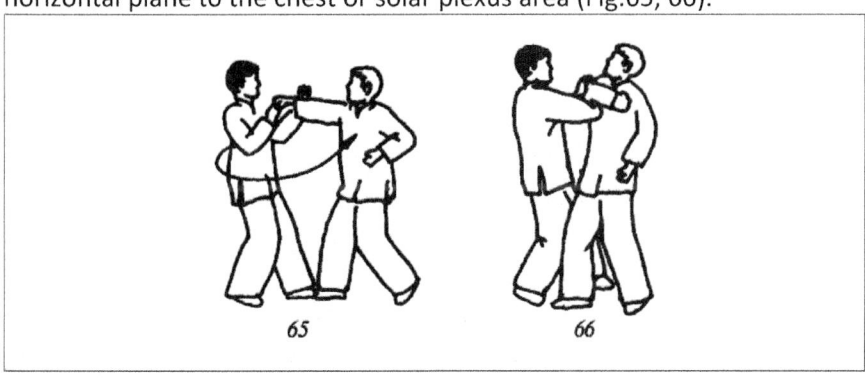

65 *66*

5. Backward elbow strike

The opponent grabs you from behind. Quickly bend your knees and make a strong strike with the elbow to the stomach or the solar plexus area (Fig.67).

67

Strikes with the elbows can be trained both on the wall, and the suspended bag.

Stand sideways to the wall bag. With the left elbow make a strike to the side (Fig.68). Turn the torso to the left and make a circular strike with the right elbow (Fig.69). Then again make a strike with the left elbow to the side (Fig.70) etc.

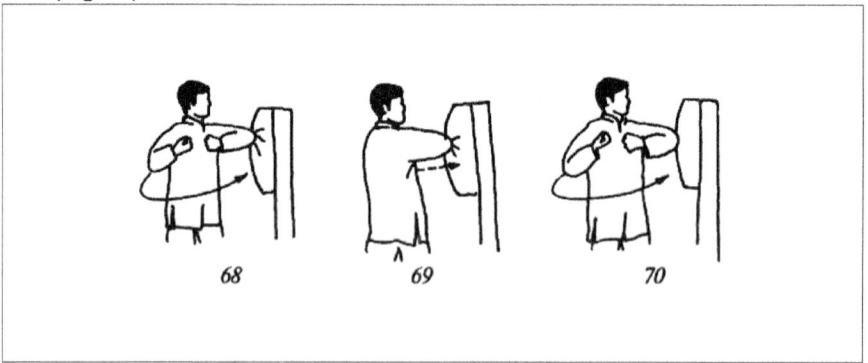
68   69   70

Kicks

Wing Chun Kuen technique does not abound with plenty of kicks and is focused on the close combat. Strikes are made not above the solar plexus, and are focused on the defeat of the vulnerabilities of the human body: lower leg, knee, groin, etc. Most of the kicks are made after you have captured with your hands the hands of the opponent. Such attacks are almost impossible to be blocked, and they are called "Invisible strikes".

Direct kick with the toe

Starting position is the Front Yee Gee Kim Yuen Ma stance. Lift up the bent at the knee right leg. The hip is parallel to the floor. Straightening the leg at the knee, make a forward direct kick at the abdomen level. The toe of the kicking leg is stretched forward (Fig.71). Bend the leg at the knee again and lower it down to the starting position.

71

Repeat the kick with the other leg.

After you make this kick mastered enough on the spot, you can start to train the attack in movement.

Take the right-hand or left-hand Ching San Ma stance. Next, make a direct kick with the toe of the backward foot forward and lower the attacking leg down forward. Then make the same kick with the other leg. Thus, you train kicking with the back leg in combination with the moving forward.

The next stage is training in kicking with the forward foot in combination with movement forward.

Direct kick with the heel

The kick is similar to the previous, with the only difference that the impact surface is the heel (Fig.72).

The objective of direct kicks are usually the knees, groin (Fig.73), abdomen and sometimes the solar plexus area of the opponent.

72   73

Direct locking kicks

This kick is usually used to stop the attack by making the stopping strike to the supporting leg or torso of the opponent.

Starting position is the Stand Yee Gee Kim Yuen Ma stance. Lift the bent at the knee right leg. The hip is parallel to the floor. Turn the foot so that the fingers were directed to the right-up. Straightening the knee, make a kick forward and down. At the moment of the kick the toe of the kicking foot is not directed straight up but slightly outwards. The impact surface is the foot (Fig.74). The objective of the attack is the knee joint or the lower leg (Fig.75).

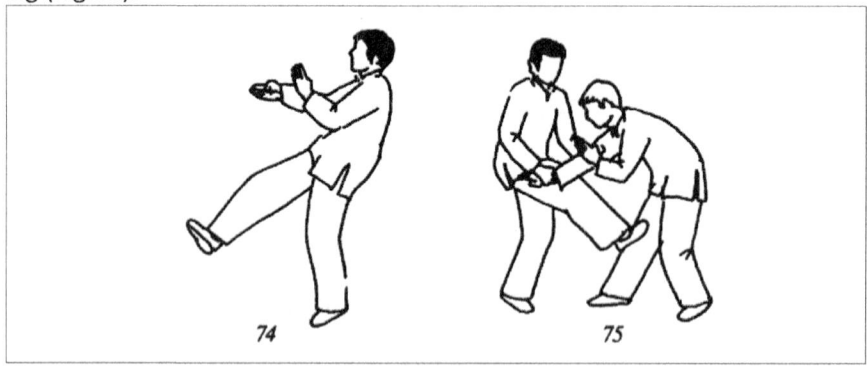

74   75

Side kick

Starting position is the Front Yee Gee Kim Yuen Ma stance. Lift the bent at the knee right leg upwards, hip is parallel to the floor. Slightly turn the torso to the left and straightening the knee, make a side kick with the right foot at the hip level (Fig.76). The impact surface is the foot or the edge of the foot.

The objective of this attack is the lower leg and the knee joint of the leg of the opponent (Fig.77).

76   77

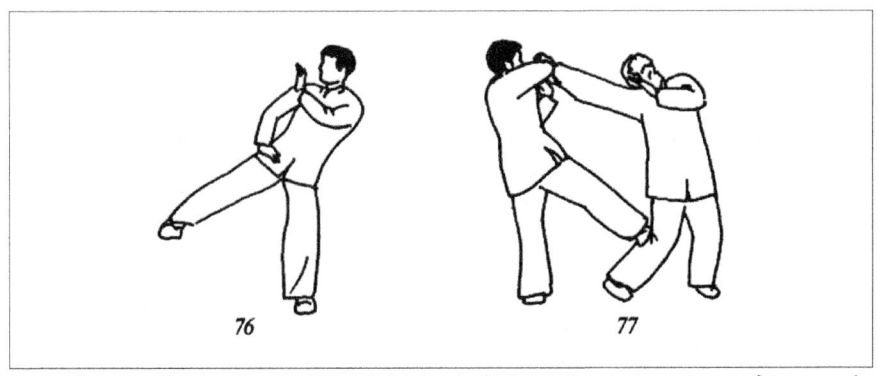

As it was already mentioned, kicks in Wing Chun Kuen are often made at the close distance, while your hands grasp and control the hands of the opponent. Such kicks are called "Invisible kicks" (Fig.78-80).

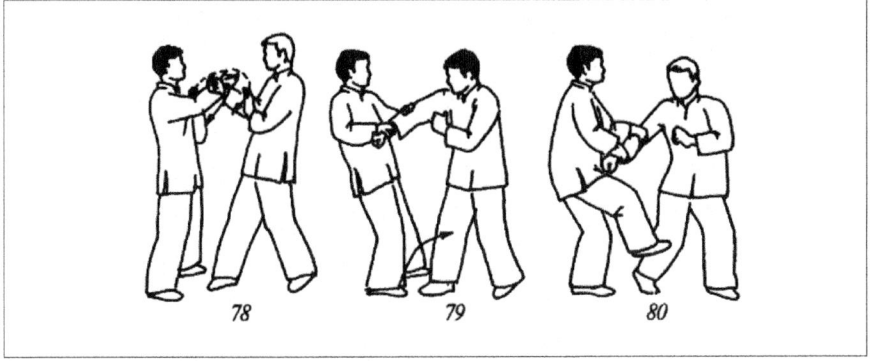

78   79   80

Often with the same foot two or more kicks are made, and the greater efficiency is achieved (Fig.81-87).

81   82   83

84   *85*   *86*   *87*

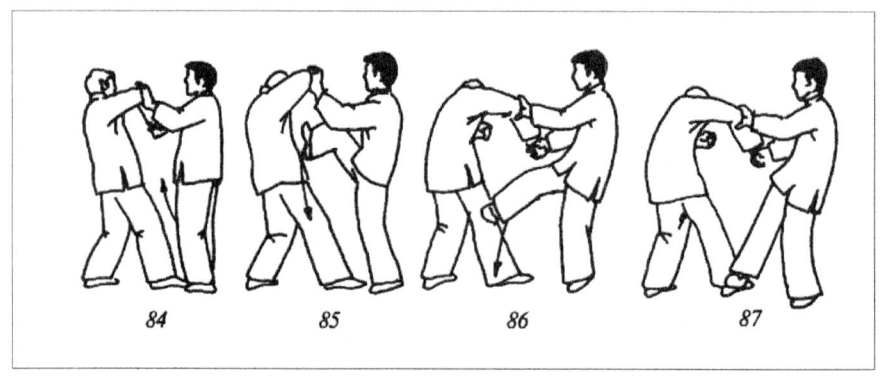

An important role is played by training the sensitiveness of the feet. This allows you to act in a fight maximally rational and with the economy of efforts. For example, your first kick to the abdomen with the right leg was blocked by the opponent (Fig.88). However, he did not control your attacking limb. Slightly bend your leg at the knee and without lowering it on the ground, make the second kick to the bending crease of the forward leg of the opponent (Fig.89).

88   *89*

Since Wing Chun Kuen is focused on the fight at the short distance, its technical arsenal includes the knee kicks, which are an effective close combat weapon. These kicks are made almost at any angle and any trajectories. They are often made after the grab of the hands of the opponent (Fig.90, 91).

90 *91*

The force of kicks is worked out at the three-sectional wall bag (Fig.92-95) and on the wooden poles (Fig.96-98).

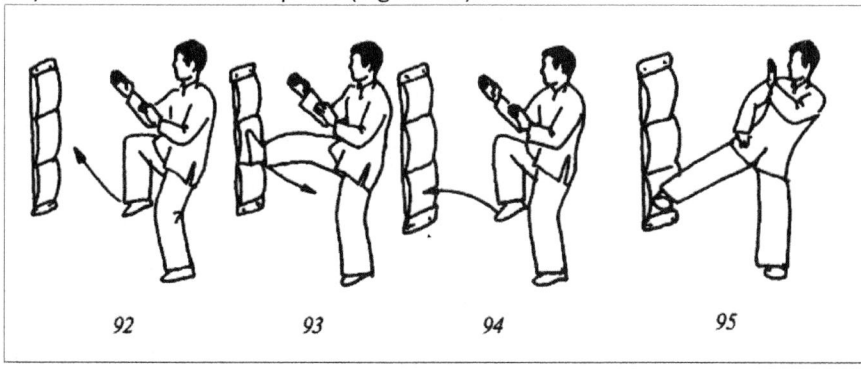

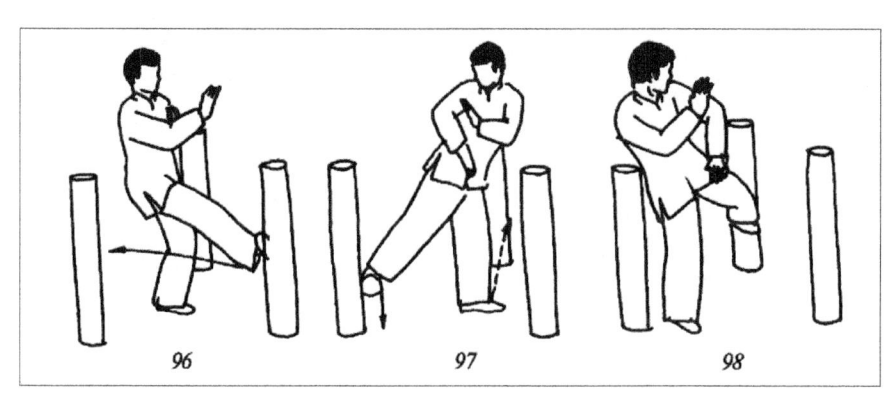

92 *93* *94* *95*

96 *97* *98*

Chapter 5
Defense technique

The objective of the defense is to prevent the attack of the opponent to reach its final phase by diverting it to the side or making stopping kicks. The effectiveness of the protection is considered to be in a high level, if it allows you quickly, without pausing to go to the counterattack and to finish the fight.

Defence stance

At the beginning of the fight Wing Chun fighters take the Yee Gee Kim Yuen Ma, Pien San Ma or Ching San Ma stances, facing the opponent. The hands are located in front of themselves.

One hand is stretched fingers forward towards the opponent, the palm is vertical. Elbow is half-bent, slightly in front of the body. The frontal hand is called Man Sau.

The other hand is in the position with the fingers directed upwards. Elbow is located at the torso. This hand protects the torso and is called Wu Sau. In this position of the hands they can be used equally effectively both in defense and attack (Fig. 1).

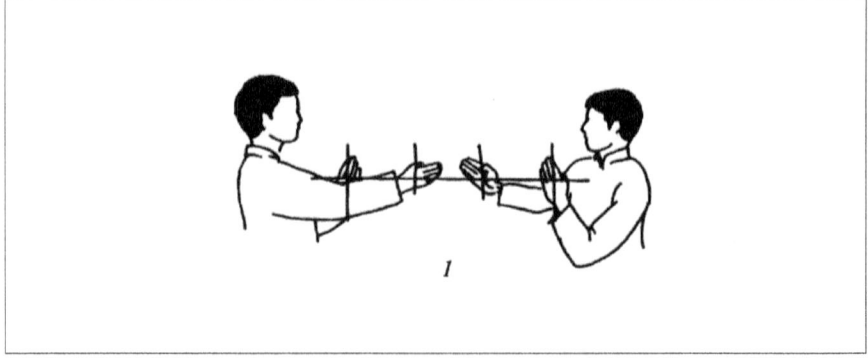

1

The outstretched hand defends its so-called outer area (Fig. 2). The second hand defends the inner area (Fig. 3).

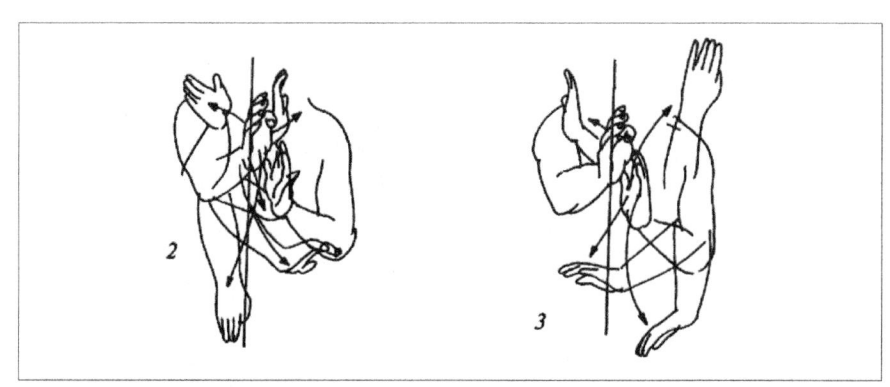

At such a distribution of zones of defense, the arms can instantly cover any area of the body. It is enough the slightest movement of the forearm to make an effective block.

Important points:
- *The basic principle of defence in Wing Chun Kuen is the principle of economy of movements,*
- *The center for most of the movements in the defense is the elbow,*
- *During most of blocking movements, it is necessary to ensure that the elbow is fixed,*
- *It is necessary to ensure that during the training of blocks, the hands would not go far beyond the body limits. "Aerobatics" is considered the diverting of the attacking limb of the opponent in millimeters from your own body.*

Block from the inside out - Tan Sau

Tan Sau is the blocking movement of the outer part of the forearm from the inside - outside (Fig. 4). First the hand is displayed forward, meeting the attacking limb of the opponent, then, due to the rotation of the forearm, the hand turns palm up and diverts the opponent's strike to the outside. The movement is enhanced by turning of the torso.

It is important to watch the blocking angle would be such that the arm of the opponent would pass literally in millimeters away from your body (Fig. 5, 6).

Tan Sau usually used to neutralize attacks directed at the upper torso. Fighters Wing Chun at the same time blocking frequently used counter-attack in the side (Figure 7).

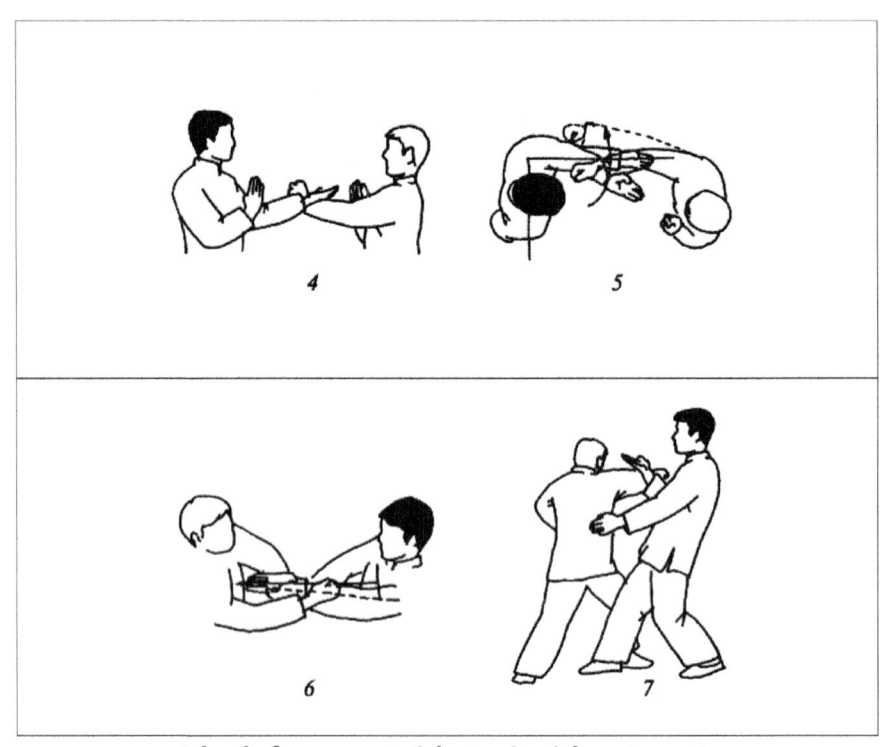

Block from outside to inside - Jum Sao

The punch is countered with the inside part of the forearm and the edge of the hand, movement from the shoulder to the center. When the attack is moved inwards, not outside, it is better to remain sideways to the opponent (Fig. 8, 9).

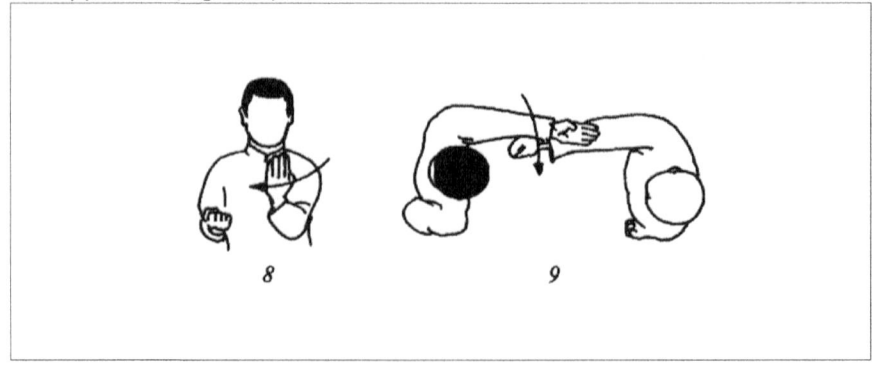

Side block with the palm - Pak Sau

Pak Sau - this is a very sharp shout block with the open palm. Fingers are directed upwards. The push with the hand is made from outside to inside from the vertical of the other shoulder, passing horizontally by the chest (Fig.10).

Pak Sau is a knocking block with the palm, often used to neutralize the attack to the head and upper part of the body. It is necessary that the palm would not go beyond the body limits.

As many other techniques of Wing Chun Kuen, this block is very conveniently combined with a simultaneous counter-attack (Fig. 11).

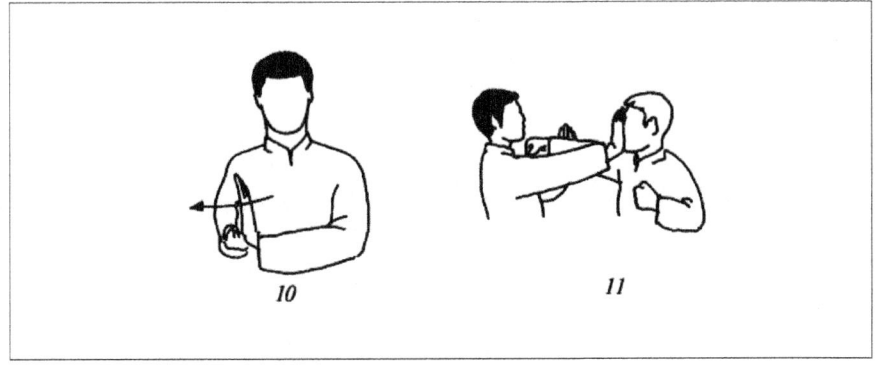

10

11

Wing block - Bong Sau

This block is made with the outer part of the forearm from elbow to outstretched fingers. During the protection the elbow rises up, like a bird opening its wing. The forearm is directed downwards and sideways in the direction of the opponent. The other hand is at the chest, securing against possible second attack (Fig. 12 - 16).

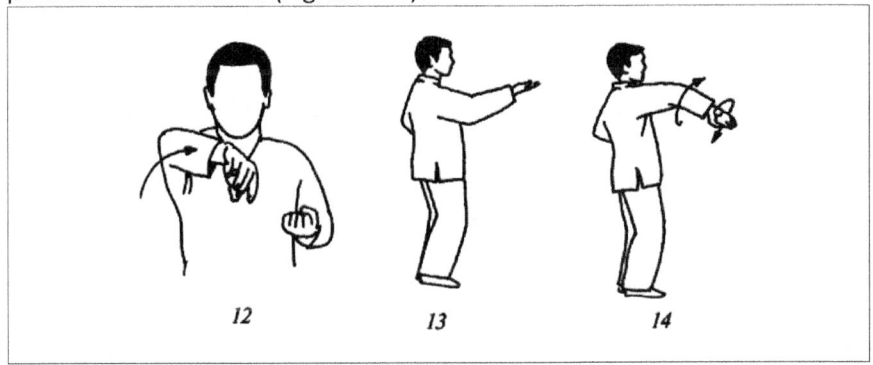

12

13

14

15 *16*

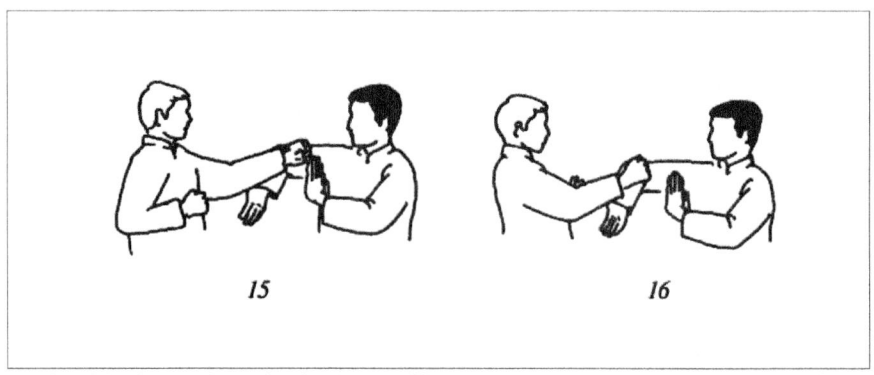

This block reaches the highest efficiency in conjunction with turn of the torso and the side step to the side (Fig.17, 18).

17 *18*

Blocking down with the forearm - Gan Sau

Gan Sau - is a divertive block from the inside out with the outside of the forearm. It is used to neutralize the direct and side strikes to the lower part of the body (Fig. 19).

This block is very easy to combine with a simultaneous counter-attack (Fig. 20).

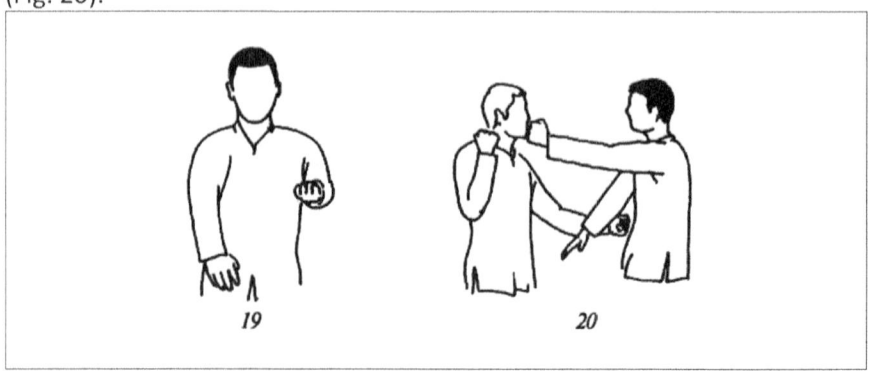

19 *20*

Pressing palm block - Gum Sau

Gum Sau is a block with the palm from downwards - upwards (Fig. 21). It is used to neutralize direct strikes to the lower part of the body. This protection is conveniently combined with the turn of the body and side-step to the side (Fig. 22).

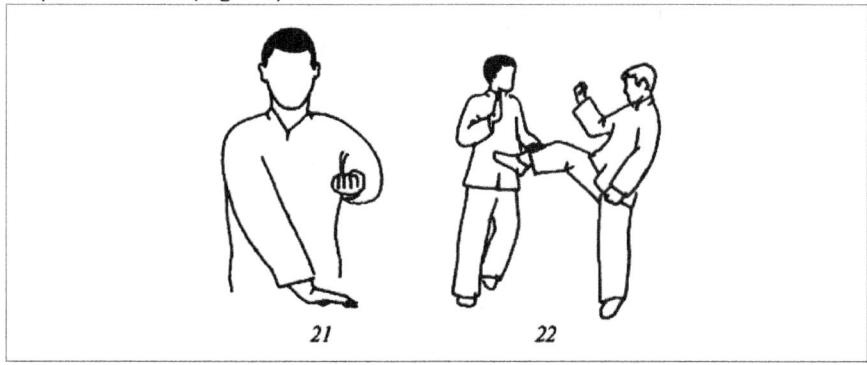

The divertive wrist block - Huen Sau

Huen Sau is a divertive outward block with the inside part of the wrist. It is used to neutralize strikes to the middle part of the torso and diverting to the side of the attacking limb of the opponent. With this movement you open the opponent's body for your own attack (Fig. 23, 24).

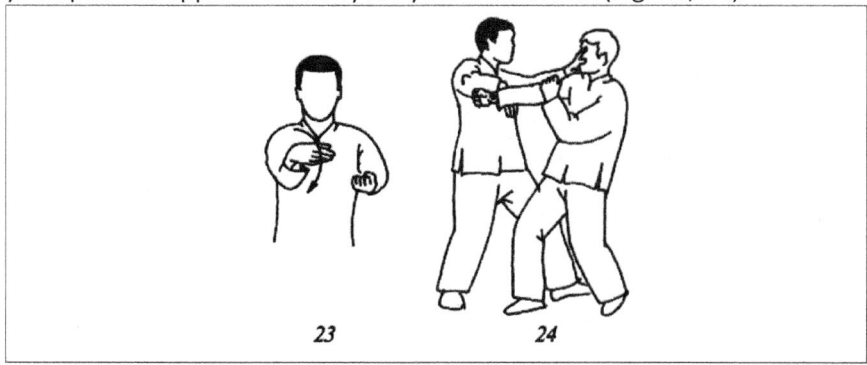

Double block - Jum / Gan Sau

Jum / Gan Sau is a double block consisting of two protecting movements. One hand makes Gan Sau, while the other hand simultaneously makes Jum Sau.

This block is used for defense against the direct and circular strikes to the head, upper and middle part of the body (Fig. 25).

The defense must be made in conjunction with the turn of the body in the appropriate direction.

During the defense from circular kicking it is advisable to block the leg of the opponent in the hip area, and not in the lower leg area, as the amplitude and speed of the lower leg is faster and therefore the force directed to the point of contact, will be more too (Fig.26).

25

26

Upward block - Man Sau

Man Sau - is a divertive block upwards with the outer part of the forearm. It is used to neutralize strikes to the head. During the defense, the arm moves upwards and simultaneously rotates along its longitudinal axis (Fig.27, 28).

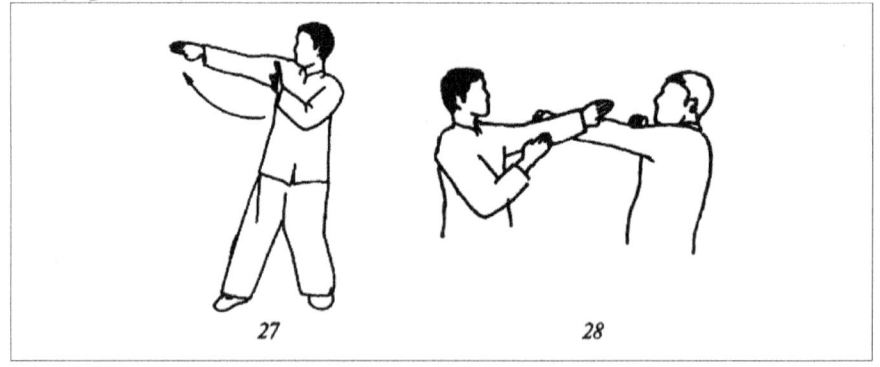

27

28

"Five defenses" form

One of the types of practicing of defense is to train special forms in which all the blocks are presented in a certain logical sequence. In the presented to our readers form five blocks are practiced, which are the most commonly used in the style of Wing Chun Kuen. The shape may be trained both single or with the partner.

Single form training

Starting position is the Front Yee Gee Kim Yuen Ma stance. Hands are in the main defence position (Fig. 29). Turn 45 degrees to the left and take the right-hand side Pien San Ma (Cheun Ma) stance. At the same time with the turn, make the Bong Sau at the lower level with the right hand. The left hand is taken to the chest in the Wu Sau position (Fig. 30). Return to the starting position and make the Tan Sau block with the same hand (Fig. 31).

Turn 45 degrees to the right, taking the left-hand side stance. At the same time with the rotation, make the Gan Sau block with the right hand (Fig. 32). Turn 90 degrees to the left and take the right-hand side stance. At the same time with the right hand make the defense Jum Sau movement (Fig. 33).

Return to the starting frontal Yee Gee Kim Yuen Ma stance. At the same time with the right hand make the Wu Sau block, which is an oppressive movement with the hand forwards. The hand is vertical, palm is facing inwards, fingers - upwards (Fig.34).

Take back the arms to the starting defensive position (Fig. 35).

29   30   31   32

33   *34*   *35*

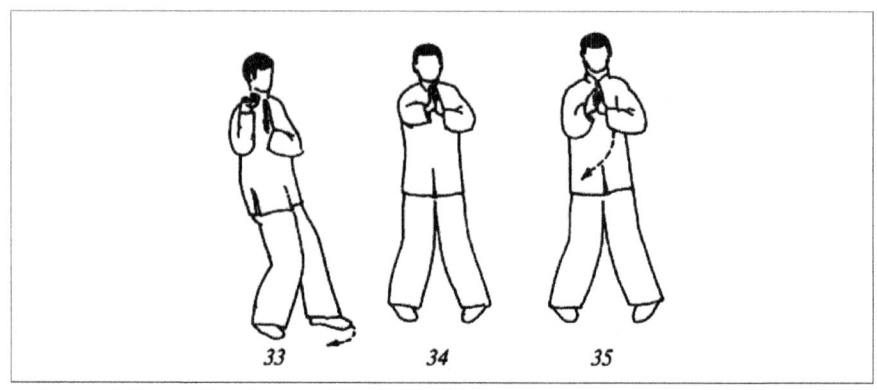

Repeat the entire form with the left hand.

Pair form training

Partners take the frontal stances at arm's length from each other. Turning to the left at the same time they make the lower Bong Sau making punches with wrists to each other (Fig. 36). Then, taking the frontal stances partners make the Tan Sau block (Fig. 37). Then the Gan Sau block follows (Fig. 38), Jum Sau (Fig. 39) and, finally, Wu Sau (Fig.40).

36   *37*

38   *39*   *40*

In addition to the training of the defense technique, the training of the "Five defenses" form, strengthens the wrists and forearm of the partners, thus preparing the limbs to the conditions of the hard fight.

Blocks with the leg

This technique is developed in details in the Wing Chun Kuen and is adapted for the close combat. With its help you can reliably defense your lower part of the body from various attacks.

Legs blocks are divided into two large groups:
- Divertive movements
- Stopping strikes.

Despite the apparent simplicity, these methods are necessary to be worked out carefully for quite a long period of time.

The divertive block from the inside out - Tan Gerk

Starting position is the Front Yee Gee Kim Yuen Ma stance. Lift the bent at the knee right leg. The toe of the foot is directed to the right. The movement is made forward and slightly to the right (Fig. 41). As a rule, this block is used to neutralize the attacks made by the same name leg of the opponent (Fig.42).

41 42

Wing block - Bong Gerk

Starting position is the Front Yee Gee Kim Yuen Ma stance. Lift the bent at the knee leg. The toe of the foot is directed to the left. The movement is made forward and slightly to the left (Fig.43). This defense is used to neutralize attacks of heteronymic foot of the opponent (Fig.44).

43 *44*

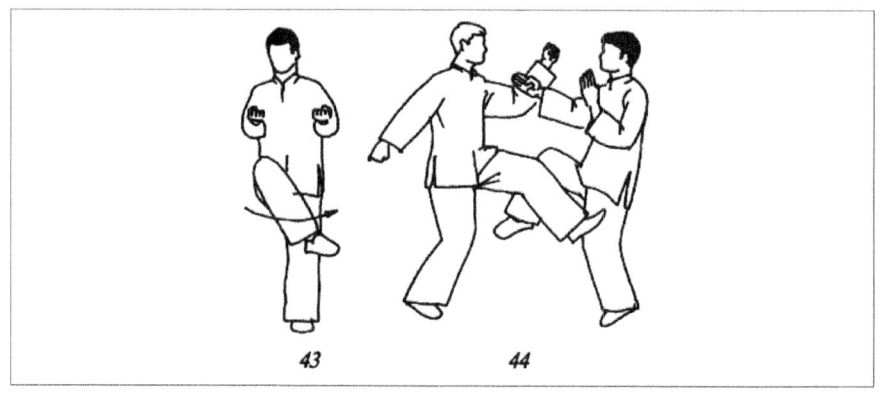

Stopping block with the leg

This block is a locking kick with the rib of the foot forward and down. The movement is universal as it can be used both in defense and in attack. The main condition of the movement is that the stopping block should be made ahead of the curve, i.e., at a time when the opponent is preparing to attack (Fig.45).

45

Chapter 6
Throws and grabs

Despite the primacy of strikes throws and grabs are actively used in Wing Chun Kuen. With their help it is relatively easy to put the opponent in a position where he will not be able to continue the fight. There are not many methods of wrestling in the style compared to, for example Judo, but they are easy and reliable in actual use.

This book covers only methods of unbalance the opponent, thawing him, but without the final phase of the decisive counter-attack when he is already lying helpless on the ground.

Throw with the grab of the arm at the shoulder
(Option # 1 - the entrance to the method from the outside)

The opponent makes a direct punch to the head with the left fist. Block his attack with the left forearm (Fig. 1). With the right hand grab his arm, while with the left palm make a direct punch to the head (Fig. 2). If the opponent made a block with his right hand, grab quickly his limb with your left hand (Fig. 3). Step to the right foot to the right forward foot of the opponent, turn left 90 degrees and make a steep with the left foot. At the same time, place his left hand on your right shoulder (in the space between the shoulder and elbow joints). With your left hand grab his arm at the elbow area (Fig. 4).

Bend forward - downward, increasing the movement with a sharp rise of the pelvis up, throw the opponent over the back downwards (Fig. 5).

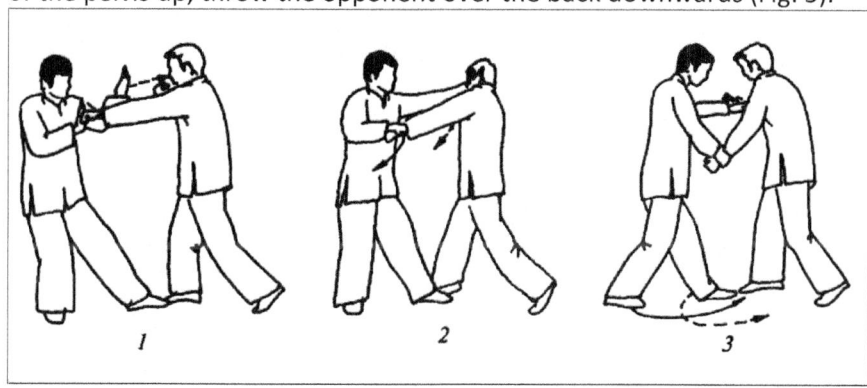

4   5

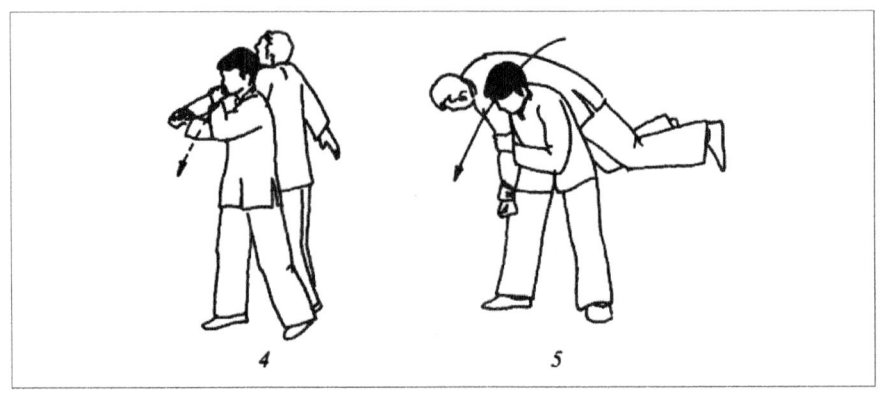

Throw with the grab of the hand on the shoulder
(Option # 2 - the entrance to the method from the inside)

The opponent makes a punch with the right fist to the head. With the left hand block the attack. Along with defense, make a counter-attack with the right palm (Fig. 6). Move the right foot to the right forward foot of the opponent, turn around and step back with the left foot. At the same time grab the opponent's limb and place it on your right shoulder (Fig. 7). Sit down. Then, straightening your knees, lift your pelvis up and bend down the torso. Throw your opponent over the back on the ground (Fig. 8).

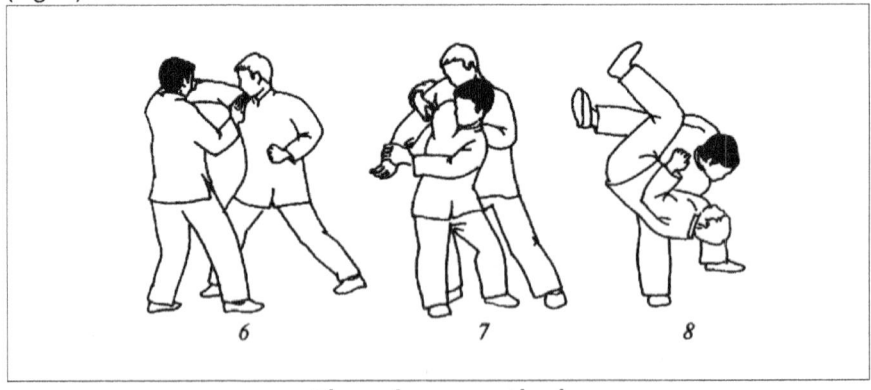

6   7   8

Throwing over the leg

The opponent makes a direct punch to the head with the right fist. With the right hand, make the Tan Sau block. Then, using the side step forward, step with the right foot forward behind the opponent's legs and throw him back down over your leg (Fig. 9, 10).

                                   9   10

Back trip-up

The opponent makes a circle kick to the head with the right leg. With the hands make the Jum / Gun Sau block with both hands and grab his leg. Move your right foot to his supporting leg and place it on the toe. With a fast movement lower the right hill on the ground, tripping-up the opponent's leg and pushing him with the right palm to the chest, tilt him on the ground (Fig.11-13).

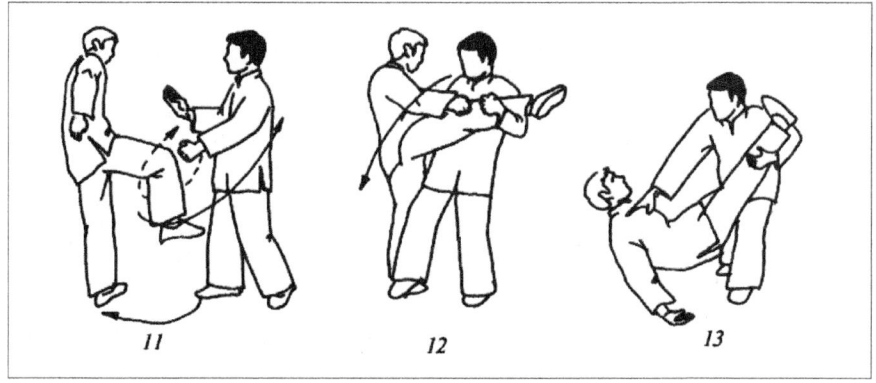

                   11   12   13

Side trip-up

The opponent makes a direct punch to the head with the right fist. Make the Pak Sau block with the left palm and neutralize the attack. Using the side step, step with the left foot behind the right forward leg of the opponent and make a trip-up. With the left hand, make a push, enhancing the effect of the throw (Fig. 14, 15).

14 *15*

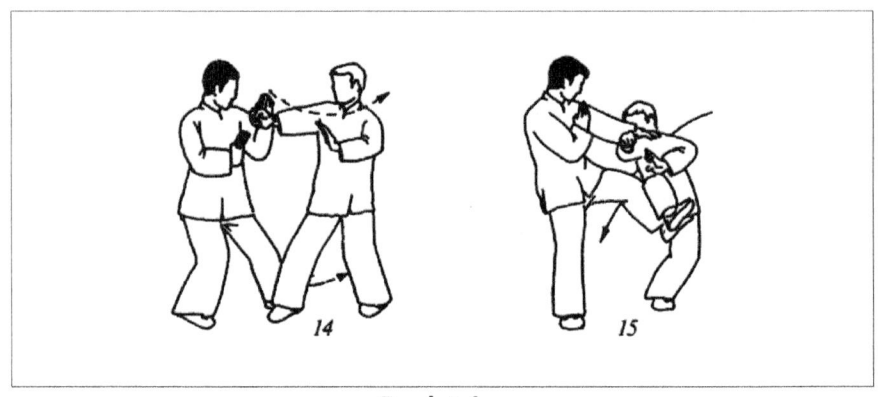

Back trip-up

The opponent makes a reverse circle kick to the head with the left foot. With both hands neutralize the attack and fix the attacking limb with your left hand. Using a side step get closer to him and step with the right leg behind his supporting leg. Moving your right leg backwards, make the trip-up. To enhance the effect, at the same time push him away forwards with the right hand (Fig.16-18).

16 *17* *18*

Elbow lever
(Option #1)

The opponent makes a direct punch to the head with the right fist. Turn right and make the Bong Sau block with the left hand. With the right hand grab the attacking limb. With the right foot step back and turn right. With the left forearm push his elbow in the direction of the turn and down. Due to the inertia of the movement of his body and the impact of pain on the elbow, the opponent will be forced to lower down on the ground (Fig.19-21).

                    19   20   21

Elbow lever (Option #2)

The opponent makes a direct punch to the head with the right fist. Turn right and make the Jum Sau block with the left hand. With the right hand grab the attacking limb. With the right foot make a small step back and turn to the right more. With the left forearm push his elbow in the direction of the turn and down. Due to the inertia of the movement of his body and the impact of pain on the elbow, the opponent will be forced to lower down on the ground (Fig.22-25).

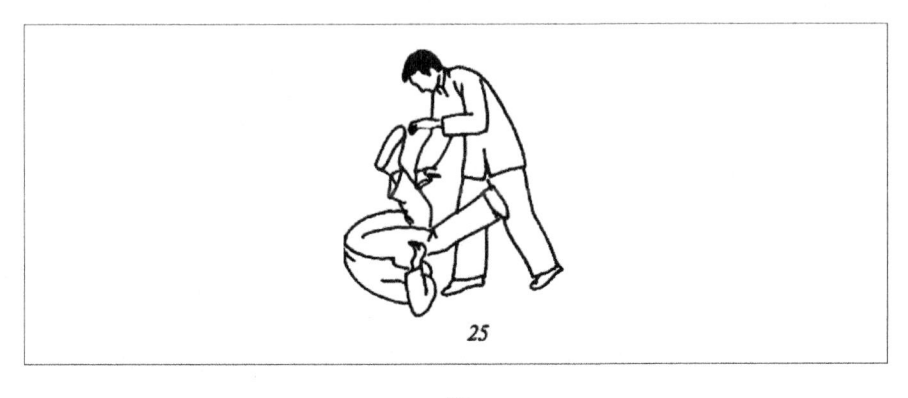

                    22   23   24

                                                 25

Chapter 7
Training combinations

The study of training combinations is a very important stage in understanding of the intricacies of the Wing Chun Kuen art. They exactly contain the nuances of the style and display the manner of the fight. Before you start learning the combinations, you must thoroughly study and master almost all the elements of the basic technique of the school.

Tan Sau - Chung Chui

Starting position is the Front Yee Gee Kim Yuen Ma stance. Hands are in the main defence position: the right arm is directed forward, left - at the chest (Fig. 1). Turn right 45 degrees. Simultaneously with the rotation make the Tan Sau block with the right hand, and make the Chung Chui punch with the left fist (Fig. 2). Return to the starting position, only now the left arm is directed forward and right - at the chest (Fig.3). Turn 45 degrees to the left and repeat the exercise to the other side.

Repeat the combination 20 times in each direction. After some time, the initial phase position can be omitted. As a result, during the exercise, you will make turns 90 degrees to the left and right.

This combination is the defense and counter-attack at the same time (Fig. 4).

4

After studying hand movements during turning on the spot quite well, you can pass to the working out of the combination in conjunction with the side step.

Starting position is the left-hand combat Ching San Ma stance (Fig. 5). With the left foot make a side step forward. At the same time with the left hand make the Tan Sau block and with the right fist make the Chung Chui punch (Fig. 6). Make one more side step forward. At the same time with your right hand make the Tan Sau block, and with the right fist - Chung Chui punch (Fig. 7).

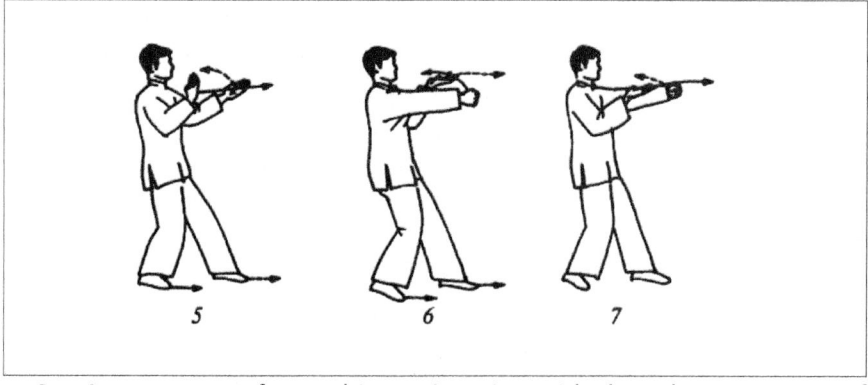

5   6   7

Continue to move forward in conjunction with the relevant actions of the hands.

The next step in the study of this combination is its working out in conjunction with the movement in side step backwards.

Gan Sau - Chung Chui

Starting position is the Front Yee Gee Kim Yuen Ma stance. The right hand is directed forward, the left - at the chest (Fig. 8). Turn 45 degrees to the right. At the same time with the right hand make the Gan Sau block and with the left fist make the Chung Chui punch (Fig. 9). Get back to the starting position, but now the left hand is in front, and right - at the chest (Fig. 10).

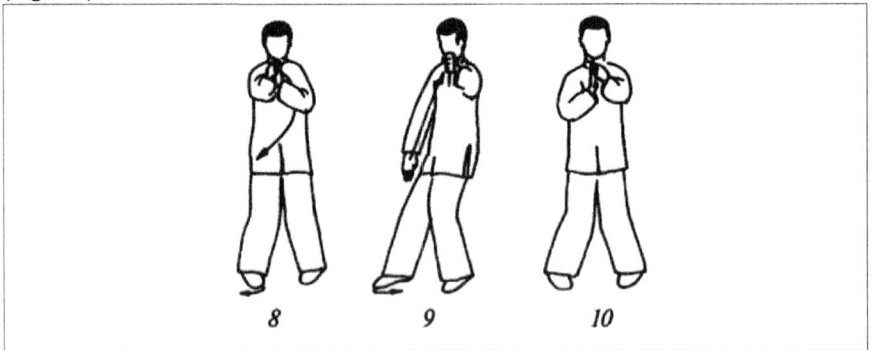

8 9 10

Repeat the exercise to the other side.

This combination is the defense of the lower part of the body and counterattack at the same time (Fig. 11).

11

The next step is the training of the combination in conjunction with the side step.

Starting position is the left-hand combat Ching San Ma stance (Fig. 12). With the left foot make the side step forward. At the same time with the left hand make the Gan Sau block and with the right fist make the Chung Chui punch (Fig. 13). Make one more side step forward. With the right hand make the Gan Sau block, with the left fist make the Chung Chui punch (Fig. 14).

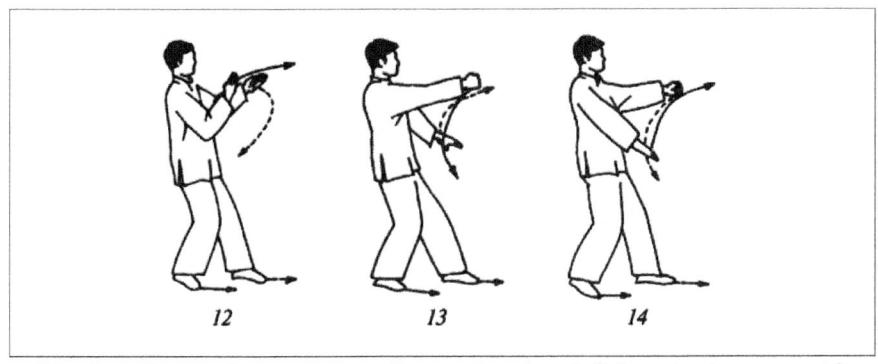

12 *13* *14*

Moving forward, you are always in the left-hand stance. After completing a number of such movements, turn 180 degrees, take the right-hand Ching San Ma stance and repeat the combination, moving in the opposite direction.

Lop Sau - Chung Chui

Starting position is the Front Yee Gee Kim Yuen Ma stance. The right hand is directed forward, left – at the chest (Fig.15). With the right palm make the covering and grabbing downward Lop Sau movement (Fig. 16). With the left fist, make a direct Chung Chui punch (Fig. 17).

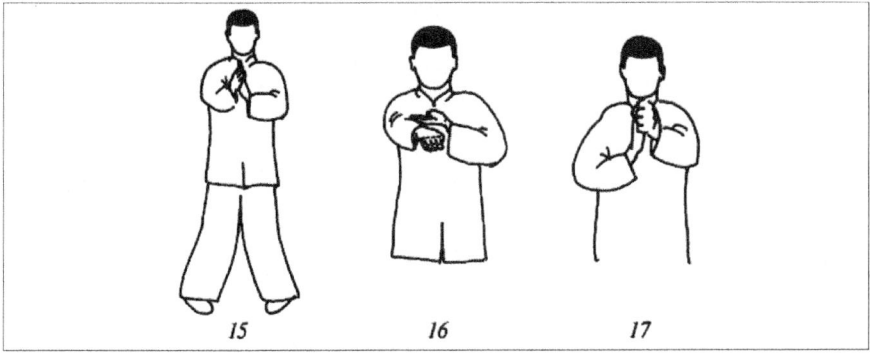

15 *16* *17*

Repeat the exercise with the other hand. Repeat the combination 20 times with each hand.

The next step is the implementation of the combination in conjunction with the side step.

Starting position is the Front Yee Gee Kim Yuen Ma stance (Fig. 18). With the palm hand make the Lop Sau punch (Fig. 19). With the right foot step forward, step up with the left foot while making the Chung Chui punch with the left fist forward at the chest or head levels (Fig. 20).

18 19 20

Return to the starting position and repeat the combination again. Repeat this exercise 20 times.

Make the combination, making a step with the left foot and making the Chung Chui punch with the right hand.

Make the combination with a partner:

From the starting position (Fig. 21) take a step forward with his right foot quickly and with the right palm cover the exposed forward left hand of the opponent (Fig. 22). Step up with the left foot and make the Chung Chui punch with the left fist (Fig. 23).

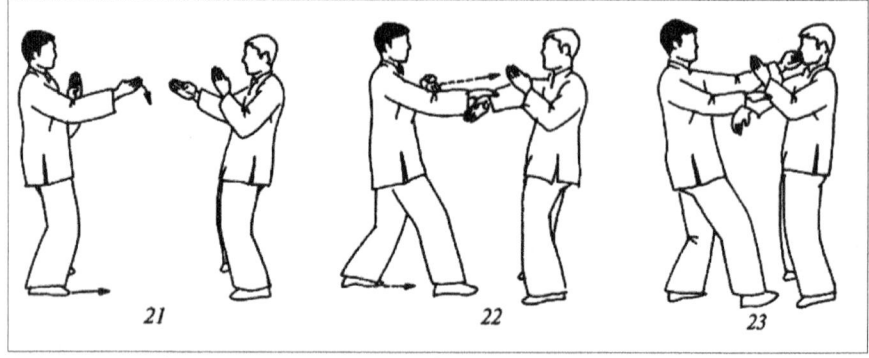

21 22 23

Return to the starting position and repeat the combination again. Then change places with the partner.

Pak Sau - Chung Chui

Starting position is the Front Yee Gee Kim Yuen Ma stance. The right arm is stretched forward, the left is located at the chest (Fig. 24). With the right hand, make the Pak Sau block at the middle level. At the same time with the left fist, make a direct Chung Chui punch forward (Fig. 25).

Return to the starting position. Take the right hand to the chest and the left moves forward (Fig.26).

24　　　　25　　　　26

Repeat the exercise with the other arm.

The next stage is the implementation of the combination in conjunction with the movement forward.

Take the starting position (Fig.27). With the right foot, make the side step forward and take the right-hand Ching San Ma stance. With the left hand, make the Pak Sau block, at the same time with the right fist make the direct Chung Chui punch forward (Fig. 28).

With the left foot make the side step back and return to the starting position (Fig. 29).

27　　　　28　　　　29

Repeat the exercise the necessary number of times.

Make the combination with the partner:

From the starting position (Fig. 30) with the right foot, make the side step forward. Simultaneously, with the left hand divert the right hand of the opponent downwards and to the side. With the right fist make the Chung Chui punch (Fig. 31).

30 *31*

Return to the starting position and repeat the combination the necessary number of times.

Double block Jum / Gan Sau

This combination represents the implementation of movement, which is the Jum Sau block with one hand and Gan Sau with the other hand, in conjunction with the turns of the body to the right and to the left (Fig.32-34).

32 *33* *34*

This exercise can be made in the movement.

Starting position is the Front Yee Gee Kim Yuen Ma stance (Fig. 35). With the right foot, make a side step forward and take the right-hand stance. The body is twisted to the left. Make the double Jum / Gan Sau block with the hands (Fig. 36). With the right foot make another side step forward. With both hands, make the chopping movement in the horizontal plane (Fig. 37).

35 36 37

Return to the starting position and repeat the exercise necessary number of times.

Make the combination with the partner:

From the starting position (Fig. 38) the opponent makes a circle strike to the head. With the right foot, make the side step forward and make a double block with the hands (Fig. 39). Make the counterattack with the chopping movements of two hands (Fig.40).

38 39 40

Lop Sau - locking kick - Chung Chui

Starting position is the Front Yee Gee Kim Yuen Ma stance (Fig. 41). With the right hand make the Lop Sau movement. With the right foot make the locking kick on the level of the knee. At the same time, with the left hand make the Chung Chui punch (Fig.42). Lower the right foot on the ground and step up with the left foot. You are in the right-hand stance. At the same time make the Lop Sau movement with the left hand, and with the right fist make a direct Chung Chui punch (Fig.43). Return to the starting position.

41　　　　　　　42　　　　　　　43

Make the combination with a partner:
From the starting position (Fig.44) the opponent makes a step with the right foot forward, making a direct punch to the head with the right fist. With the Lop Sau movement you neutralize this attack. At the same time with the right foot, make the locking kick to the knee and with the left fist - a direct punch to the head (Fig.45). Finish the counterattack with the right Chung Chui to the head. With the left hand control the right hand of the opponent (Fig. 46).

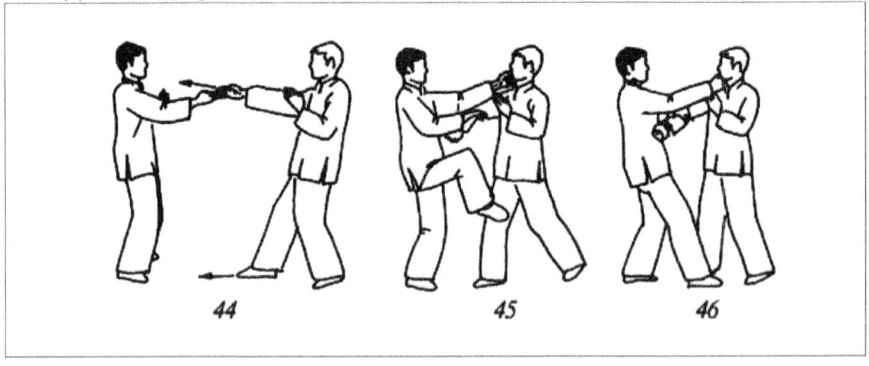

44　　　　　　　45　　　　　　　46

Man Sau - side kick

Starting position is the Front Yee Gee Kim Yuen Ma stance (Fig.47). With the left foot make a step to the left. At the same time make the Man Sao movement with the right hand (Fig.48). Immediately after this, make kick to the right with the right foot (Fig.49). Return to the starting position and make the movement in the other direction.

47   48   49

Make the combination with a partner:

The opponent attacks you with a direct punch with the right fist to the head. Make a step with the left foot back and to the side, brake the distance between you. At the same time, with the right hand make the Man Sau block, then make a counterattack with the right foot to the ribs or to the knee (Fig.50, 51).

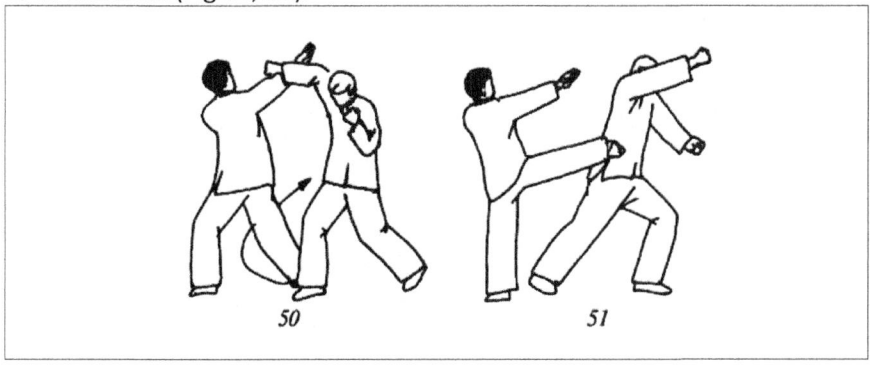

50   51

Chapter 8
Methods of attack

In many styles of Chinese martial arts, techniques of the start of combat are based on the fact that the opponent is the first to start the attack, the adept defences and conducts his own counterattack. That's right morally, but it is profoundly mistaken in terms of the harsh reality. It is known in Wing Chun Kuen that before to start the defence, we must learn to attack.

The methods of attack are divided into two major groups:
- *Attack with the strike to the "open" area of the opponent,*
- *"Opening" of the opponent and the subsequent attack.*

Methods of the first group are based on the fact that the opponent in his fighting stance created a "hole", for example, he lowered his hand, leaned back, etc. It is here the first lightning strike is made, which is either terminating, or is followed by a specific combination.

Methods of the second group are based on the fact that the opponent is in a closed combat stance, respectively, it is important some way to make him to take such a position in which any of parts of his body will be available for your attack.

Consider a few examples.

Methods of the first group:

Example # 1

The opponent lowered the hands

In this case, the open area is his head, where you can make either a direct or a side punch (Fig. 1, 2).

Example # 2

The opponent moves the elbows far from the torso

In this case, the open area is the entire lower part of the body. It is possible to make direct punches, upward strikes (Fig. 3), and kicks.

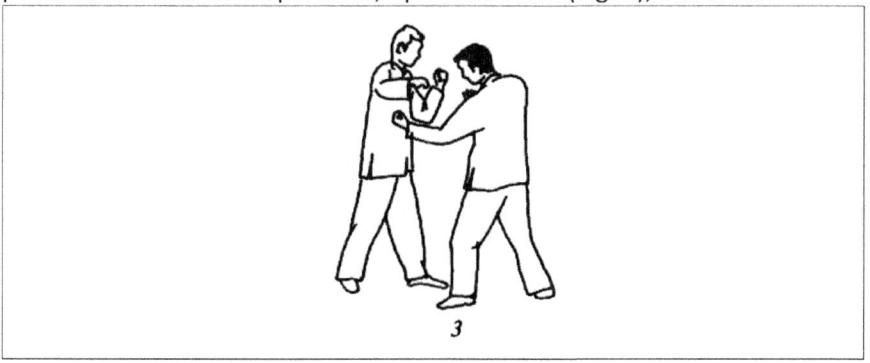

Example # 3

Opponent leans back

It is convenient to start the fight with a kick to the groin, knees or lower part of abdomen (Fig. 4).

4

Methods of the second group:
Example # 1

To "open" the head area for your attack, you can grab the hand located in front of the opponent and pull it towards you and down. Then make a direct punch to the head with the other hand (Fig.5-7).

5 *6* *7*

Example # 2

To "open" the body for your attack, you can raise with your hand the frontal hand of the opponent and fix it with your second hand. In this case, the entire lower part of his body will be open for your attack (Fig. 8, 9).

8 *9*

Example # 3

In order to create an opportunity for the attack of the opponent's legs, you can grab his arm and pull it down with a force. He will lean forward and will carry the weight on the forward leg. At this moment, you can make a kick to his supporting leg (Fig. 10, 11).

10 *11*

Example # 4

Since Wing Chun is actively used in the close combat, a special place is occupied by the attacks, performed after the grab of the neck of the opponent. In this case it is convenient to make strikes with the elbows (Fig. 12, 13) or knee (Fig. 14, 15).

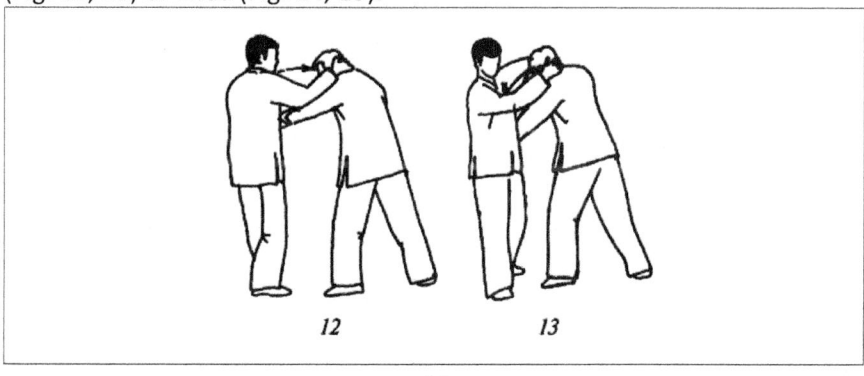

12 *13*

14 *15*

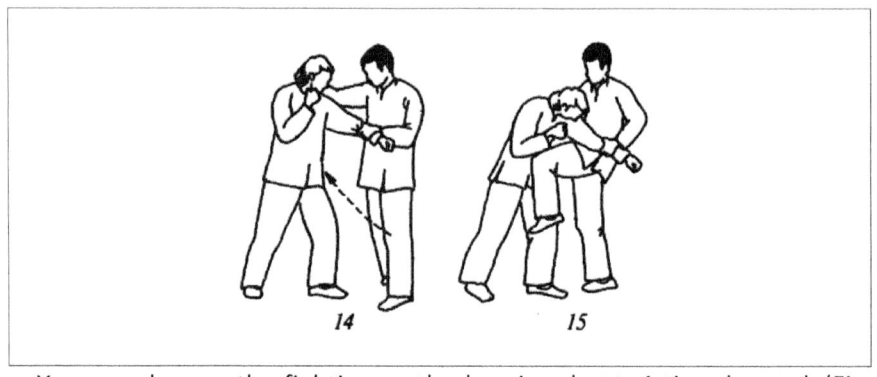

You can also use the fighting methods, aimed at twisting the neck (Fig. 16 -18).

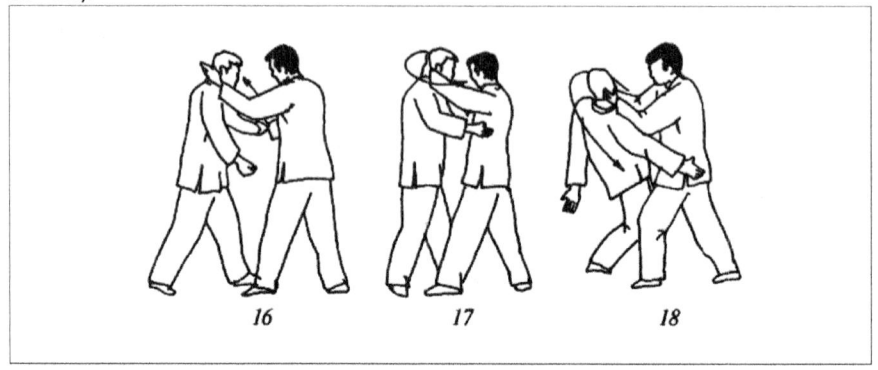

16 *17* *18*

Technique of combination attack

During the fight every strike has to be effective and should be aimed to strike the opponent with a single strike. However, this is not always possible, so we have often to make a series of strikes in order to "break" the defense of the opponent, and disable him.

There are many attacking combinations, including 2-3 strikes and throwing techniques and techniques of the pain control.

The volume of the book does not allow to consider the whole vast arsenal of attacking techniques of Wing Chun, in this regard, we will focus primarily on the two-strikes combinations.

You should not think that the first strike is only for opening of the opponent. It should be made with a real speed and force, and in the case of hitting the target, to carry a real threat.

Consider the specific attack combinations.

Combination 1

Attack starts with the punch with fingers to the eyes (Fig. 19). The opponent will be forced to neutralize the attack, raising one hand and leaning the head back. In this case, he opens the solar plexus area (zone 3), where immediately, is made the direct punch with the right fist (Fig. 20).

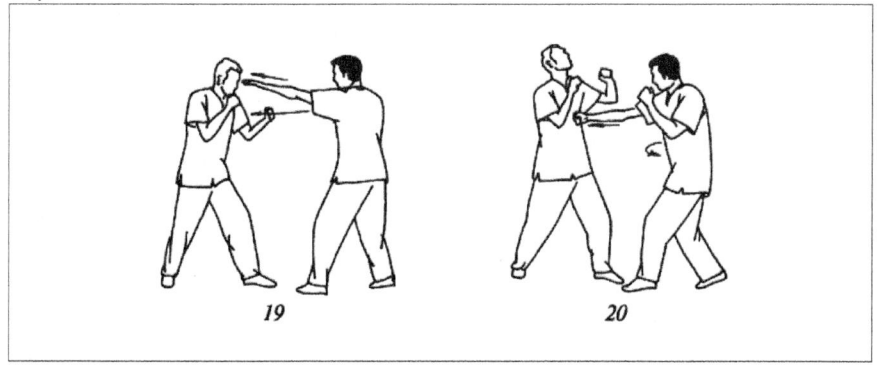

19   *20*

Combination 2

From the starting position (Fig. 21) make a punch with the fingers of the left hand to the solar plexus. The opponent will try to defense by making the downward block of the left hand (Fig. 22). Grab this hand of the opponent at the wrist with the left hand and pull it to the left. At the same time, make a direct punch with the right fist to the head (Fig. 23).

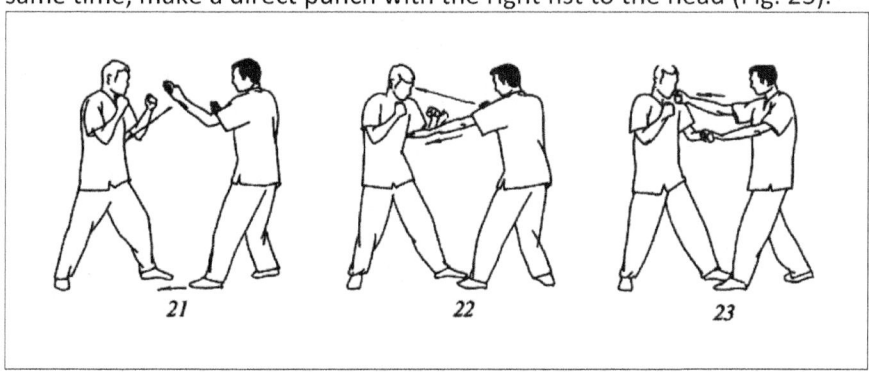

21   *22*   *23*

Combination 3

Attack starts, as in the previous variant, with the punch of the fingers to the solar plexus, which the opponent neutralizes with the downward block (Fig. 24). Put the right palm on the opponent's left forearm and push the arm down (Fig. 25). At the same time, make a direct punch with the left fist to the head (Fig. 26).

                    24   25   26

If the opponent was able to neutralize the strike (Fig. 27), grab his right arm at the wrist (Fig. 28), and, making a step forward with the left foot, make a punch with the right elbow to the head (Fig. 29), and you need to push the opponent's hand down.

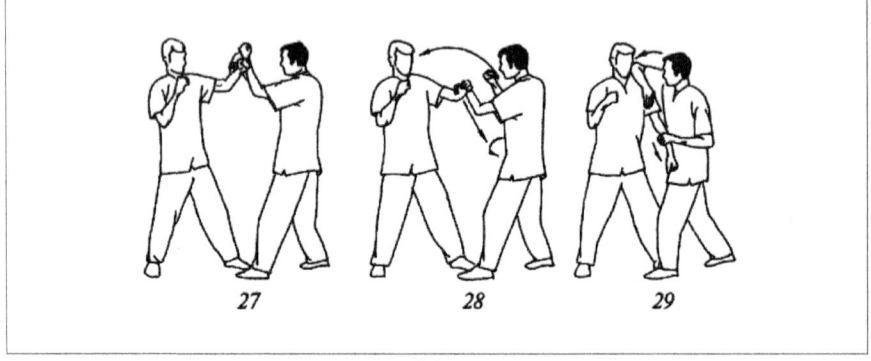

                    27   28   29

Combination 4

From the starting position (Fig. 30), start the attack, making a direct kick with the left foot to the groin (Fig. 31). And then quickly make a punch with the left hand to the eyes (Fig. 32). If the opponent was able to neutralize both strikes (Fig. 33), grab his left hand at the wrist and pull it to the left and upwards. At the same time, make a direct upward punch with the right fist to the lower ribs area (Fig. 34).

30   *31*   *32*

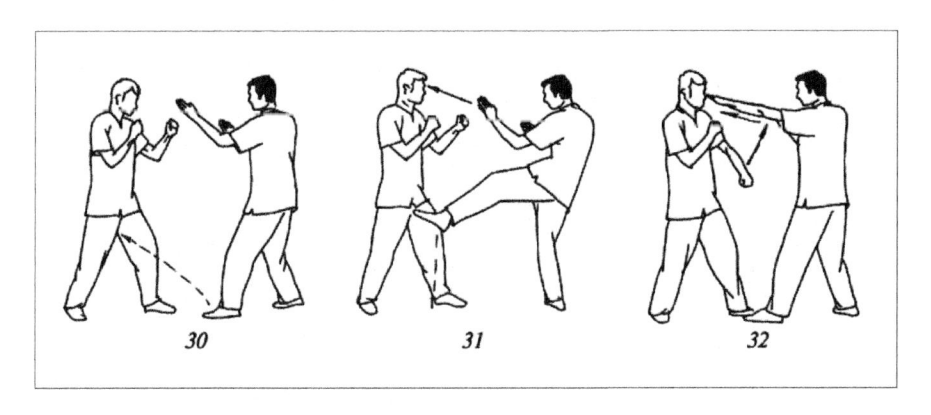

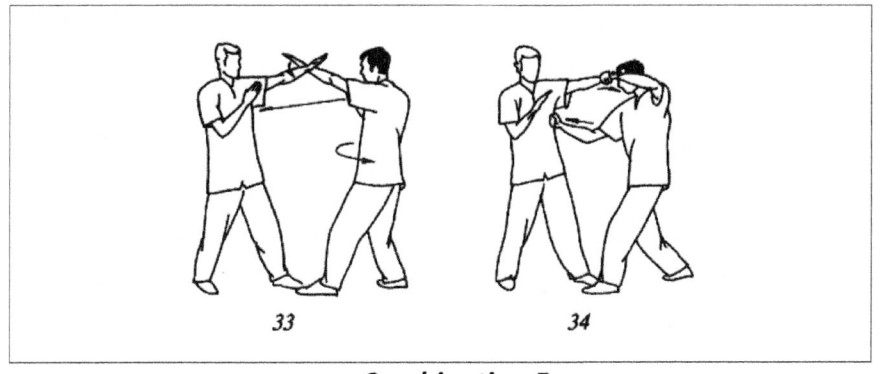

33   *34*

Combination 5

From the starting position (Fig. 35), make a direct kick with the left foot to the groin (Fig. 36). Lowering the foot on the ground and taking a step forward, make the second punch with the right fist to the head (Fig. 37). If the opponent neutralized the final strike, making a block with the left hand (Fig. 38) grab it at the wrist with your left hand and with the right — make a punch with the edge of the palm to the neck area. At the same time with the right foot tap the left foot of the opponent (Fig. 39), knocking him to the ground (Fig. 40).

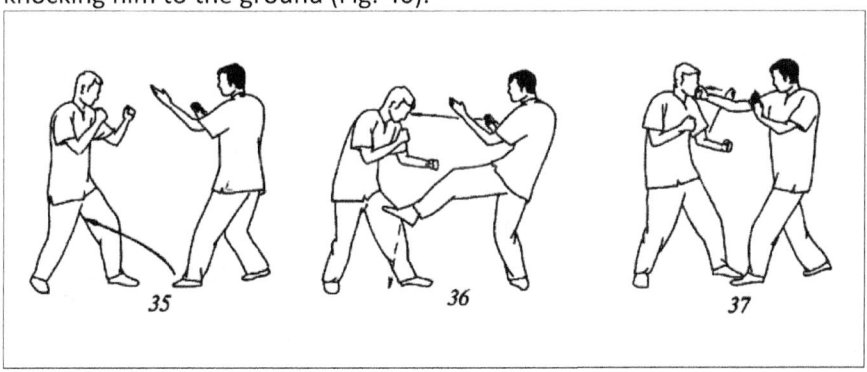

35   *36*   *37*

38 39 40

74

Chapter 9

Methods of defense and counterattack

Proper and effective defense is the main objective of all types of martial arts. In Wing Chun Kuen great attention is paid to the theoretical and practical aspects of the proper use of protective methods and counterattacks following them. The theory of defense is based on the following principles and concepts:
- *Central Line,*
- *Lower and upper levels,*
- *Principle of four gates,*
- *Principle of simultaneous defense and counterattack.*

Central line — is an imaginary vertical line passing in the middle of the body and dividing it into two parts. It is believed that along this line the most important organs of the human body are located. Therefore the Wing Chun Kuen fighters pay special attention to its defense.

If we draw an imaginary horizontal line located at the solar plexus level, it will divide the human body into two parts: upper and lower. Depending on what level the opponent is targeting his attacks, the fighter of Wing Chun Kuen chooses means and methods to neutralize them.

Central and horizontal lines divide the human body into four areas (Gates) (Fig. 1).

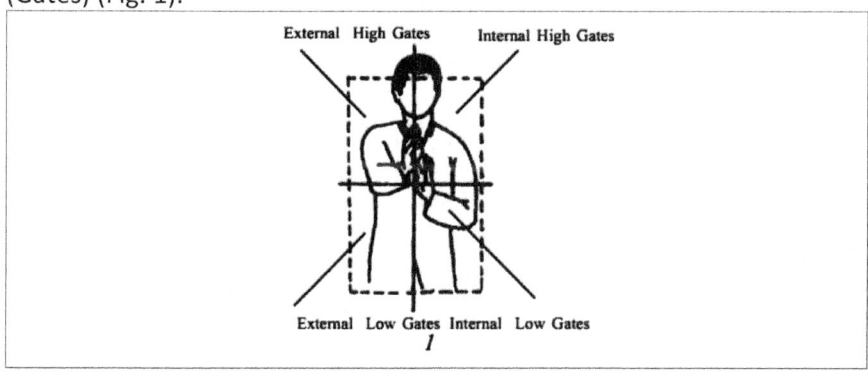

1

At the defense of these areas the whole defensive tactics of the style is built.

From the side of the stretched arm these areas are called:
- *External high "gates"*
- *External low "gates"*

From the side of the brought hand to the chest areas are called:
- *Internal high "gates"*
- *Internal low "gates"*

Based on this classification of areas of the defense, are select the most economical and efficient blocking actions. Typically, the stretched forward hand is responsible for the defense of its respective areas: external high "gates" and external low "gates". The backward hand is responsible for the defense of internal high "gates" and internal low "gates" (Fig. 2).

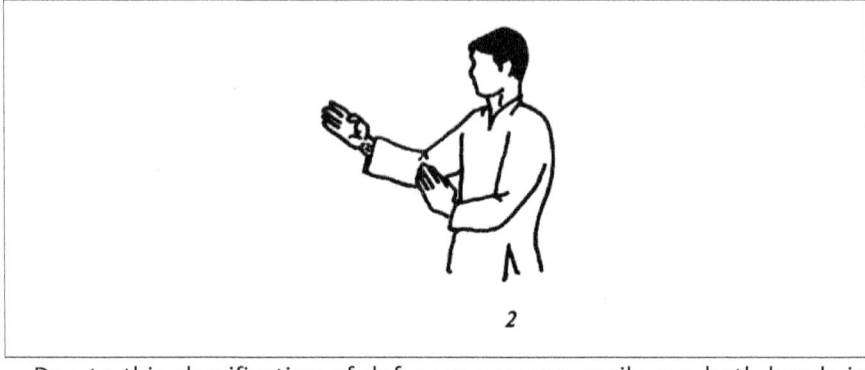

2

Due to this classification of defenses you can easily use both hands in the fight at the same time. For example, one hand makes a blocking action, and the second - the counterattack. This use of defense and attack techniques is the "hallmark" of Wing Chun Kuen.

Consider the basic techniques of the training of defense and counterattack.

Defense from single strikes
Defense from internal high "gates"

The opponent with the right fist makes a direct punch to the head. According to you, this attack is made to the inner high "gates". Turn the body to the left a little. With the left hand, make the Tan Sau block. At the same time with the right fist make a direct Chung Chui punch to the head (Fig. 3, 4).

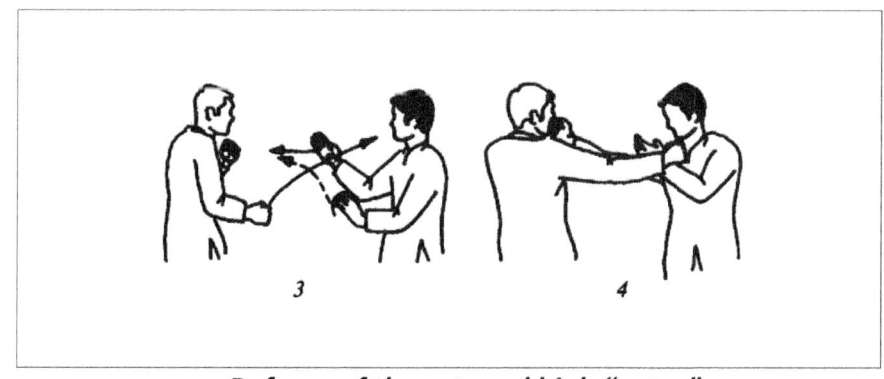

Defense of the external high "gates"

The opponent with the left fist makes a direct punch to the head. According to you, this attack is made to the external high "gates". Turn the body to the right a little. With the right hand make the Tan Sau block. At the same time make a direct punch to the head with the left fist (Fig.5-7).

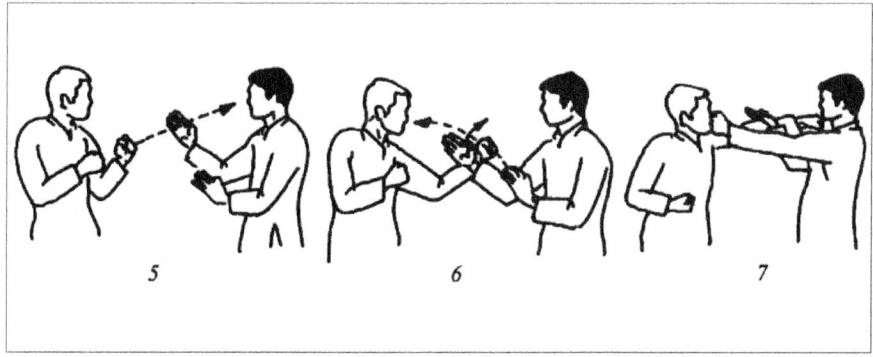

Defense of the internal low "gates"

The opponent with the right fist makes a direct punch to the stomach. With the left hand make the Gum Sau block. At the same time with the right fist make a direct punch to the head (Fig. 8, 9).

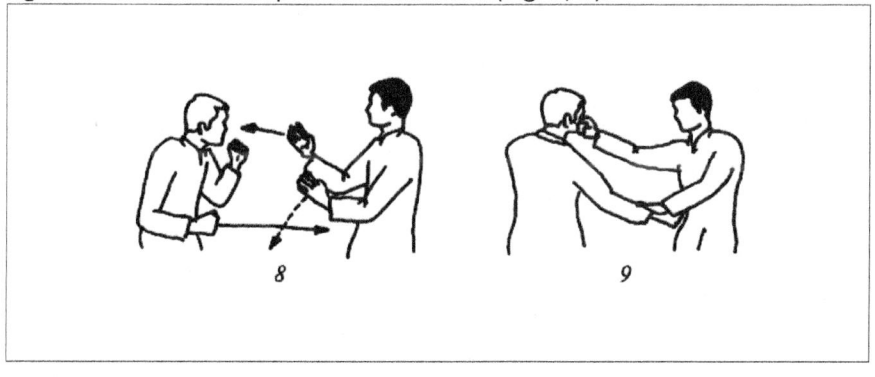

Defense of the external low "gates"

The opponent with the left fist makes a punch to the stomach or the liver area. With the right hand make the Gan Sau block. At the same time make a direct punch to the head with the left fist (Fig. 10, 11).

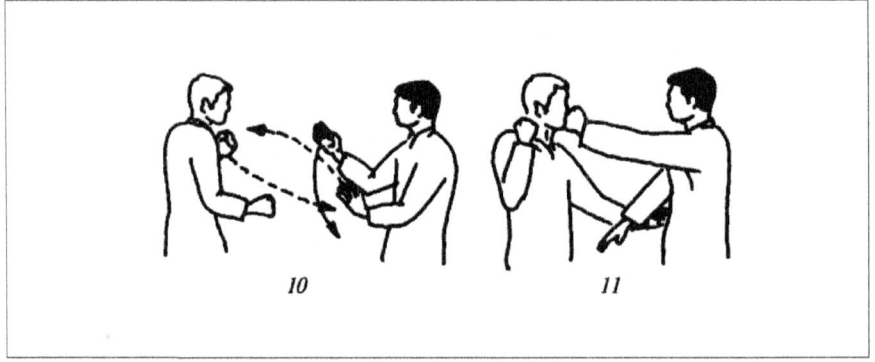

10 *11*

Despite the fact that the ideal of the style are both defense and counterattack, sometimes it appears to be effective to make the defense at first , bring the opponent off the balance and use the fact that he is in a disadvantageous position to perform his counterattack.

The opponent with the left fist makes a direct punch to the stomach. Turn left. Simultaneously with the rotation make the lower Bong Sau with the right hand. The opponent follows the direction of his attack and "falls" forward. With the left hand grab his arm and pull it back in the direction of his movement. With the back side of the right fist make a punch to the head (Fig.12-15).

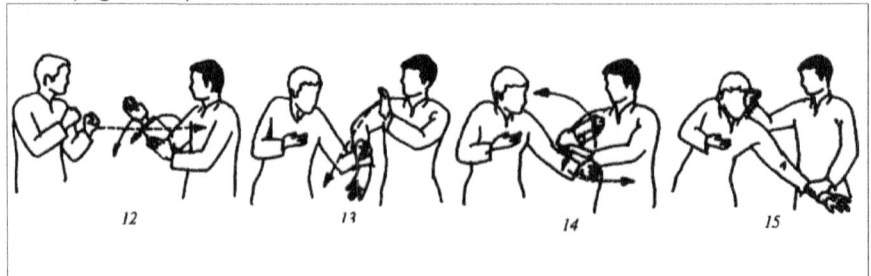

12 *13* *14* *15*

Defense from strike series

The larger part of the opponent's attack consists not of one strike, but of a series of two or three actions. The most commonly series of two strikes are used in the combat.

Defense of the high external and high internal "gates"

The opponent makes a series of punches of direct punches with the right and left hands to the head. First make the Tan Sau block with the left hand (the defense can be combined with your counterattack). From the second strike defend with the right Tan Sau and make your counterattack (Fig.16-19).

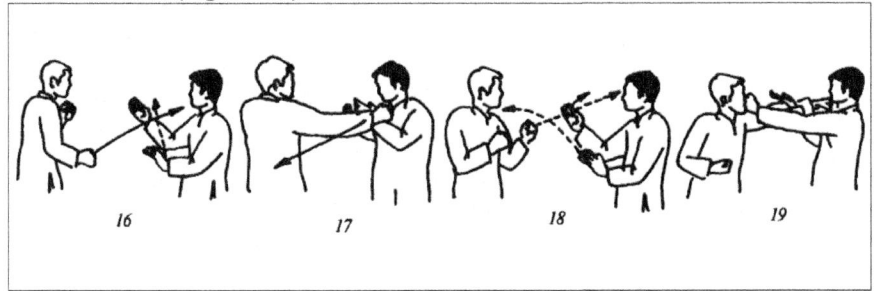

Defense of the lower external and lower internal "gates"

The opponent makes two punches with the right, then with the left fists to the stomach. Neutralize the first strike using the Gum Sau block, the second - Gan Sau. With the left fist make a direct punch to the head (Fig.20-23).

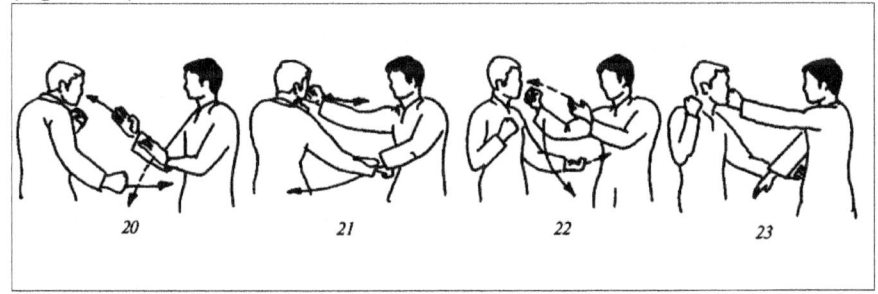

Defense of the external high and external low "gates"

The opponent makes a series of punches: with the right fist to the head and with the left fist to the stomach. From such an attack you can defend as follows. With the right Tan Sau block the first punch, then with the same hand beat off the second punch too. At the same time make a direct punch to the head with the left fist (Fig.24-26).

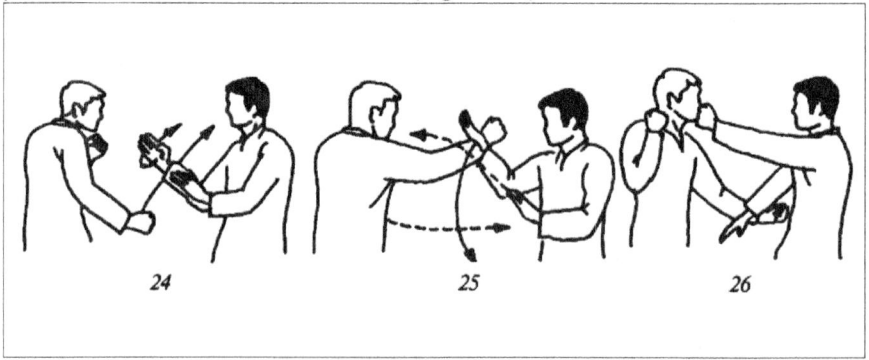

24 25 26

Defense of the internal high and external low "gates"

The opponent first makes a punch with the right fist to the head, then with the left fist to the stomach. First make Tan Sau, then the right Gan Sau and the left direct punch to the head (Fig.27-29).

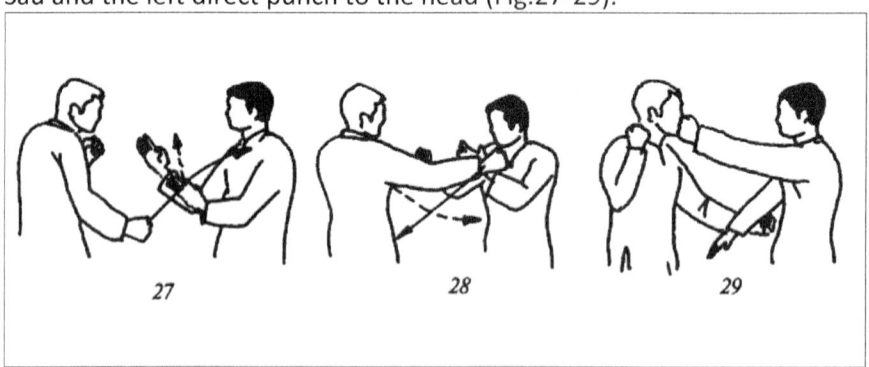

27 28 29

Defense of the external high and internal low "gates"

The opponent attacks with the left direct punch to the head and the right punch to the stomach. You defend with the right Tan Sau and the left Gum Sau. Along with the latest defense, make a direct punch to the head with the right fist (Fig.30-32).

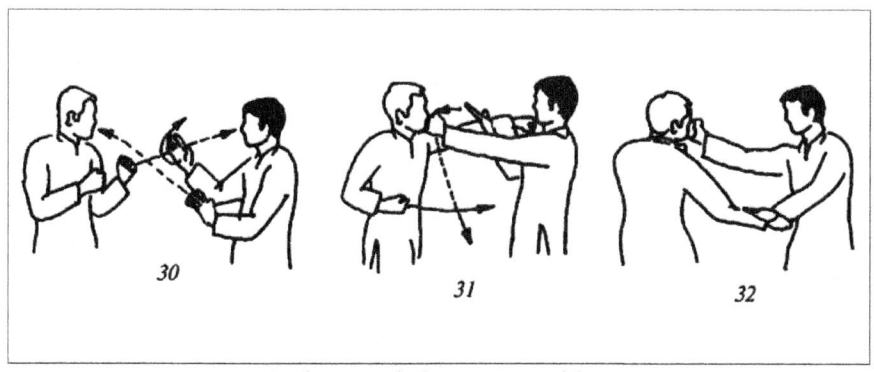

Defense of the external lower and external high "gates"

The opponent makes the direct kick to the stomach with the left foot first, then with the right fist to the head. Beat off the kick with the left Gum Sau, then make the Man Sau block. At the same time with the right fist make a punch to the stomach or the solar plexus area (Fig.33-35).

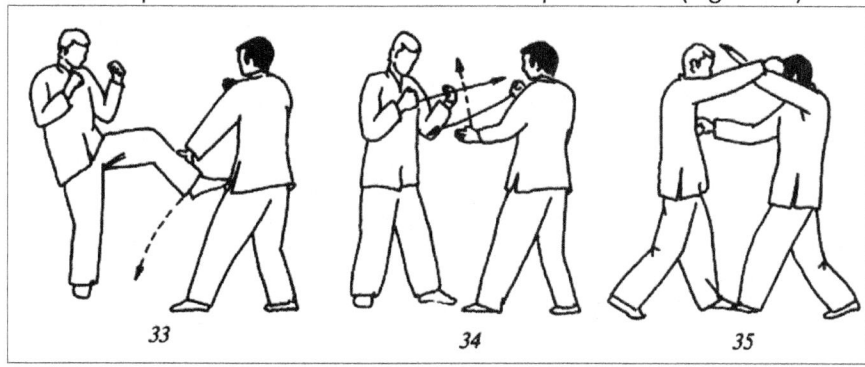

Defense of the internal low and external high "gates"

The opponent makes a series of two punches: direct kick with the right leg to the stomach and direct punch with the right fist to the head. With the right palm defend yourself from the first strike. Then turn the body to the right and to defend from the direct punch use the left Bong Sau. Intercept the attacking hand of the opponent and pull it towards you. With the left fist make a direct punch to the head (Fig.36-38).

Defense of the high internal and high external "gates"

The opponent attacks, making a direct punch to the head with the left fist. Neutralize the attack with the left hand, making the Pak Sau block (Fig. 39). Continuing the attack, the opponent makes a direct punch to the head with the right fist. For the defense, use the Bong Sau movement, which is made with the left hand (Fig. 40). Grab the attacking opponent's hand at the wrist with the right hand (Lop Sau) and pull it to you (Fig. 41). At the same time make the counterattack, making the punch with the other side of the fist to the head (Fig. 42). If the opponent reacted to your strike, putting his left hand (Fig. 43), immediately grab it (Fig. 44) and pull down, thus restricting the movement of both hands. At the same time make a strike with the right elbow to the head (Fig. 45).

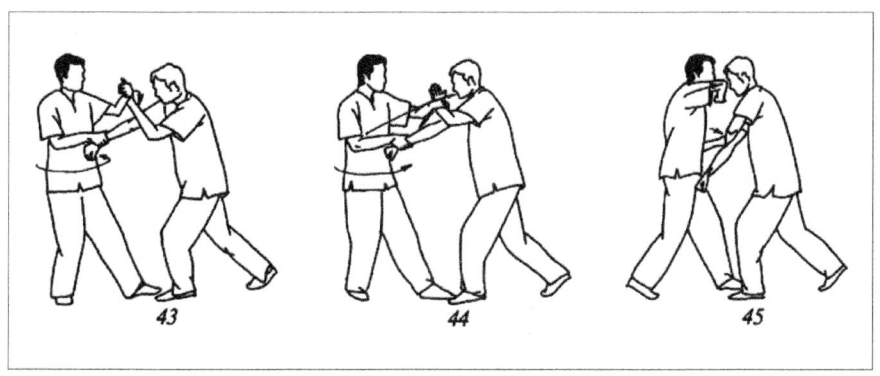

Defense of the internal high and external high "gates"

From the starting position (Fig. 46) the opponent attacks with the left fist, making a direct punch to the head. Grab the attacking limb of the opponent at the forearm with the left hand and pull down (Fig. 47.48). The opponent continues to attack with the direct punch with the right fist to the head (Fig. 49). With the right hand grab his attacking arm at the wrist and pull it towards you and down (Fig.50). Crossing the arms of the opponent and pushing them to the body, with the right palm (Fig. 51), make a direct punch with the left fist to the head (Fig. 52).

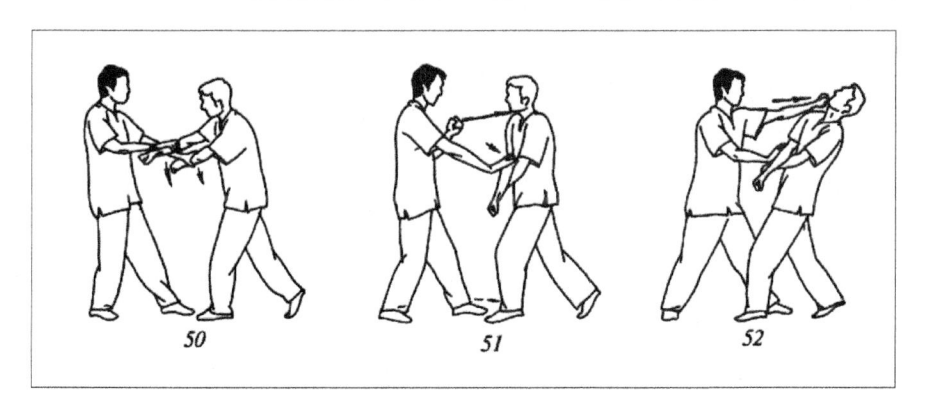

Defense of the internal high and external high "gates"

The opponent attacks, making a direct punch to the head with the left fist. Neutralize the attack with the Pak Sau block with the right hand (Fig. 53). The opponent continues to attack by a direct punch with his right fist to the head, which is blocked by you with the left hand using the Pak Sau movement (Fig. 54). Cross the hands of the opponent, pressing them to the body (Fig. 55) and counterattack with a direct punch with the right fist to the head (Fig. 56.57).

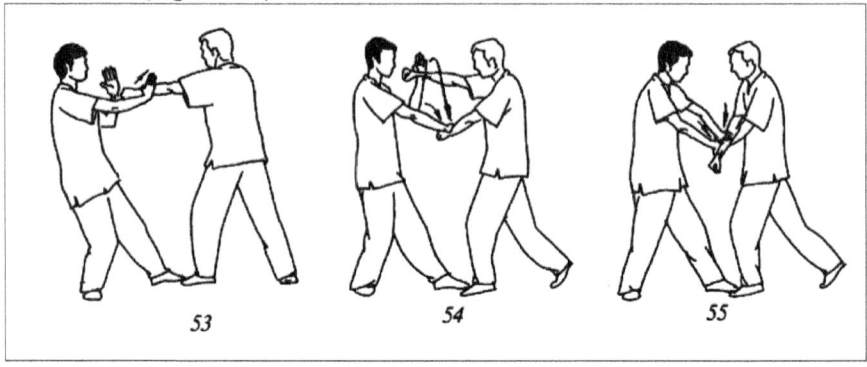

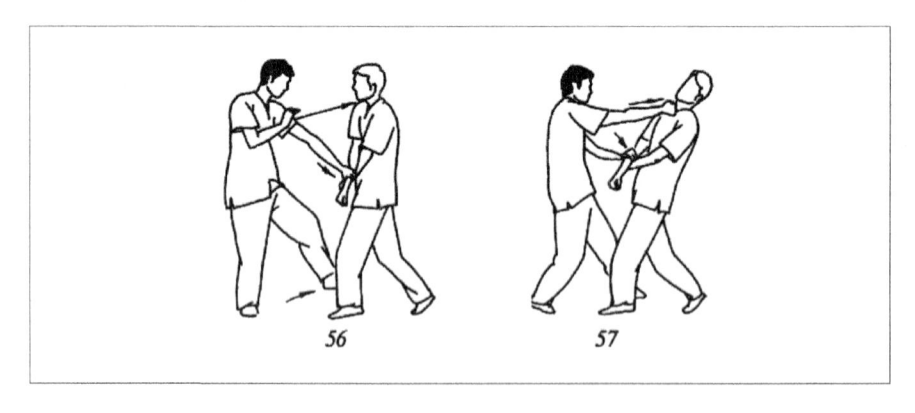

53

54

55

56

57

Defense of the high external and high internal "gates"

The opponent attacks, making a direct punch to the head with the right fist. Neutralize the attack with the Pak Sau block with the left hand (Fig. 58). Continuing the combination, the opponent makes a direct punch to the head with the left fist, which you block with your right hand, using the Pak Sau movement (Fig. 59). With the left hand grab the attacking limb of the opponent at the wrist and pull it towards you while counterattacking with a direct kick with the toe of the left foot to the groin (Fig. 60.61). Then lower your leg on the ground and make a direct punch to the head with the right fist, still holding the left hand of the opponent in the grab (Fig. 62).

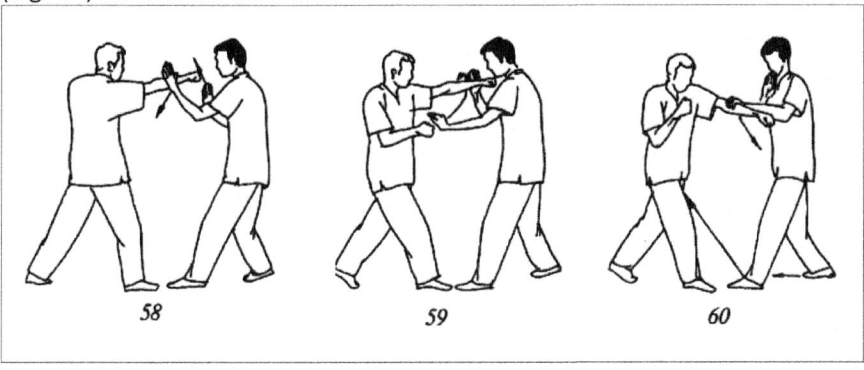

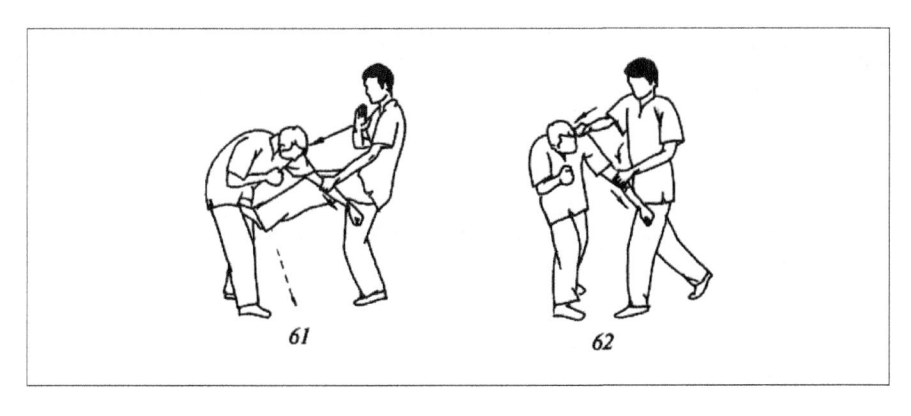

Defense of the high internal and low external "gates"

The opponent is attacking with a direct punch with the left fist to the head. Neutralize the attack with the right hand, making the Pak Sau block (Fig. 63). Continuing moving forward, the opponent makes a direct punch with the right fist to the middle part of the body which you block with the left hand. Make the Bong Sau movement (Fig. 64). Without stopping, with the right hand make the Lop Sau movement and with the left – make the counterpunch with the back side of the fist to the head (Fig. 65.66).

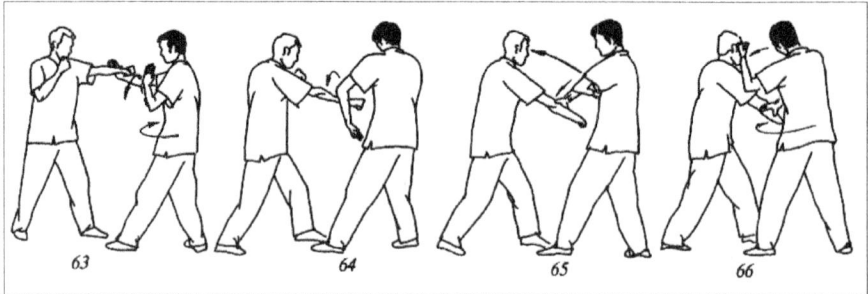

Defense of the high external and low internal "gates"

The opponent is attacking with a direct punch with the left fist to the head. Neutralize the attack with the Jum Sau block with the left hand (Fig. 67). The opponent makes the second direct punch with the right fist to the middle part of the body which you block with the left elbow, lowering it down (Fig. 68). Make the counterattack instantly, making a punch with the fingers the eye (Fig. 69).

If the opponent can defend with the left hand (Fig. 70) and try to counterattack with the right, in this case, grab his right arm by the wrist (Fig. 71) and making the Fook Sau movement (Fig. 72), make a punch with the edge of the right hand to the solar plexus (Fig.73,74).

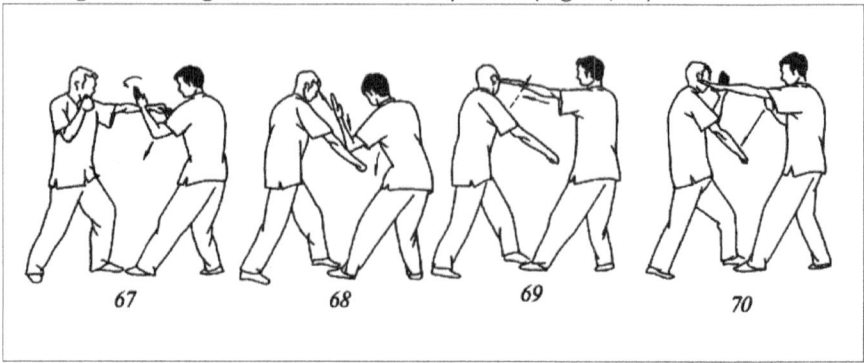

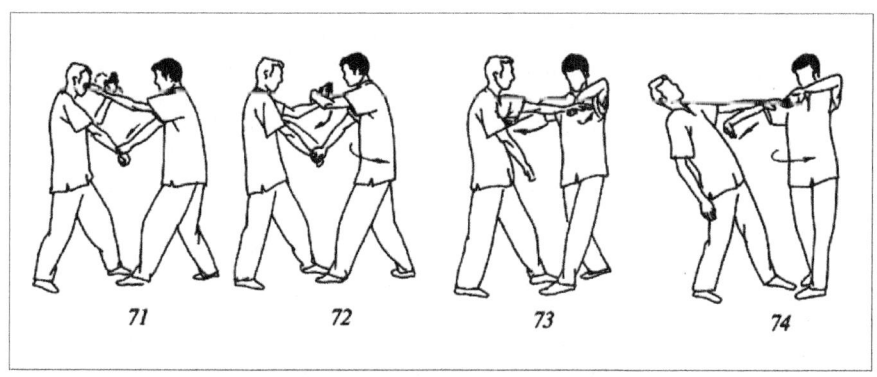

71 *72* *73* *74*

Defense of the low external and high internal "gates"

The opponent is attacking with the direct kick with the left foot to the lower part of the body. Making a step with the right foot to the right, neutralize the attack with the Gan Sau block with the left hand (Fig. 75). Lowering the foot on the ground, the opponent makes a direct punch to the head with the right fist, which you block with the right hand, making the Jum Sau movement (Fig. 76, 77). Grab the right hand of the opponent at the wrist with the left hand and pull it toward you while counterattacking with the edge right palm to the throat (Fig. 78). Continuing to pull the opponent at the grabbed hand, make a kick with the left foot to the knee joint of his left leg (Fig. 79).

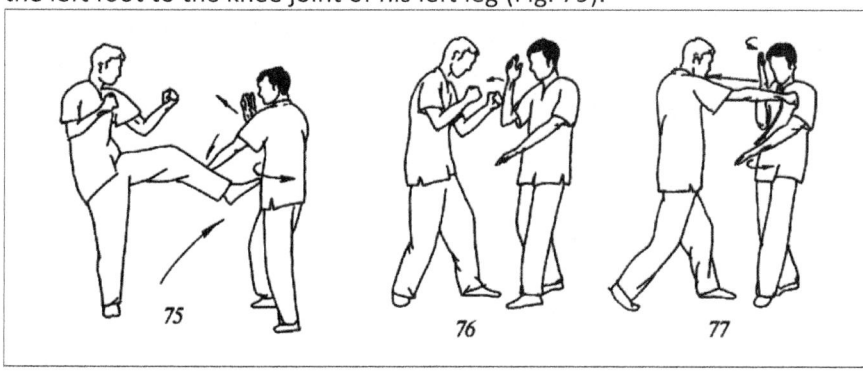

75 *76* *77*

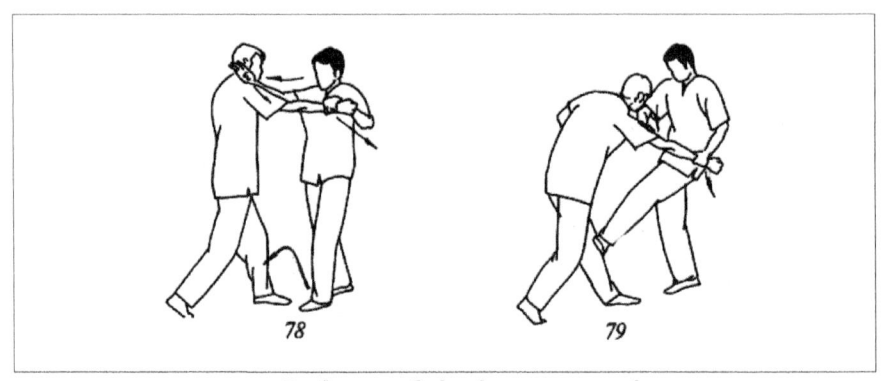

Defense of the low external and high internal "gates"

From the starting position (Fig. 80) the opponent attacks, making a direct kick with the left foot to the lower part of the torso. Neutralize attack with the left hand, making the Gum Sau block (Fig. 81). Lowering the foot on the ground and making a step forward (Fig. 82), the opponent makes the circle kick with the right leg to the hip area of the forward leg. Raise your left leg up, blocking the kick (Fig.83), and then, making a step with the left foot forward, counterattack with a direct punch with the left fist to the head (Fig. 84). Make a direct punch with the right hand to the head (Fig.85).

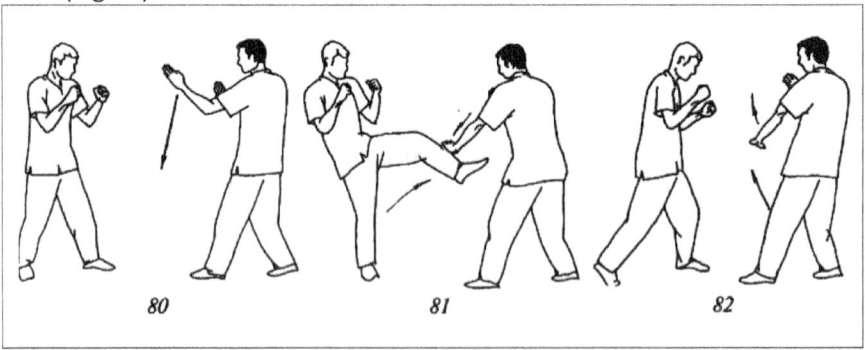

83 *84* *85*

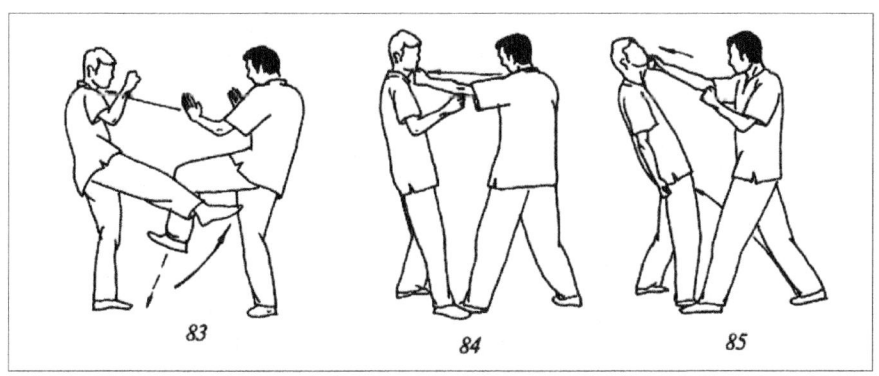

    This chapter provides only the simplest options of attack and defense, which adequately illustrate the principles of the material. After a sufficient study of the presented combinations, you can start up composing your own combinations.

Important points:

- At the first stage of training you should slowly learn the training combinations,
- At the second stage, all movements are made with force and quickly,
- At the third stage all technique movements are worked out at the sparring. The task of the attacker is to make the pre-agreed combination at the free movement. The task of defender is to be able to protect and make a certain counterattack.
- At the fourth stage. The attacker in the sparring can use pre-agreed combinations only. The defender firstly makes the defending actions, but in his counterattack can also use a series of strikes, throws, grabbs etc.
- The fifth stage is a freestyle fight.

Chapter 10
Sticky hands - Chi Sau

Chi Sau (in Chinese "sticky hands") - these exercises develop the ability to feel and control the hands of the opponent. The sensitivity of the forearms reaches such a degree that allows guessing instinctively your opponent's next movement. The Chi Sau gives the impression of a continuous movement consisting of the wave and flow of internal energy and a complete mental relaxation where the body is given the opportunity to anticipate the disclosure in the defense of the opponent. The constant practice of these exercises allows the fighter of Wing Chun instantly, reflexively make an adequate movement in response to any action of the opponent.

There are two basic types of Chi Sau:
1). Dang Chi Sau,
2). Shuang Chi Sau,

The first type includes the exercises made with one hand. It is studied at the initial stage of mastering the technique of Wing Chun Kuen and creates the basis for mastering of more complex types of "Sticky hands".

The basic idea of **Dang Chi Sau** is to "stick" with the forearm to the hand of your opponent and to try to grab the control over the central line.

Shuang Chi Sau - is a more complex form of "Sticky hands". The exercises included in this group teach the simultaneous actions of two hands. They help to develop a sense of contact, learn the correct application of force and the proper use of the angles of its use.

Dang Chi Sau

Starting position: partners are located opposite each other at the arm's length in the frontal Yee Gee Kim Yuen Ma stance. You keep the right hand in the Tan Sau position, and your partner keeps his left hand in the Fook Sau position (Fig. 1). Make a slow punch with the right vertical palm forwards. Your partner blocks this movement, making the Gum Sau downwards. It is necessary to try to ensure that during this movement the hands would not lose the contact with each other (Fig. 2). Without stopping the opponent makes a direct punch with the left fist to the face or chest. Without breaking the contact of the hands, make the Bong Sau block (Fig. 3). Return to the starting position (Fig. 4).

Further the cycle is repeated. Having repeated the exercise a number of times, change roles with your partner. Then make the exercise with other hands.

There are ways which help to learn the making of instant attacks at the time of appearing of the voids in the defense of the opponent.

Exercise

Partners are located opposite each other and train the Dang Chi Sau exercise (Fig.5). At some point, the opponent breaks the connection of your hands to strike the lower part of your body (Fig. 6). Feeling no pressure from his hand, instantly make a strike to his chest (Fig. 7).

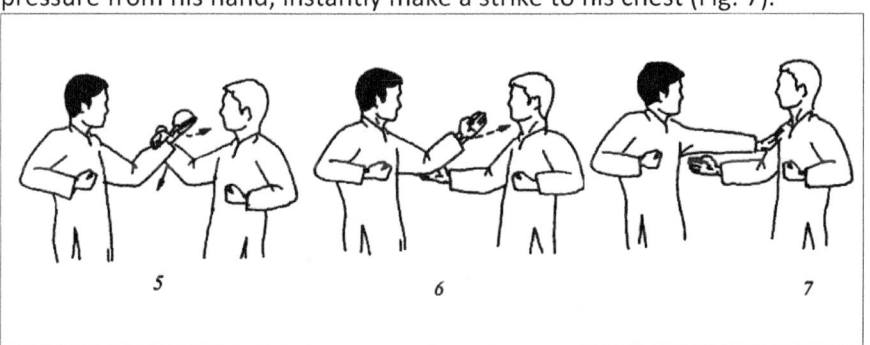

For a thorough training of the Chi Sau technique in Wing Chun Kuen special tools are often use. This simulator is a straight rod with a diameter of 3 cm, clipped to the horizontal axis, or to the ceiling, by the harness. To one end of the rod a weight of 1-2 kg is attached. (Fig. 8-10).

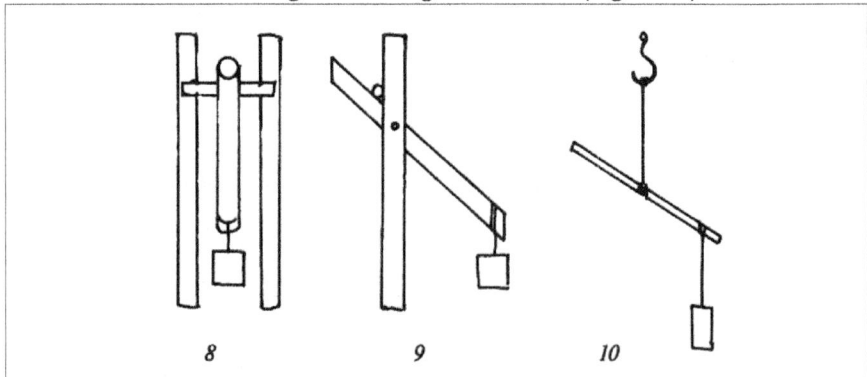

In such a simulator it is convenient to practice the Dang Chi Sau exercises in the absence of a partner (Fig.11-14).

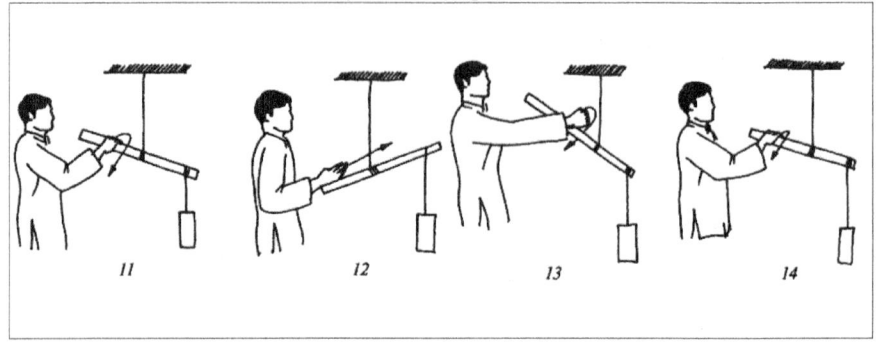

Shuang Chi Sau

Shuang Chi Sau consists of several groups of exercises. Initially the Poon Sau technique is studied, which in Chinese means "Rotating arms".

Starting position: partners are located opposite each other at arm's length in the frontal Yee Gee Kim Yuen Ma stance. You keep the right hand in the Bong Sau position, and the left - in the Tan Sau position. Your partner keeps both hands in the Fook Sau position (Fig. 15).

The exercise begins with the change of the position of your hands on the opposite, i.e. the right hand takes the Tan Sau position, and the left - the Bong Sau position. Your partner does not change the position of his hands, he just follows your movements (Fig. 16). You change the position of the hands again to the initial one. He sticks with his hands to your hands and continues to follow your movements (Fig. 17).

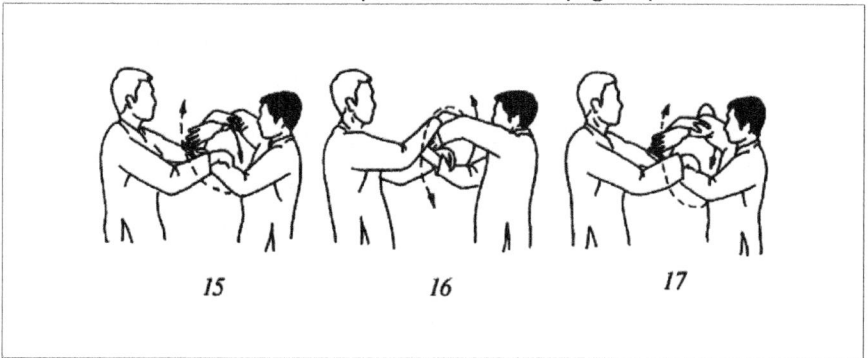

15   *16*   *17*

Repeat the cycle a number of times, then change roles with your partner.

Poon Sau Exercise with attacks

Partners are located opposite each other and make the Shuang Chi Sau exercise (Fig. 18). Your partner suddenly makes a punch with the palm forward. You feel the movement of his hands and without breaking the contact with the attacking limb, make the Gum Sau block (Fig. 19). With the left fist make a direct punch to the head or chest. The opponent without breaking the contact with your left hand makes the Tan Sau block (Fig. 20).

You make the Shuang Chi Sau exercises again (Fig. 21). After a while, without negotiating one partner makes his attack with the palm forwards, etc.

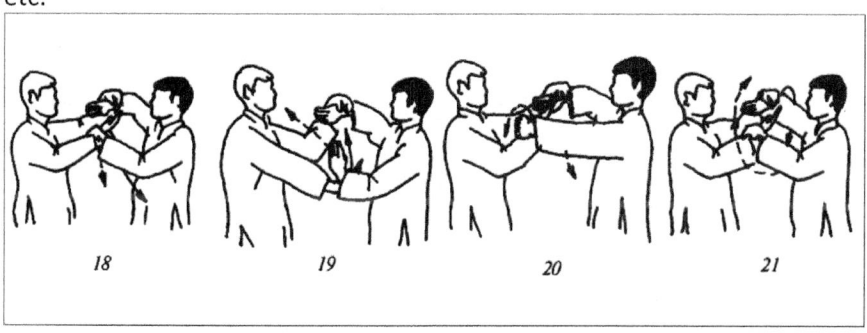

18   *19*   *20*   *21*

Exercises "Sticky legs" - Chi Gerk

The "Sticky legs" technique is a set of paired exercises, the meaning of which is similar to the Chi Sau exercises, and allows using effectively the legs in the close combat. These techniques are unique and are an integral part of the Wing Chun Kuen style.

It is very important to solve two problems in any fight:

1). It is important to monitor the opponent's legs constantly, to prevent him to make movement, kicks, and steps or sweeps.

2). If the opponent kicks at the close distance, it is often becomes impossible to make a standard hand block. The fighter of Wing Chun blocks the attack with his leg and then strikes back with it. Thereby restoring the balance.

These problems are solved with the help of the Chi Gerk exercises, which gives a huge advantage in the close combat.

Exercise # 1

Starting position: take the position in front of each other at arm's length, which are connected at the lock (Fig.22). Make a direct kick with the right foot at the abdomen level. The partner blocks the kick with the Tan Gerk movement from the outside - inside (Fig.23). Blocking is not rigid, but a mild diversion of the attacking limb to the side. Then the partner makes a side kick to your supporting leg. Moving the foot down take the foot down and to the side (Fig.24).

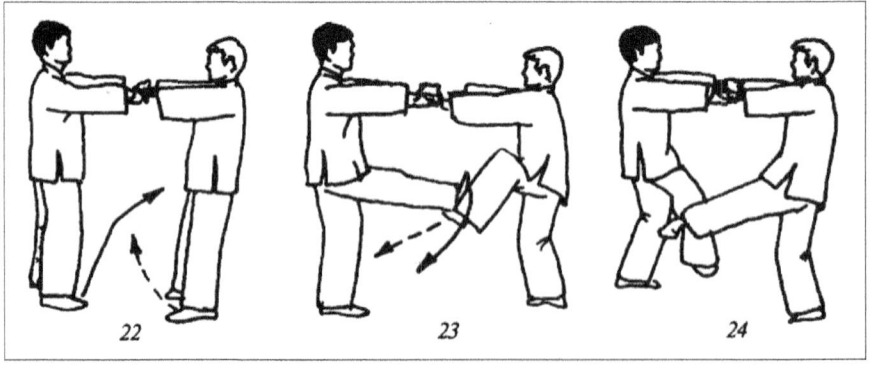

22   23   24

Make a direct kick with your right foot again and repeat the whole cycle of the exercise one more time.

Exercise # 2

Take the starting position (Fig.25). Partner makes a direct kick. To neutralize this attack, use the Tan Gerk block. The toe of your right foot should be turned outwards. The block is made from the inside - outside (Fig.26). After blocking make a side kick to the knee of the supporting leg of the opponent. Directing the force down and to the right, the partner neutralizes your attack (Fig.27).

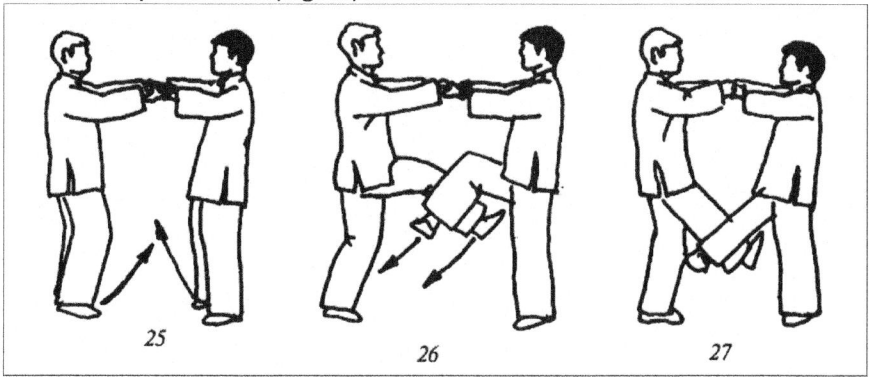

25
26
27

Without lowering the leg on the ground, repeat the exercise 10-15 times, then change the roles.

During the "Sticky legs" exercises you must ensure that the contact between your legs was never interrupted.

The skills acquired in the Chi Gerk exercises are very useful and are often used in the combat (Fig. 28, 29).

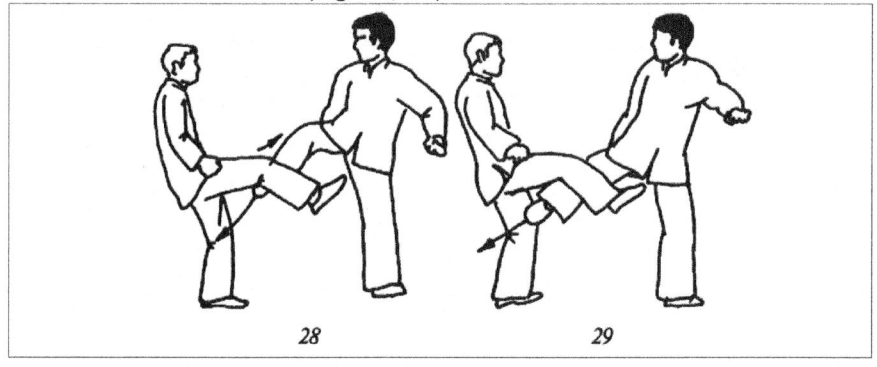

28
29

Chapter 11
Special exercises

In Wing Chun Kuen Lop Sau – "Grabbing hands" and Fon Sau – "Tiding hands" are the special exercises.

Lop Sau – is the exercise, aimed at developing the skills at grabbing the opponent's hands. This ability is extremely useful in a close combat as it allows fully control the hands of the opponent.

Fon Sau – is the exercises that can help you to learn how to tie the hands of the opponent. If during the conduct of the fight, you will be able to pin down the opponent's hands, his ability to defend and attack significantly decrease. This technique is generally used against those who are accustomed to block first and then to counterattack.

Lop Sau

Basic exercises

Starting position: partners are located opposite each other at arm's length in the frontal Yee Gee Kim Yuen Ma stance.

The partner with his right hand presses on your right hand and removes it downwards. Immediately thereafter, he lands a direct punch to the face with his left fist. You use the right Bong Sau to neutralize this attack. Hedge with the left hand against the second possible attack (Fig. 1).

With the left hand intercept the attacking limb and pull it down. Immediately afterwards make a direct punch with the right fist to the face. The opponent makes the left Bong Sau and blocks your attack (Fig.2).

With the right hand he intercepts your attacking limb and pulls it down. Immediately afterwards he makes a direct punch with the left fist to the head. You block again this punch with the right Bong Sau (Fig. 4).

| 1 | 2 | 3 | 4 |

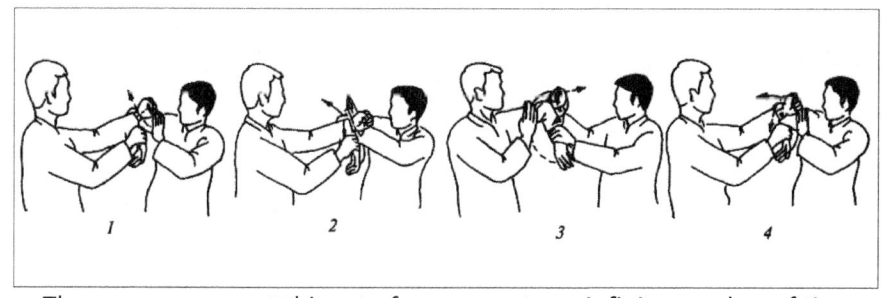

Thus you can repeat this set of movements an infinite number of times.

On the basis of the basic exercise all the other Lop Sau techniques are built. Consider the most common ones:

Exercise # 1

From the starting position the opponent makes a direct punch to the face with his right fist. Make the left Bong Sau (Fig. 5). Turn the torso to the left and with the right hand make the Biu Sau movement – poking movement with the fingers forward - up from under your left hand. In order to defend from your attack the opponent and stretches his right arm forward, and unclenching the fist, makes the Biu Sau movement (Fig. 6). Grab your opponent's right hand with your right hand and pull it down. At the same time make a direct punch to the face with the left fist. He puts under the punch his left hand, thus making the Wu Sau block (Fig. 7). With the left hand grab his left arm and take it down. With the right fist make a direct punch to the face. The opponent turns to the right and makes the left Bong Sau, blocks your attack (Fig. 8). With his right hand he catches your right hand and lowers it down (Fig. 9). With the left fist he makes a direct punch to the head. Turn left and make the right Bong Sau (Fig. 10).

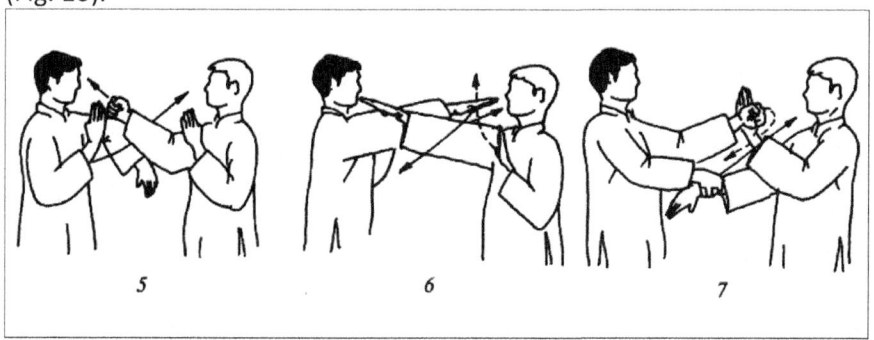

| 5 | 6 | 7 |

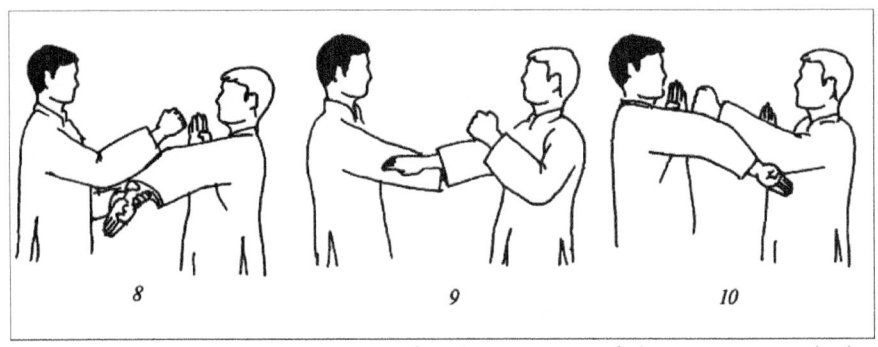

You are in the starting position for the training of the exercise with the other hand. Repeat this set of movements a number of times, and then change the roles with your partner.

Exercise # 2

From the starting position the opponent makes a direct punch to the face with the right fist. Make the left Bong Sau (Fig. 11). With the right hand intercept the attacking limb and lower it down (Fig. 12). Moving the left arm in an arc, make the side chopping punch to the neck of the opponent with the edge of the hand. With the left hand he makes the Pak Sau block and neutralizes your attack (Fig. 13). With the left fist the opponent makes a direct punch to the face. Turn left and make the right Bong Sau (Fig. 14).

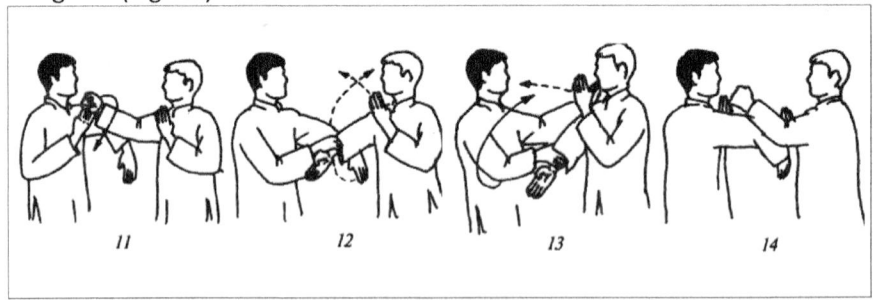

You are in the starting position for training the exercise with the other arm. Repeat this set of movements a number of times, then change the roles with your partner.

Exercise # 3

With the left fist make a direct punch to the face. The opponent makes the right Bong Sau (Fig. 15). With the left hand grab his left arm (Fig. 16). Pull down the grabbed limb and to yourself (Fig. 17). With the right fist make a direct punch to the face. The opponent makes the left Bong Sau (Fig. 18). Make this exercise with the other hand.

15 16 17 18

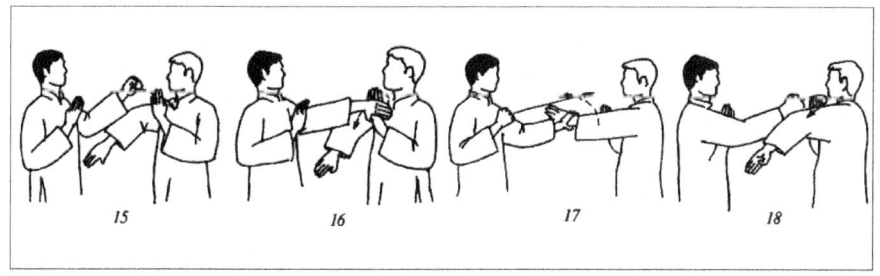

Repeat this set of movements a number of times, then change the roles with your partner.

Fon Sau

The techniques of Fon Sau are effective only when the opponent makes the block first and then the counterattack. If he defends and attacks at the same time, the shackling of his hands is quite difficult.

These techniques are appropriate to apply, in condition of a constant practice of Chi Sau and Lop Sau.

This chapter provides two basic Fon Sau methods, on the basis of which it is possible to build more complex forms of snare of the opponent's hands.

Exercise # 1

With the right fist make a direct punch to the face of the opponent (Fig. 19). To neutralize your attack he uses the right Tan Sau (Fig. 20). With the right hand grab his arm and lower it down. At the same time make a direct punch to the face with the left fist. The opponent makes the Tan Sau block again with the left hand (Fig. 21). With the left hand grab his arm and lower it down. Your opponent's hands will be crossed with each other. After that, with the right fist make a direct punch to the head (Fig. 22).

19 20 21 22

Exercise # 2

With the right fist make a direct punch to the face. The opponent blocks the attack with the left Pak Sau (Fig. 23). With his left hand he grabs your right arm and lowers it down (Fig. 24). With his left hand intercept his arm. At the same time take your right hand to you, and then make a punch to the face with the right fist. He blocks the attack with the right hand (Fig. 25). Grab his right hand with your right hand and lower it down, crossing his hands. At the same time, make a direct punch to the face with the left fist (Fig. 26).

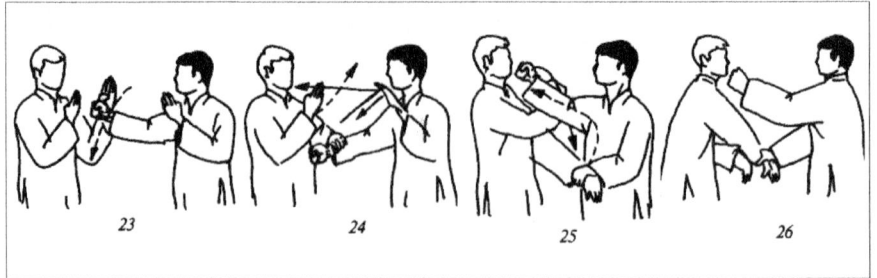

Chapter 12
Forms

In the arsenal of almost any style of Wushu are forms (Tao-lu), playing the role of technical and tactical training of the fighter. They are a set of strikes, selected by taking into account the increasing of complexity of training and change of tactical missions in the combat.

InWing Chun all the Tao-lu are not as spectacular as the forms of other styles, but they have very practical meaning and are designed to fulfill the clearly marked tactical tasks. In the Siu Lim Tao form the basic principles and the technical elements of defense and counterattack are worked out. The Chum Kiu trains the entry into the opponent's defense and work against several attackers. In the Biu Jee form the secrets of attacks on vulnerable points on the human body are revealed and the angles of their application are practiced.

Siu Lim Tao
"The Form of a Small Idea"

Siu Lim Tao - is the most famous form in Wing Chun Kuen. It presents the basic techniques and principles of the defense of the central line and counterattack techniques. Almost all the movements are made in a slightly slow pace. It is necessary to watch that the movement would be made smoothly without jerking and excessive muscle tension. After the complex is well developed, it can be trained standing on one leg.

Siu Lim Tao consists of ten parts:
1). Initial form;
2). Crossing of arms;
3). Direct punch - rotating hand;
4). Three bows to the Buddha;
5). Gum Sau - Biu Jee poke with fingers;
6). Pak Sau - a direct punch with the palm;
7). Tan Sau - Gan Sau;
8). Bong Sau;
9). Freeing hand - "Three Stars" Strike;
10).The final form.

Part 1
Initial form

Starting position: stand straight, the toes are brought together, arms down at the sides (Fig. 1). Squeeze the hands into fists and raise them to the chest (Fig.2,3). Bend your knees (Fig. 4). Dilute the toes outwardly at an angle of 90 degrees. Heels remain on the place (Fig. 5). Spread the heels to the external sides. You are in the Yee Gee Kim Yuen Ma stance (Fig. 6, 7).

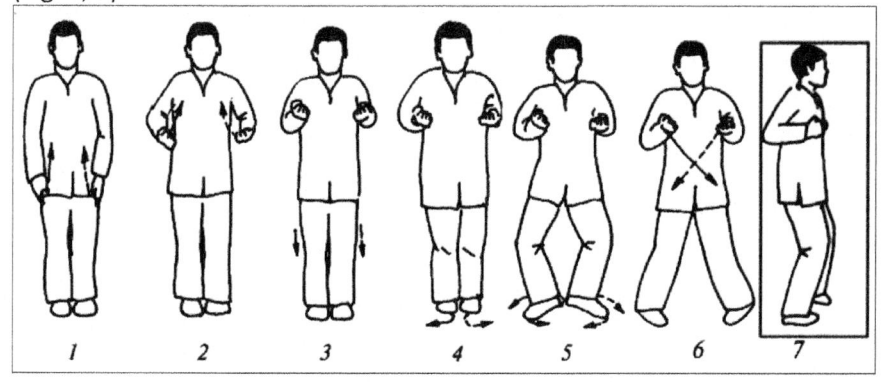

Part 2
Crossing hands

Unclench the fists and move both hands from the chest down. During the movement, the forearms are crossed with each other, the left hand is over the right hand (Fig. 8). Lift up the crossed hands, fingertips are on the same level with the nose (Fig. 9). Squeeze the hand into fists and move them to the chest (Fig. 10).

Part 3
Direct punch with the fist - rotating hand

Move the left fist to the middle part of the chest and moving it forward, make a direct punch to the face (Fig. 11, 12). Unclench the fist and turn the palm up (Fig.13, 14). Make the rotational movement of the hand clockwise, squeeze it into a fist and move to the chest (Fig.15-18).

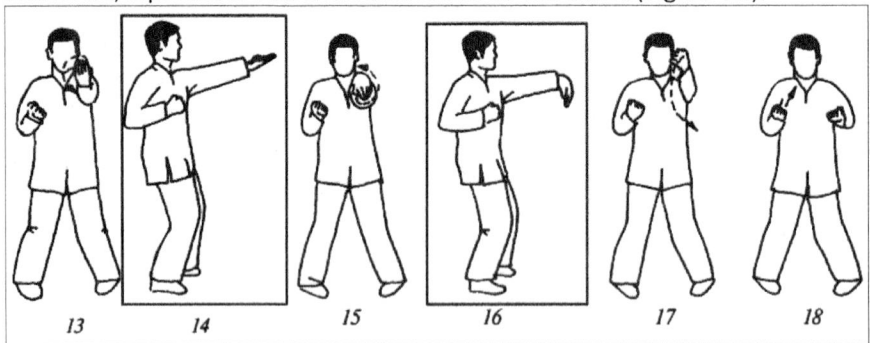

Repeat all the movements of this part of the form with the right hand (Fig.19-23).

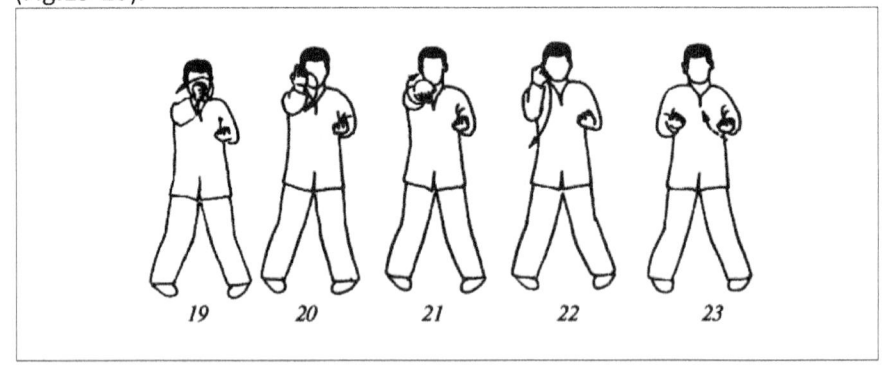

Part 4
Three bows to Buddha

Unclench the left fist and slowly moving the hand from the chest forward make the Tan Sau block (Fig.24-26). Rotating the hand clockwise, make the Huen Sau block and fix the hand in the vertical Wu Sau position (Fig.27, 28). Without changing the position, move the hand to the chest (Fig.29-31). Bend the arm at the wrist. The hand takes the Fook Sau position. Without changing the position, move the hand forward (Fig.32-34). The hand is rotating clockwise and takes the Wu Sau position (Fig. 35). Take the hand to the chest (Fig. 36). Bend your arm at the wrist. The hand takes the Fook Sau position. Without changing the position, move the hand forward (Fig.37, 38). The hand is rotating clockwise and takes the Wu Sau position (Fig. 39). Take the hand to the chest (Fig. 40).

From the middle part of the chest make the Pak Sau block with the left palm. Ensure that your hand does not go beyond the line of the body (Fig. 41). Bring the hand to the middle part of the chest (Fig.42). Straighten the arm at the elbow and make a direct punch with the left palm forward at the face level (Fig.43). Expand the palm up (Fig.44). Rotate the hand in the wrist in a clockwise direction, and then squeeze it into a fist and move to the chest (Fig.44-47).

24 25 26 27 28 29

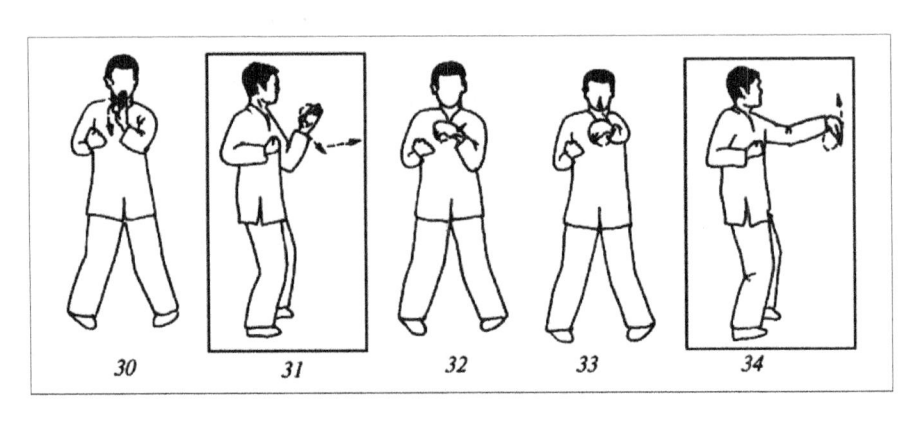

30   31   32   33   34

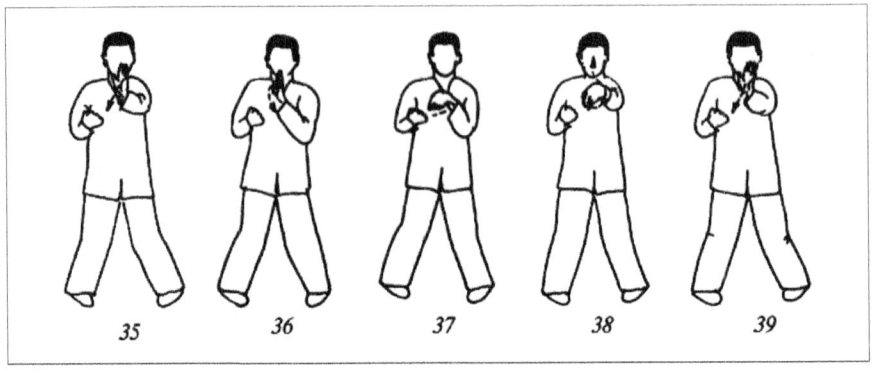

35   36   37   38   39

40   41   42   43   44

106

45 46 47

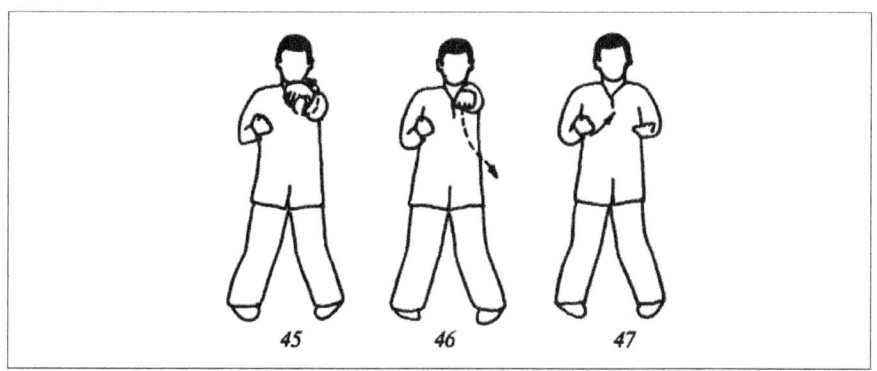

Repeat all the movements of this part of the form with the right hand (Fig.48-67).

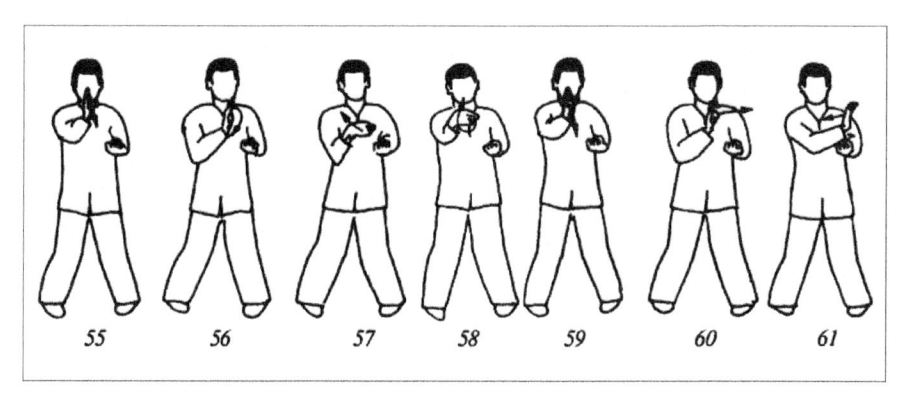

48 49 50 51 52 53 54

55 56 57 58 59 60 61

| 62 | 63 | 64 | 65 | 66 | 67 |

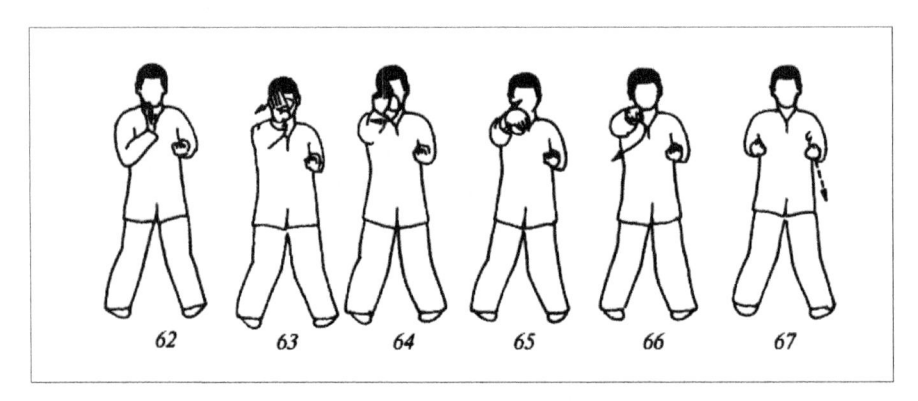

Part 5

Gum Sau – Biu Jee poke with fingers

Lower the left arm down, making the Gum Sau block from the side (Fig.68). Make a similar movement with the right hand (Fig.69).

Bend the elbows to swing then simultaneously make the push with the palms back-down (Fig.70-72). Raise both hands along the sides to the chest (Fig.73). With both hands make the blocking Gum Sau movement down in front of you (Fig.74, 75).

Raise both arms, bend your elbows and place them horizontally in front of the chest. The left hand is placed over the right hand (Fig.76).

Spread both hands to the sides at the shoulder level (Fig.77).

Place the bent at the elbows arms in front of the chest. The right hand is over the left hand (Fig.78). Through the crossed position the hands take the position with fingers forward (Fig.79). Expand the hands, palms up, and place them at the level of the chin (Fig.80, 81). With both hands make the covering movement, turning them down (Fig.82, 83).

With the stretched fingers of both hands, make a poking movement forward at the face level (Fig.84, 85). Make the low block with both palms down in front of you (Fig.86, 87). Give both hands the "Hook" form and lift to the chin level (Fig.88, 89). Squeeze the hands into fists and move them to the chest (Fig.90, 91).

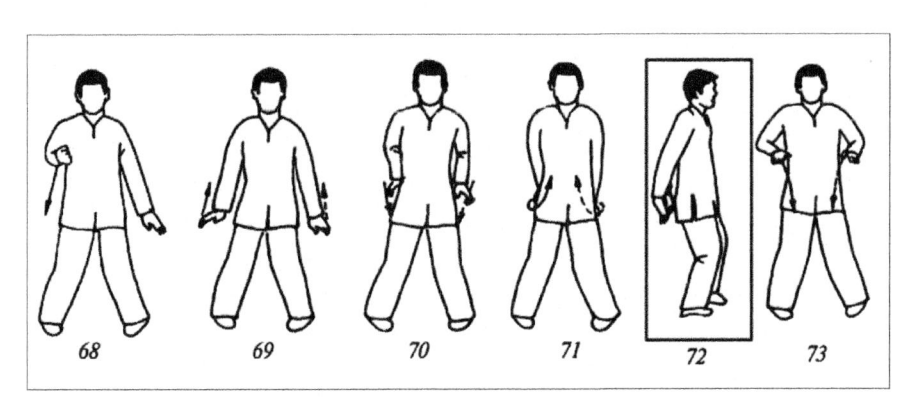

68 69 70 71 72 73

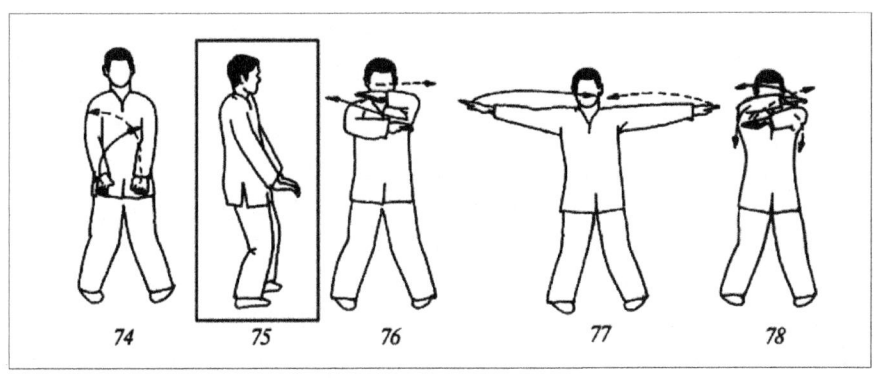

74 75 76 77 78

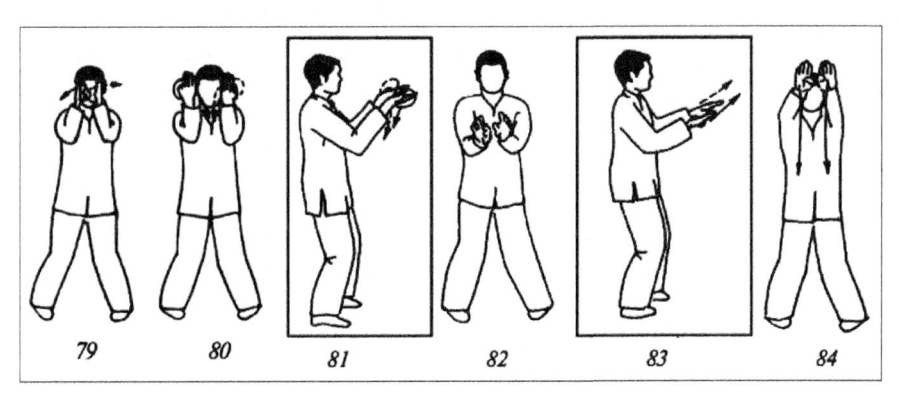

79 80 81 82 83 84

109

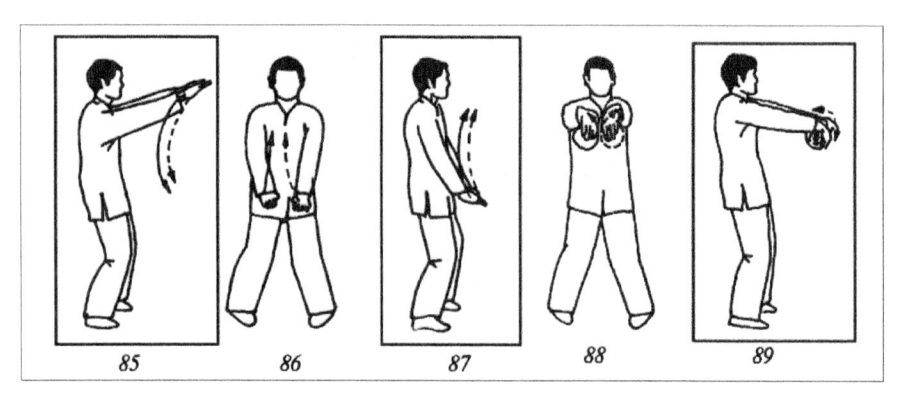

Part 6
Pak Sau - a direct punch with the palm

With the left palm, make the Pak Sau block to the right (Fig.92). Move the hand to the left shoulder (Fig.93). From this position, with the left palm make a direct punch forward at the face level. The fingers are directed to the left (Fig.94, 95).

Expand the palm up (Fig.96). Rotate the hand clockwise, squeeze it into a fist and move to the chest (Fig.97-99).

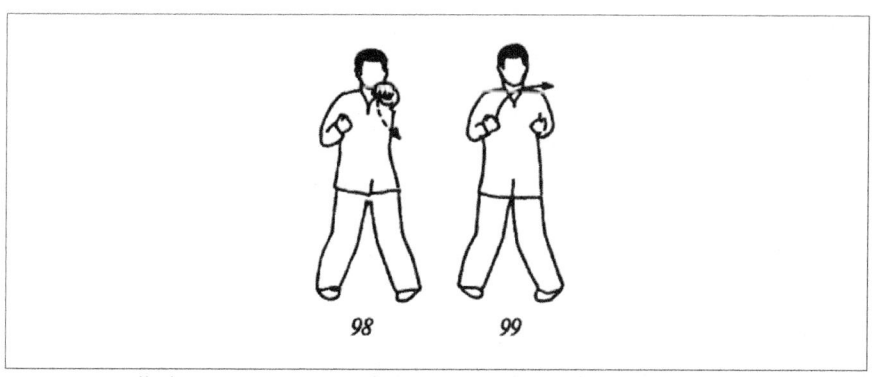

98   99

Repeat all the movements of this part of the form with the right hand (Fig.100-105).

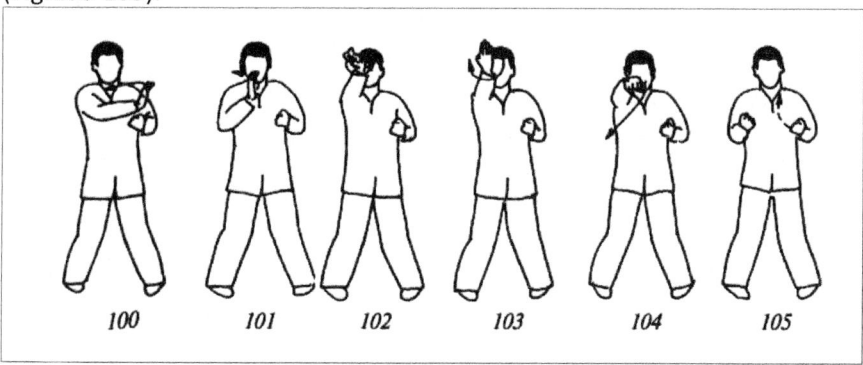

100   101   102   103   104   105

Part 7

Tan Sau - Gan Sau

With the left hand, make the Tan Sau block (Fig.106, 107). Lower the arm down and make the Gan Sau block (Fig.108, 109). Moving the left forearm from the outside upwards make the Jum Sau block (Fig.110, 111). Rotate the hand at the wrist clockwise then make a direct punch with the palm forward at the face level. Fingers are directed to the left during the punch (Fig.112, 113).

The left hand takes the Tan Sau form (Fig.114). Rotate the hand clockwise, then squeeze it into a fist and move to the chest (Fig.114-117).

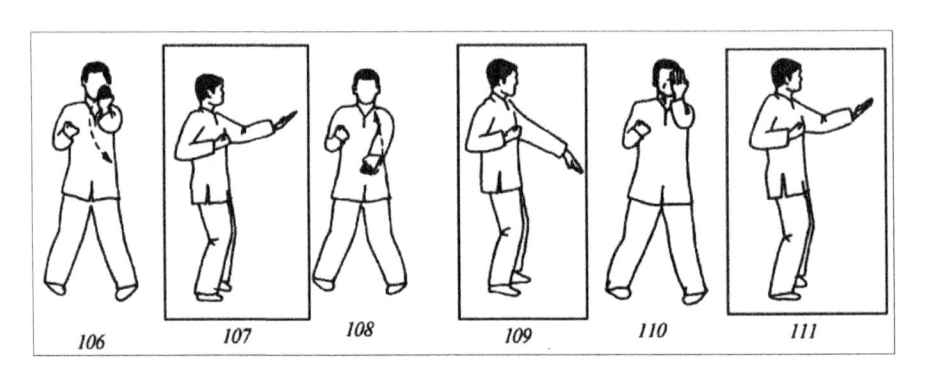

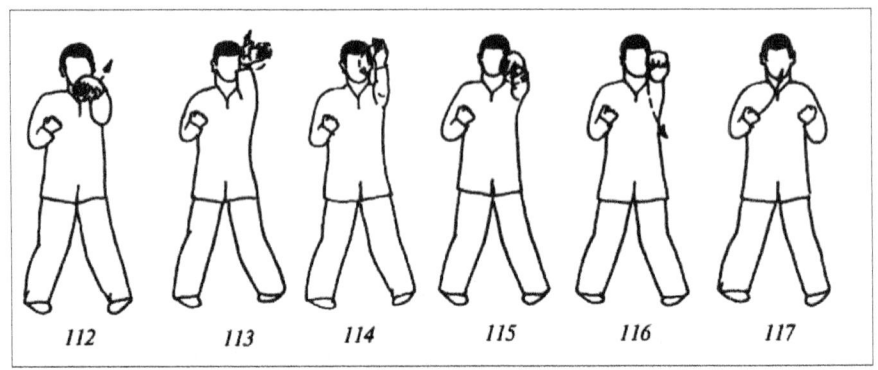

Repeat all the movements of this part of the form with the right hand (Fig.118-125).

Part 8

Bong Sau

With the left hand make the Bong Sau block (Fig.126, 127). Lower the left elbow down and make the left Tan Sau (Fig.128). Straighten the arm at the elbow and make a direct punch with the palm at the face level. Fingers are directed downwards (Fig.129, 130).

Rotate the hand clockwise, then squeeze it into a fist and move to the chest (Fig.131-133).

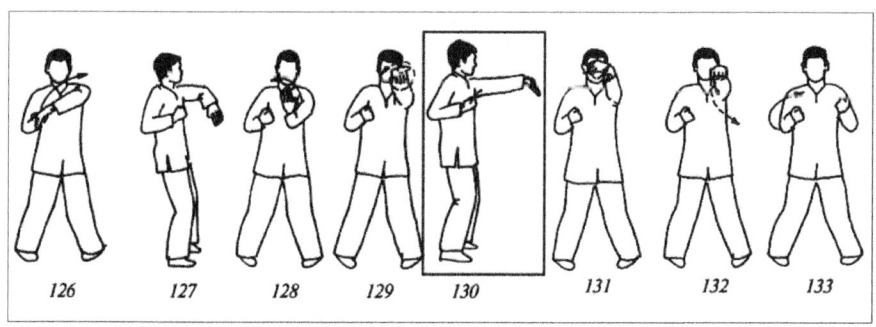

| 126 | 127 | 128 | 129 | 130 | 131 | 132 | 133 |

Repeat all the movements of this part of the form with the right hand (Fig.134-139).

| 134 | 135 | 136 | 137 | 138 | 139 |

Part 9

Freeing hand - "Three Stars" strike

With the left hand, make the Gan Sau block (Fig.140, 141). With the right arm make the sweeping movement along the left arm (Fig.142, 143). Make a similar movement with the left arm (Fig.144, 145). Make a similar movement with the right arm (Fig.146, 147).

With his left hand, make a series of three punches with the fists forward at the face level (Fig.148-150).

Expand the left hand palm up (Fig.151). Rotate the left hand clockwise, then squeeze into a fist and move to the chest (Fig.152-154).

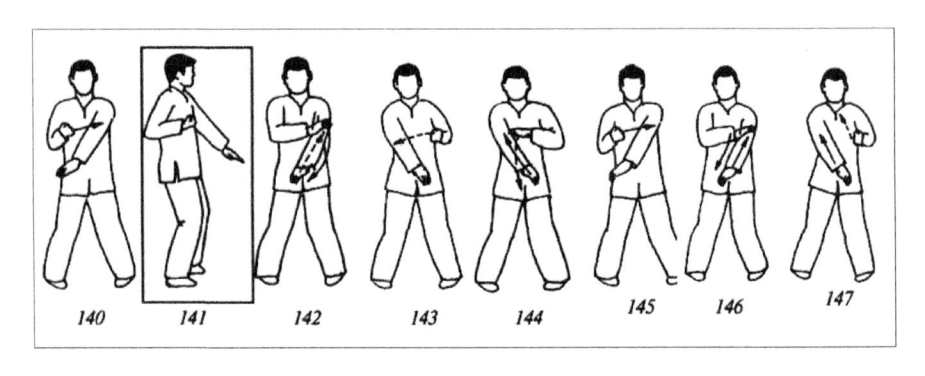

Part 10
The final form

Bring your heels together, and then move the toes to each other. Straighten the knees. Lower down the arms to the sides (Fig.155-157).

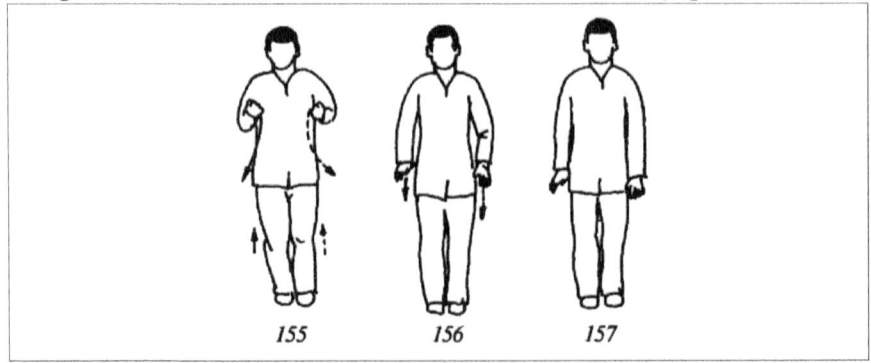

Martial combinations

Martial combinations, related to the Siu Lim Tao complex, are a base of the application technique of the school and lay the foundation for further progress in the study of Wing Chun Kuen. Before the study, it is important to master good enough the basic techniques of the style: stances, movements, strikes, defenses, and to develop the basic skills in Chi Sau and special exercises. A summary of the movements of this form, initially proposed by Master Leung Ting is given below.

Gan Sau - Chung Chui

You and your opponent are in front of each other in the same stances. The opponent takes a step with the right foot forwards and at the same time makes a direct punch with the right fist to the abdomen. With the left hand make the Gan Sau block, taking his attacking limb outwards from you. At the same time with the right fist make a direct punch to the head of the opponent (Fig.158-160).

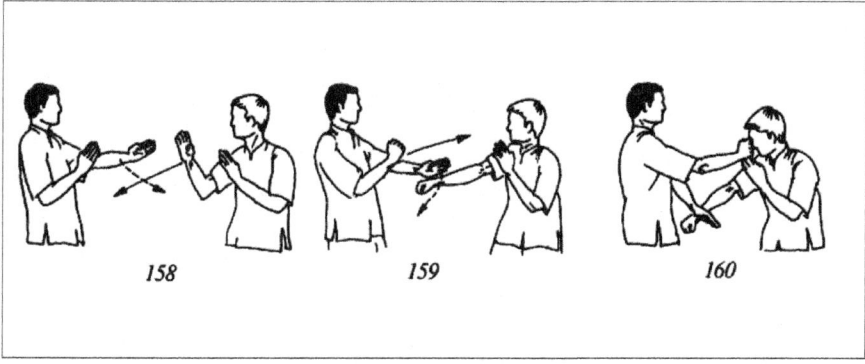

158 *159* *160*

Bong Sau - Tan Sau

You and your opponent are in front of each other in the same stances. He brings his hands to your hands from the outside, intercepts them near the wrists, and with a pressing movement lowers them down. After that, with the left hand he controls your right hand, and with the right fist makes a direct punch to the chest.

With the forearms of your hands, "stick" to the limbs of the opponent. Turn the torso to the left. With the right hand make the Bong Sau block, and with the left hand - Tan Sau. Thus you redirect the attacking force of the opponent by yourself (Fig.161-164).

161   *162*   *163*   *164*

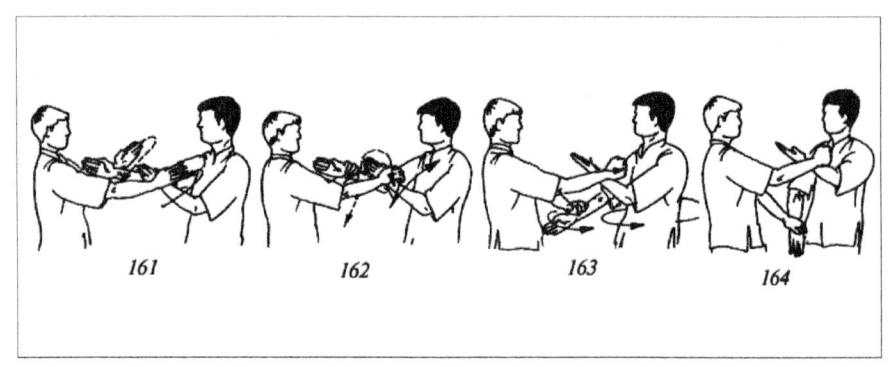

Tan Sau - Chung Chui

You and your opponent are in front of each other in the same stances. With the tight fist he makes a direct punch to the head. With the left hand make the Tan Sau block, moving the attack of the opponent by yourself. At the same time with the right fist make a direct punch to his the head. Squeeze the left hand in a fist and continuing the counterattack, make a direct punch with the left fist to the head (Fig.165-168).

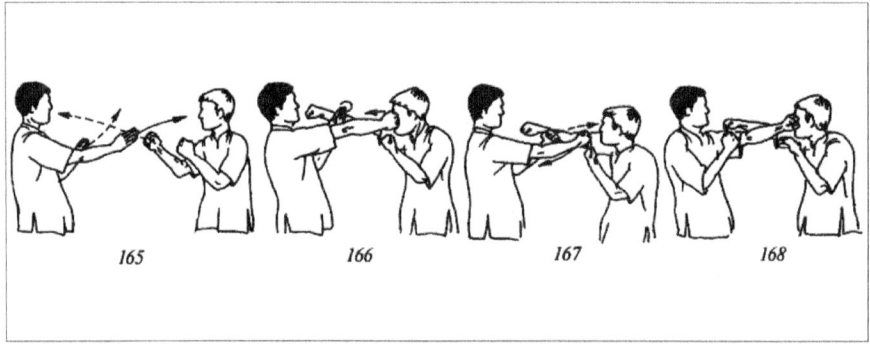

165   *166*   *167*   *168*

Chung Chui – the strike with the elbow backwards

One of the opponents is located in front of you, and makes a direct punch to the head with the right fist. At the same time another opponent approaches from behind and tries to embrace you over the arms. With the left hand, make the Tan Sau block, taking to the outside the attacking limb of the standing in front of you opponent. With the right fist make a direct Chung Chui punch to the head. After that, without stopping, bend your right arm at the elbow, turn the torso to the right and make a strike with the elbow backwards to the behind standing opponent to the solar plexus (Fig.169-172).

169   *170*

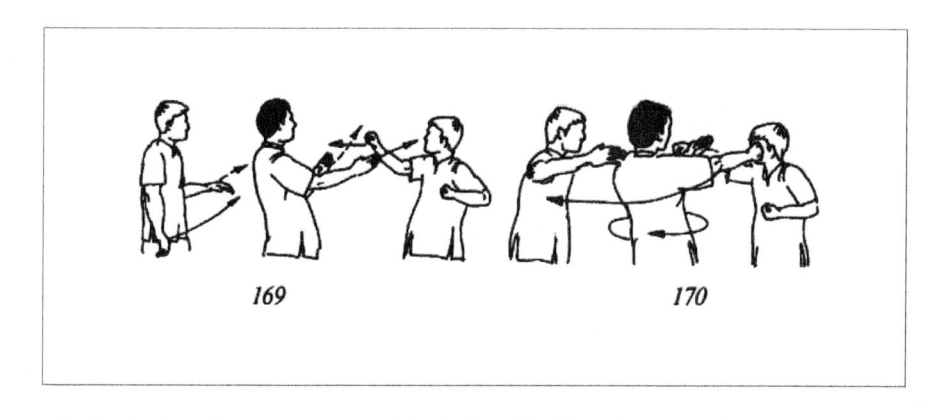

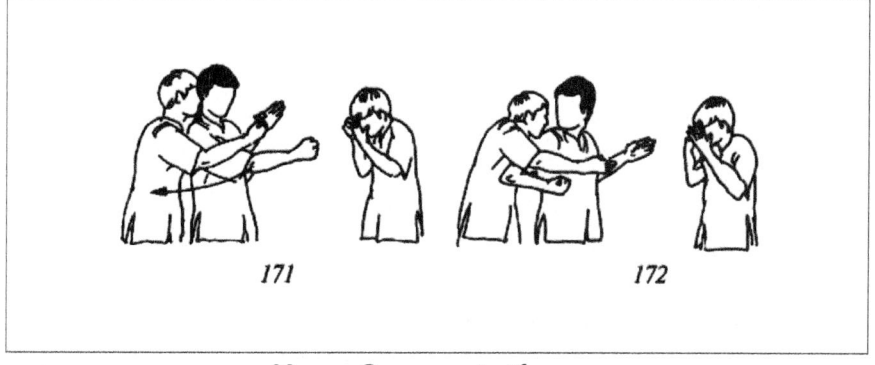

171   *172*

Huen Sau - rotating arm

This movement is the basis for the freeing from the grab of the wrists. Since in the real fights the opponent grabs your hands very often, you need to work out the suggested to your attention techniques quite well.

Option # 1

Your partner grabbed your right hand at the wrist below with his left hand. Rotating your hand inwards in a counterclockwise direction, you make an impact in the direction of the thumb of the attacking hand of the opponent. Since the thumb is the "weak link" of almost any grab, you with a minimum of efforts, free your limb. After this, in turn, make the grab of the limb of the opponent (Fig.173-177).

173 *174* *175* *176*

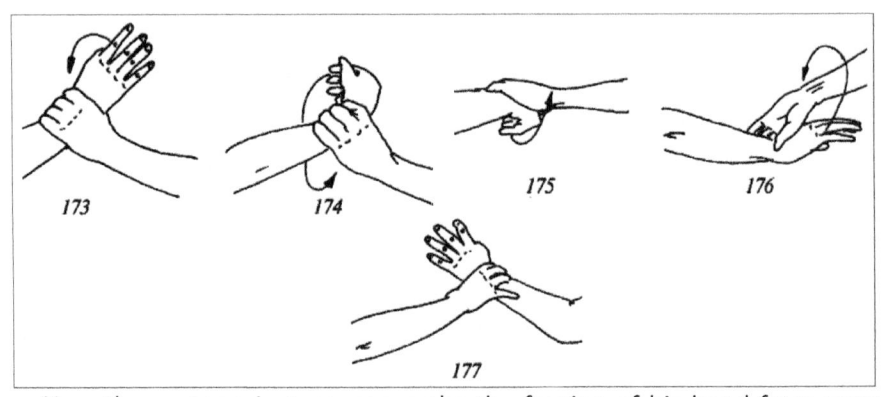

177

Now the partner, in turn, can make the freeing of his hand from your capture. Thus, it is possible to train for a long time without interruption, constantly changing roles with your partner.

Option # 2

Your partner grabbed on top your left hand at the wrist with his right hand. Rotating your wrist outwards in a counterclockwise direction, you make an impact in the direction of the thumb of the attacking hand of the opponent, and free from the grab. Then you grab the limb of the opponent (Fig.178-182). Now the partner, in turn, can make the freeing of his hand from your grab. Thus, it is possible to train for a long time without interruption, constantly changing roles with your partner.

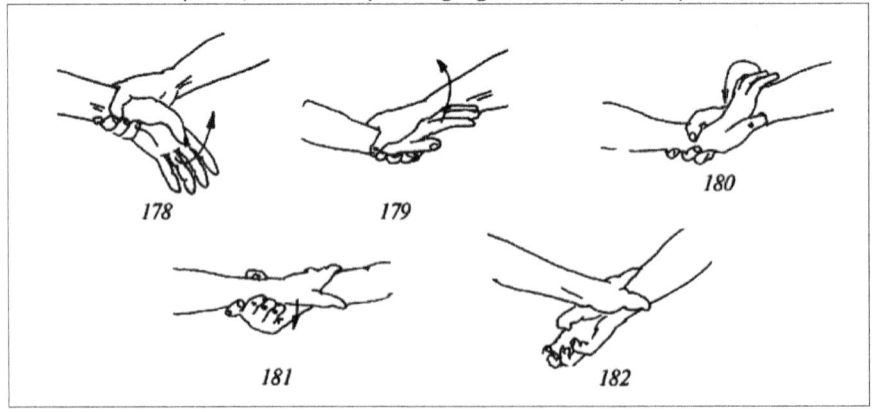

178 *179* *180*

181 *182*

Option # 3

Your partner grabbed on top your right hand with his right hand. Rotating your wrist outwards in a clockwise direction, you will reach the point to make the opponent to turn the hand with the edge of his palm up. Then, with a sharp movement lower the hand from downwards-upwards, and press down on his wrist. This will cause severe pain in his hand and force him to release the grab. You can then, in turn, grab the opponent's hand (Fig.183-187). Repeat the exercise, change roles with the partner.

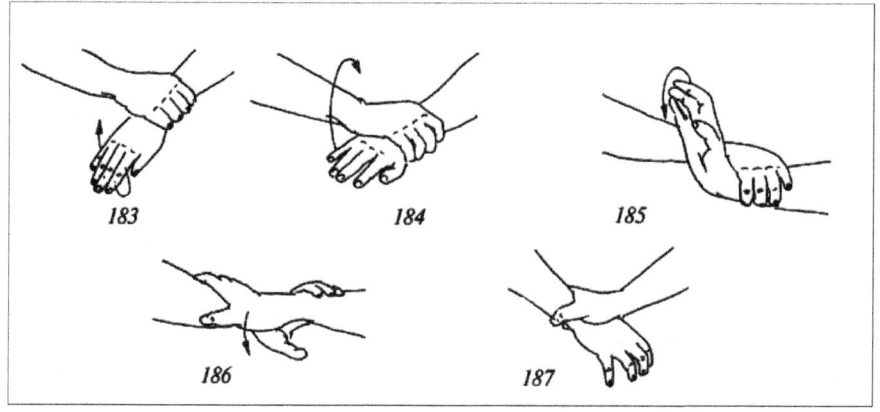

183   184   185
186   187

Option # 4

Your partner grabbed your right hand at the wrist with his right hand on top. Rotating your hand to the inside counterclockwise, you will have an impact in the direction against his thumb and free from the grab. Grab the opponent's hand, with your hand, and then repeat the exercise, changing roles with him.

Tan Sau - counterpunch
Option # 1

The opponent makes a direct punch with a vertical right fist to the head. From the starting frontal stance turn the torso to the right. Straighten forward the right hand until it touches the moving forward hand, attacking the opponent. As if you are meeting the hand of the opponent from the outside and, accompanying it in the movement, redirect the attack by yourself. This is the real Tan Sau. You use only as much force as it is necessary to divert and accompany your opponent's attacking hand. At the same time, make a direct punch with the left vertical fist to the head of the opponent (Fig.188).

Option # 2

The opponent makes a direct punch with the vertical left fist to the head. From the starting frontal stance turn the torso to the right. Straighten forward the right hand until it touches the moving forward hand, attacking the opponent. Your hand meets the opponent's hand from the inside and, accompanying it, divers the attack by yourself. At the same time, make a direct punch with the left vertical fist to the head of the opponent (Fig.189).

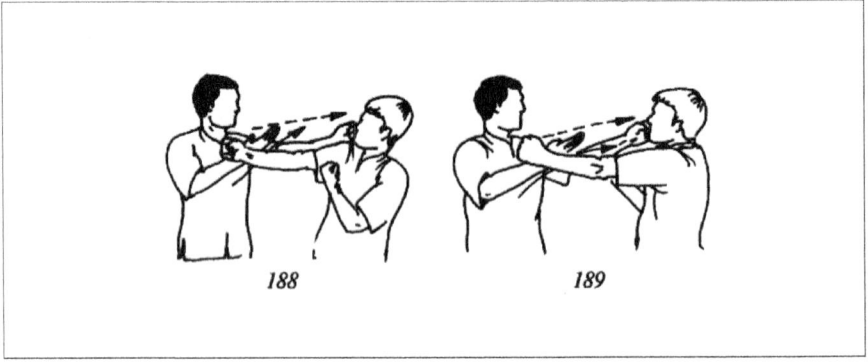

188

189

Option # 3

The opponent makes a direct punch with the vertical left fist to the head. From the starting frontal stance turn the torso to the left. With the left hand, make a diverting Tan Sau movement, thus neutralizing the attack. At the same time with the base of the right palm make a punch to his ribs at the left (Fig.190).

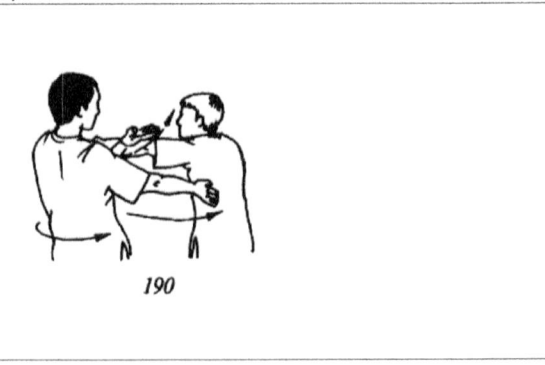

190

Fook Sau

You and your opponent stand in front of each other. The forearms touch each other, and your hand is on the outside. Bending the hand in the wrist push the limb of the opponent from the top, trying to lower it down. Immediately thereafter, with the back side of the right hand, make an upward punch from yourself to the head or neck of the opponent (Fig.191-193). This technique is effective against the fighters who are not familiar with the principles of Wing Chun. On the contrary, it will be easy to stick to your attacking limb and to make the counterattack for the master of Wing Chun Kuen, owning the methods of Chi Sau.

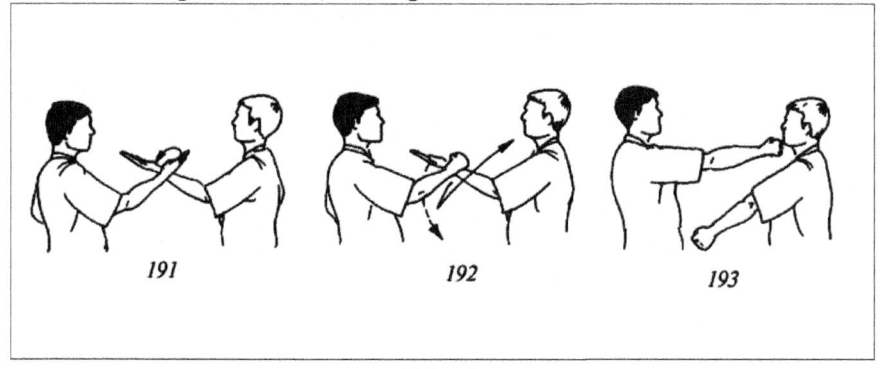

191 *192* *193*

Wu Sau

Wu Sau is one of the most important techniques of Wing Chun, the main purpose of which is to bring the opponent to a position at which it is convenient to control the attacking limb. In most cases, Wu Sau is applied in the combination with other techniques, such as Bong Sau.

The opponent makes a direct punch with the right vertical fist to the chest or head. Turn the torso to the right. With the left hand make the diverting block Bong Sau. At the same time move the right vertical hand to the outer side of his attacking hand. This is Wu Sau (Fig.194, 195). From this position you can easily control his right hand: if it is necessary, you can grab it, you can lift it down, opening the lower part of his torso for your attack, or lower it, opening the "high gates" for the subsequent counterattack.

194 *195*

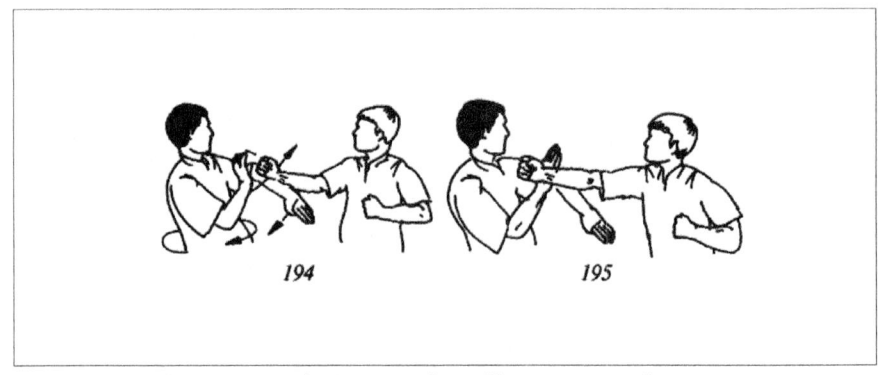

Pak Sau - The direct punch with the palm

The opponent makes a direct punch to the head with his left fist. With the right palm, make the diverting block outside – inside Pak Sau, neutralizing the opponent's attack. Then grab with the left hand his limb on top and try to lower it down, thus controlling both his hands. At the same time with the right palm make a direct punch to the face (Fig.196, 197).

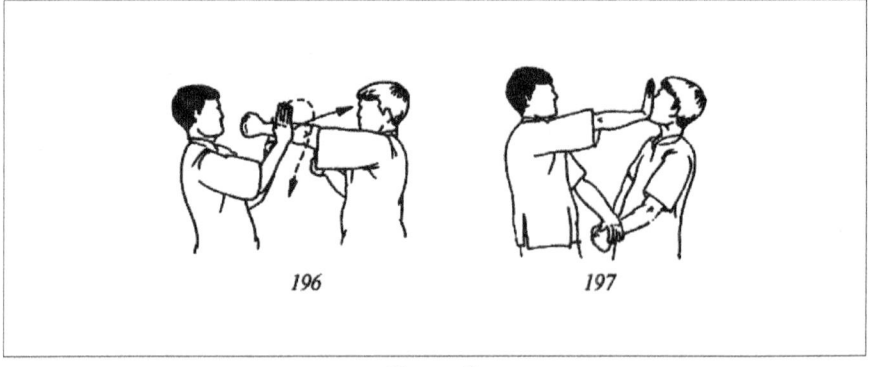

196 *197*

Gum Sau
Option # 1

The opponent came from the side and tries to make the lever of the elbow downwards. For the counteraction against this painful impact it is necessary to be proactive. Lowering the hand of the grabbed hand down, it is necessary to wrest it from the grab in the direction of the thumb of his right hand. At the same time, if the distance allows, lowering the hand down, you can make a punch with the base of the palm to the abdomen or groin (Fig.198-200).

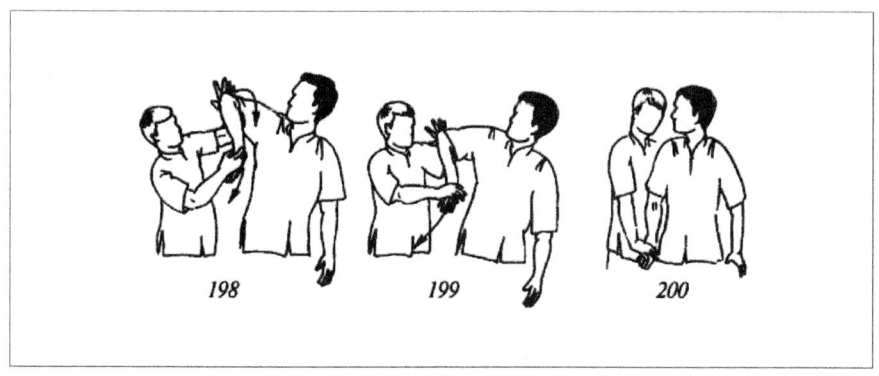

198   *199*   *200*

Option # 2

The opponent came up from behind and tries to bend the arm behind the back. For the counteraction this painful impact you must be proactive. Bend the free right arm at the elbow, and then make a punch with the base of the palm backwards to the area of the groin (Fig.201-203).

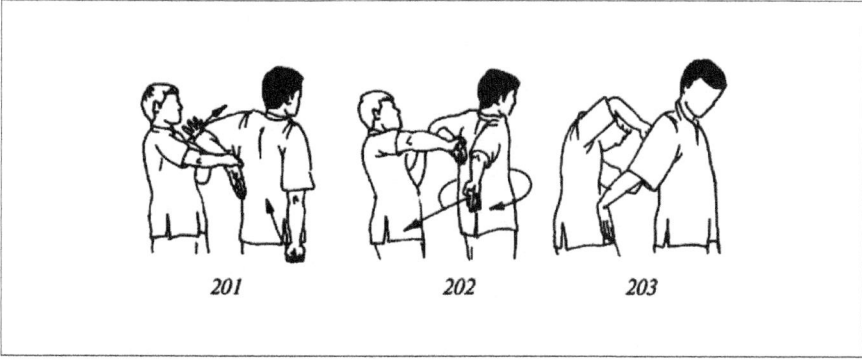

201   *202*   *203*

Option # 3

You and your opponent are in front of each other. In order to open the opponent for your attack you can circle his hands from the outside, then push quickly down and forward. Your opponent's hands, if he does not know well enough the methods of Chi Sau, will descend. This allows you to make a downward pushing punch with the bases of both palms to the chest or abdomen (Fig.204-206).

204 *205* *206*

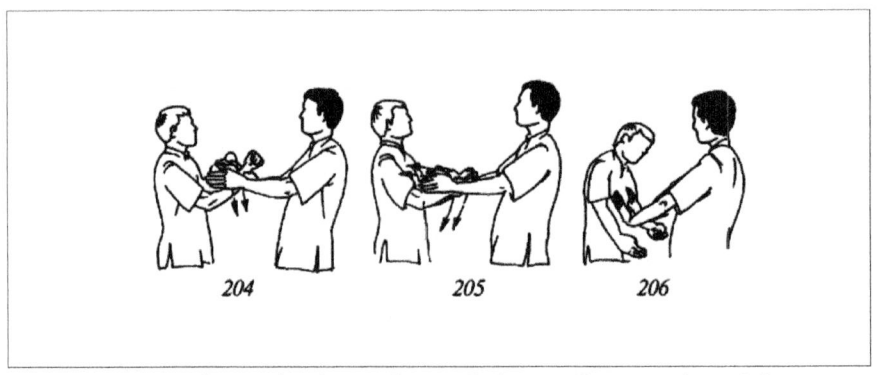

Punch with the edge of the palm to the side
Option # 1

This punch is very dangerous because of its terrible destructive force. As a rule, it must be made proactively, when the hands of the opponent will be lowered down (Fig.207).

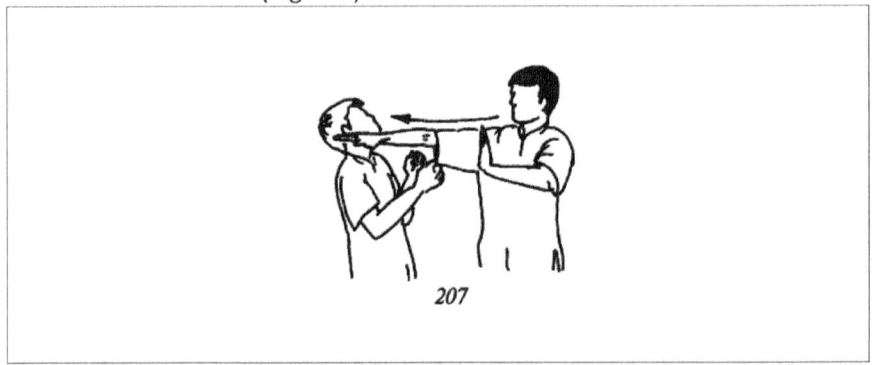

207

Option # 2

This punch can be made with the edges of both hands simultaneously in different directions. This technique is used for the simultaneous attack of two opponents located by the sides (Fig.208).

208

Jum Sau

The opponent grabbed your left arm at the Lan Sau position with his left hand (Fig.209). Trying not to change the position of the left elbow, move the forearm on a circular path in counterclockwise direction. After his attacking hand is turned upwards with the edge of the palm, lower your hand down with a sharp movement. This will cause a lot of pain in his wrist joint and force to release the grab. Then squeeze the left hand into a fist and make a direct punch to the chest or abdomen. At the same time control his left hand with the palm of the right hand (Fig.210-212).

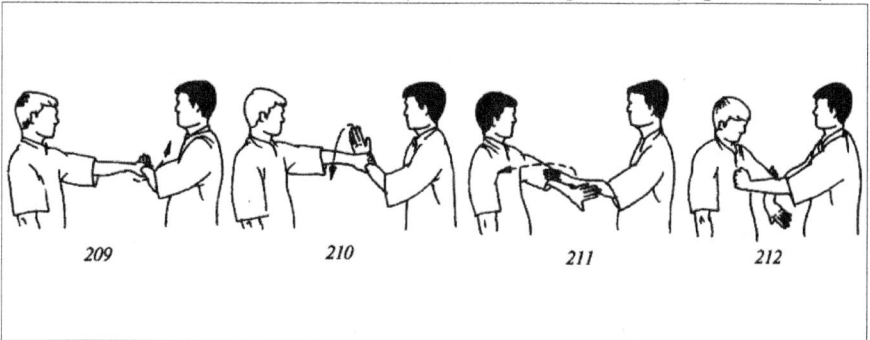

209   *210*   *211*   *212*

Tan Sau, Jut Sau and Biu Jee

The opponent makes a direct punch with the forward right fist to the head from the right-hand fighting stance. Slightly turning the upper part of the body to the right, make the Tan Sau block with the right hand and neutralize the attack. Next, turn the right hand, palm down, and make the pressing movements, removing his limb downwards. Immediately afterwards, straightening sharply the right arm at the elbow, make a direct poking punch with the fingers of the right hand to the face or throat of the opponent (Fig.213-216).

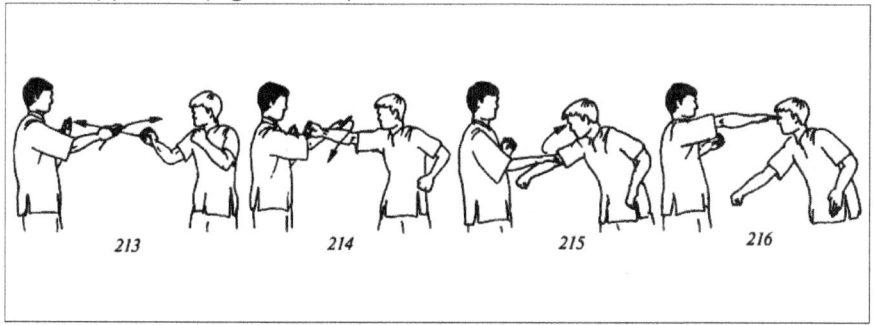

213   *214*   *215*   *216*

Double Tan Sau, double Jut Sau, double Biu Jee

You and your opponent stand in front of each other. The opponent moves both fists forwards, intending to make a strike or grab. Bring both your hands forward and make the double Tan Sau with both hands in the direction from outside to inside. You prevent the forward movement of the limbs of the opponent. Next, turn both palms down and make the pressing movement, removing his limbs downwards. Immediately thereafter, sharply straightening both arms at the elbow, make poking punches with fingers of both hands to the face or throat of the opponent (Fig. 217-220).

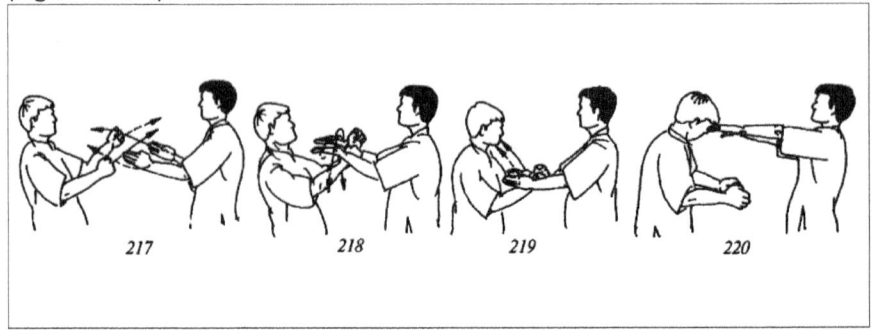

Double Gum Sau - double upward punch with the wrist

At the moment you make a double poking punch with fingers of both hands to the face, your opponent raises both hands, turning them palms up, thus preventing the implementation of your attack. Lower both hands down with a sharp movement, turning the palms down and lower the hands of the opponent. Immediately after that, raise both hands upward, making punches with the back sides of the wrists to the chin of the opponent (Fig. 221-223).

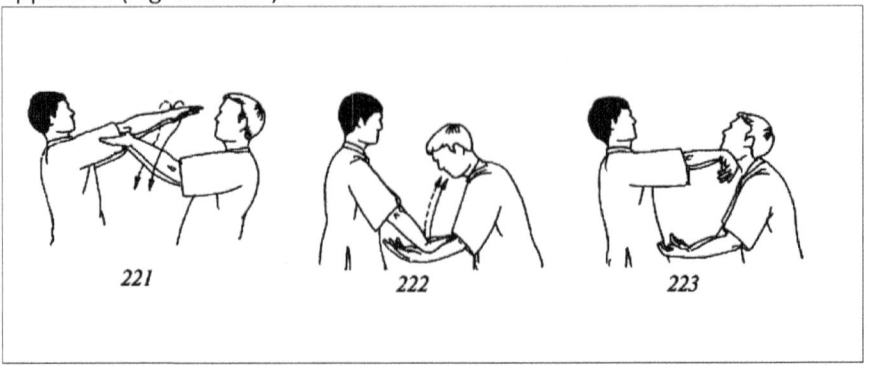

Pak Sau – punch with the palm

You and your opponent are in front of each other at arm's length. He makes a direct punch with the right fist to the head. With the left palm make a diverting Pak Sau block outwards - inwards neutralizing the attack. After that, the opponent makes another punch with the left fist. Moving the left hand in the opposite direction, take the attack to the left. With the left hand control the left hand of the opponent. With the right foot take a small step forward. With the right hand grab the opponent at the neck and pull it towards you. Simultaneously, with the base of the left palm, make a direct punch to the solar plexus (Fig.224-227).

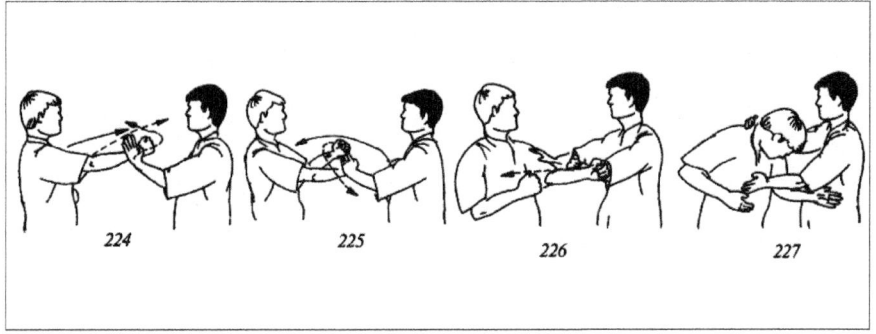

Tan Sau - punch with the fist to the face

The opponent takes a step with the right foot forward from the left-hand stance and at the same time with the right fist makes a wide amplitude side punch to the head. Turn the torso to the left and make a sopping Tan Sau block. At the same time with the right fist make a direct punch to the head (Fig.228-230).

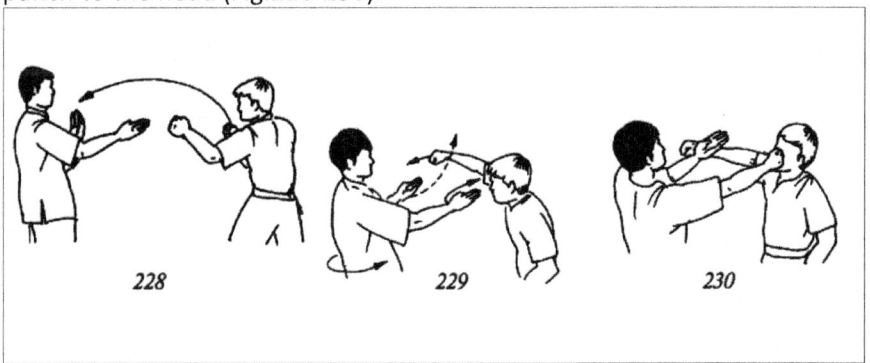

Jum Sau, Gan Sau and direct punch

The opponent takes a step with the right foot forward and at the same time moves the right hand forward, trying to grab you by the clothes. Turn the torso to the right and at the same time with your left hand make the Jum Sau block outwards - inwards neutralizing the attack. The opponent lowers the hand down quickly, trying to make another grab by the clothes near the waist. Without breaking the contact with his limb, using the Gan Sau movement, take away his hand down – to the left. With the right fist make a direct punch to the face (Fig.231-235).

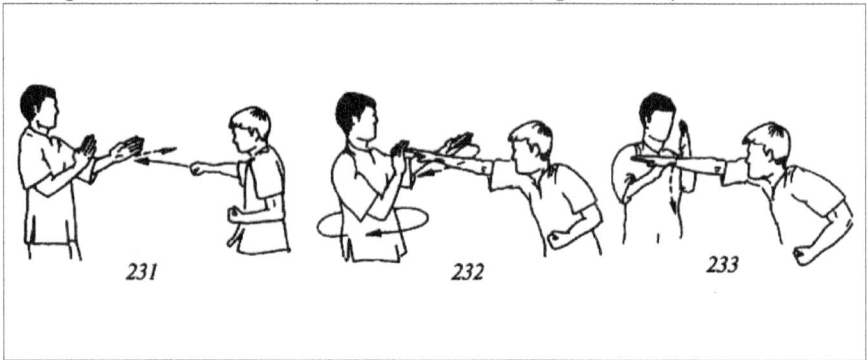

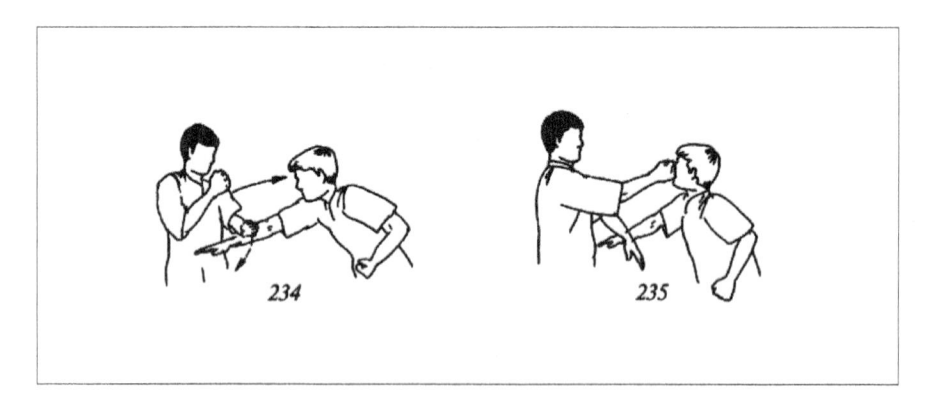

Double block - punch
with the edge of the palm

The opponent steps up with the back standing foot forwards from the right-hand stance then makes a side kick with the right foot to the chest. Turn to the right. With both hands, make a double block, neutralizing opponent's attack. After that, pick up attacking limb below with the right hand. With the right foot, make a small step forward. At the same time, with the left edge of left palm make a punch forward to the left, directed to the head of the opponent. He will lose the balance and will be overturned on the ground (Fig.235-238).

Pak Sau, Huen Sau and punch
with the base of the palm

You are in the frontal stance, and your opponent is in the left-hand combat position. With the right fist make a direct punch to the head. The opponent moves his left forearm in an arc to the left and blocks your attack inward - outward. After that, he makes a direct punch with the right fist to the head. With the left palm, make the Pak Sau block, directing his attack to the right. With the right hand make the Huen Sau movement, circle the left hand of the opponent, and then with the base of the palm of the same hand make a punch to his abdomen or solar plexus area (Fig.234-243).

239   240   241

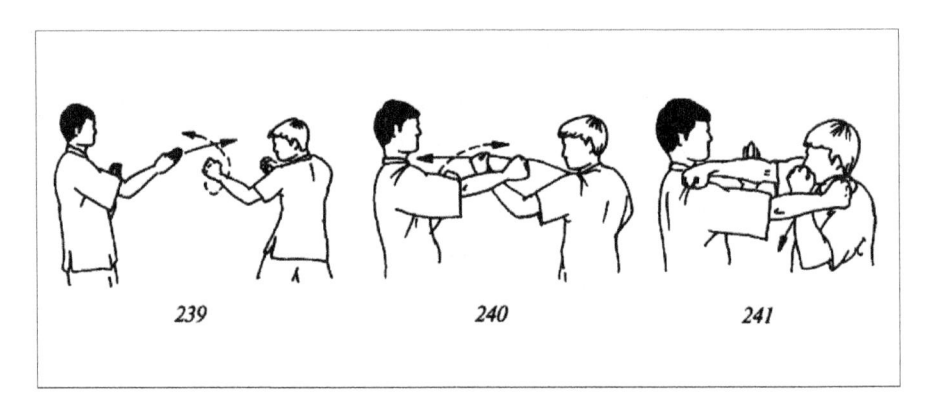

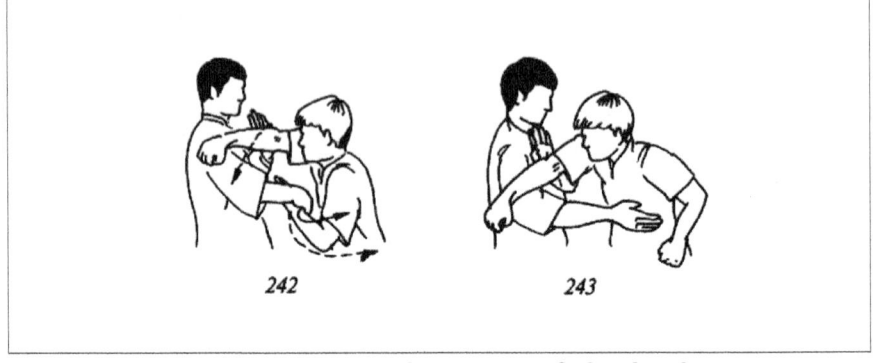

242   243

Bong Sau with a turn of the body

The opponent makes a direct punch with the right fist to the head. Move the left hand a little forward until it touches the opponent's attacking limb. Then turn the upper part of the body to the right. At the same time move your left hand to the Bong Sau position and direct the opponent's attack by yourself (Fig.244-247).

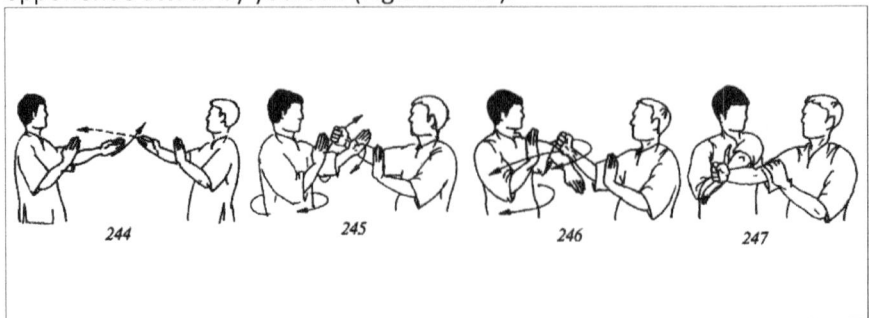

244   245   246   247

Bong Sau, Tan Sau
and punch with the palm

You and your opponent stand in front of each other in the frontal stances. He makes a direct punch to the head with the left fist. With the left hand get in contact with the attacking limb. Make the Bong Sau from outward- inward and neutralize the opponent's attack. He will have to take his hand backward. Taking advantage of this fact, move your left hand to the Tan Sau position. With the right palm control his limb at the elbow area. With the left hand circle the hand, then make a punch with the palm to the abdomen of the opponent. Fingers of the attacking hand are directed downward (Fig.248-253).

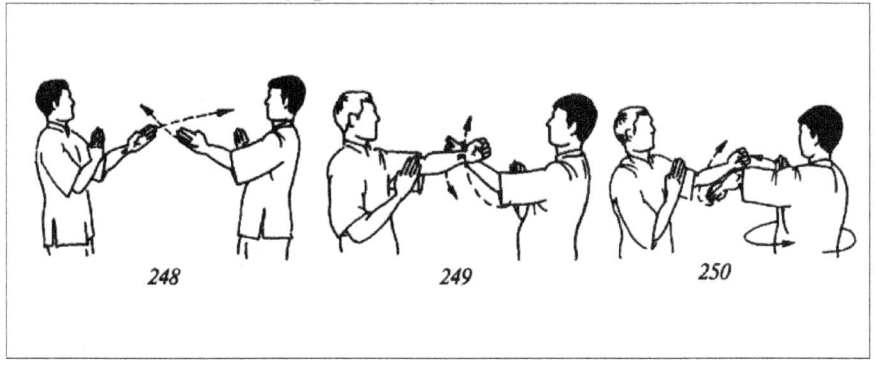

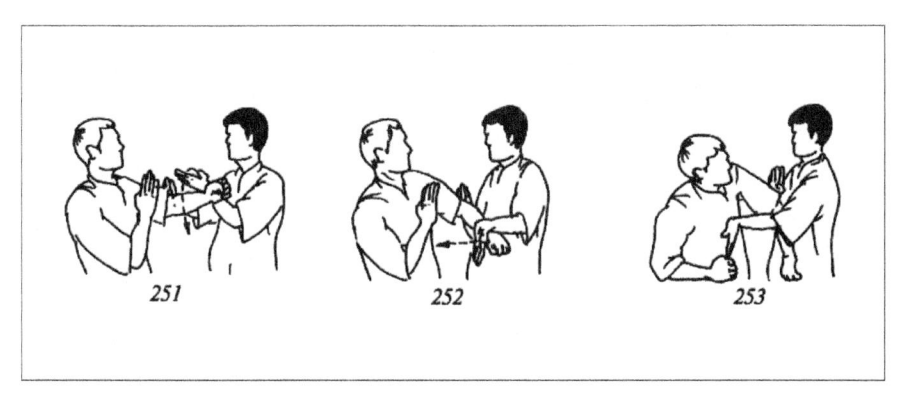

Cleaning palm - direct punch with the fist

You and your opponent stand in front of each other in the frontal stances. With the right hand he grabs your right hand. With the edge of the palm of the free left hand, make the cleaning movement forward, knocking his grab. Then with the right fist make a direct punch to the chest or the face of the opponent (Fig.254-259).

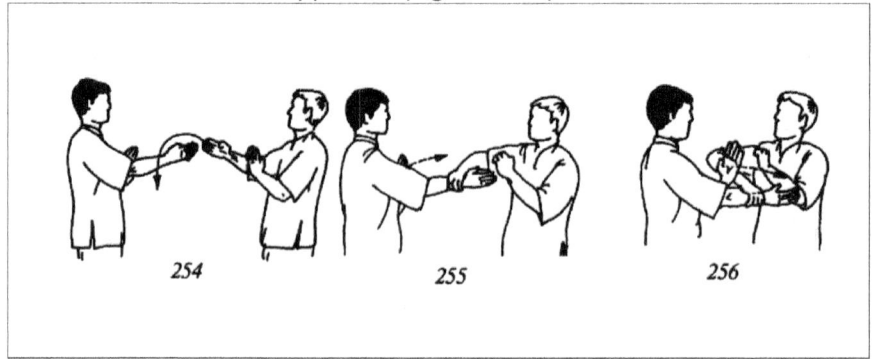

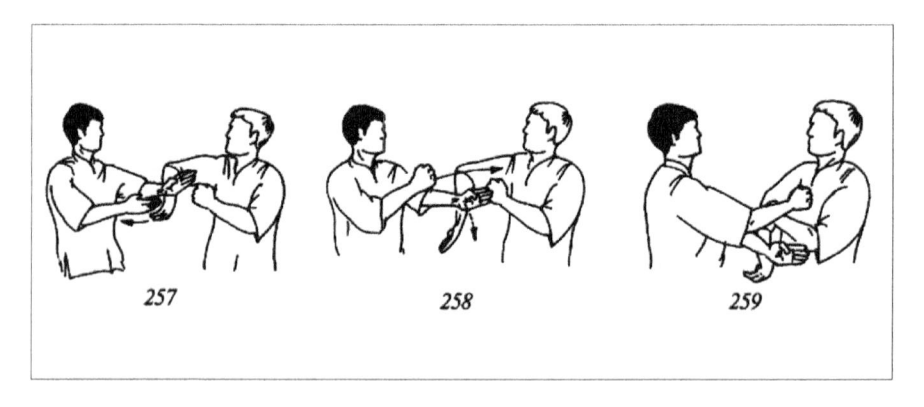

Chum Kiu
"Searching for the Bridge"

Chum Kiu – is the second form of Wing Chun Kuen. Its name reveals the meaning of this form, comprising the steps to enter into contact with the hands of the opponent, and through it to establish "bridges" into his defense.

The form is studied by those, who has mastered the Siu Lim Tao already. In his arsenal the new elements such as: steps, turns and kicks are added.

At first acquaintance with the Taolu, is struck the fact that there is a lot of attention paid to the use of the Bong Sau block, made at different levels and in combination with various turns and movements.

It is believed that there is laid the technique in the Chum Kiu, which is quite enough for a successful defense against any serious attack, and any number of attackers.

The Chum Kiu form consists of eight parts:
1). Initial form;
2). Crossing arms;
3). Direct punch - rotating hand;
4). Bong Sau - direct punch with the fist;
5). Side kick - Bong Sau - upward punch with the fist;
6). Direct Kick - lower Bong Sau – punch with the palms;
7). Gum Sau – direct punch with the fist;
8). Final form.

Part 1
Initial form

Starting position: stand straight, toes are brought together, arms down at the sides (Fig. 1). Squeeze the hands into fists and raise them to the chest (Fig. 2). Bend your knees. Dilute the toes outwardly at an angle of 90 degrees. Heels remain in place (Fig. 3). Dilute the heels to the external sides. You are in the Yee Gee Kim Yuen Ma stance (Fig. 4).

Part 2
Crossing arms

Unclench the fists and move both hands from the chest down. During the movement the forearms are crossed with each other, the left arm is over the right arm (Fig. 5). Lift up your crossed arms, fingertips are at the same level with the nose (Fig. 6). Squeeze the hands into fists and move them to the chest (Fig. 7).

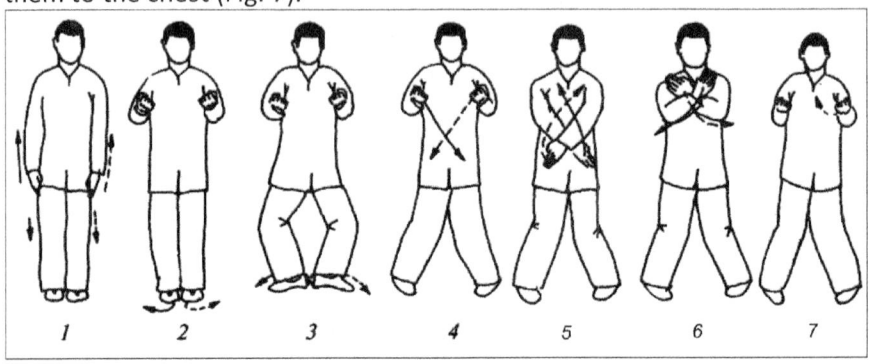

Part 3
Direct punch - rotating hand

Move the left fist to the middle of the chest and moving it forward, make a direct punch to the face (Fig. 8, 9). Unclench the fist and expand the palm upward (Fig. 10). Make a rotational movement with the hand clockwise, squeeze it into a fist and move to the chest (Fig.11-13).

8   9   10   11   12   13

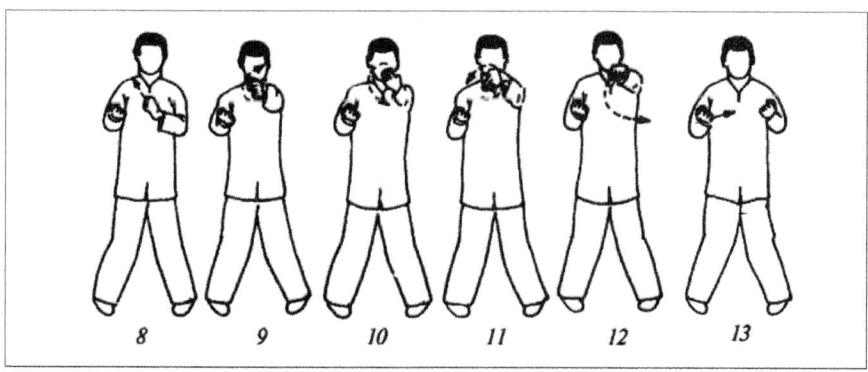

Repeat all the movements of this part of the form with the right hand part (Fig. 14-19).

14   15   16   17   18   19

Part 4
Bong Sau - direct punch with the fist

Expand both palms to each other and make a pressing downward movement in front of the chest (Fig. 20). Then quickly the poking movement with the fingers forwards (Fig. 21). Bend your elbows and place the hands in a horizontal plane in front of the chest (Fig. 22). Turn 90 degrees to the left, then 180 degrees to the right, then to the left (Fig.23-25).

Bring the arms forward, elbows are not completely straightened, palms are directed downwards (Fig. 26). With the right palm make the pressing movement on the inner side of the left forearm (Fig.27). Make a similar movement with the left palm (Fig. 28). Make a similar movement with the right palm (Fig. 29). With the right hand, make three direct punches with the palms forwards (Fig.30-32). Turn 180 degrees to the right. The right hand is in front of the chest in the Lan Sau position. At the same time make a punch backwards with the left elbow (Fig. 33). Cross the arms in front of chest, the left arm is over the right arm, palms are directed upwards (Fig.34). Turn 180 degrees to the left and make the right Bong Sau (fig. 35). Make this series of movements twice (Fig.36-42).

With the left fist make a direct punch at the face level (Fig.44).

Turn 90 degrees to the left. With the edge of the left hand, make a chopping punch to the side (Fig.45).

With the left palm make the Gum Sau block downwards (Fig. 46). With the fingers of the right hand make a direct poking punch forwards (Fig.47). Turn the right hand clockwise, squeeze into a fist and move to the chest (Fig.48, 49).

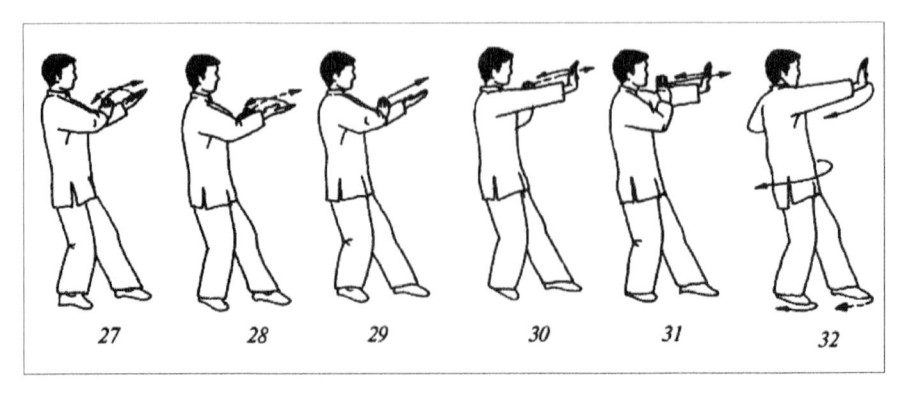

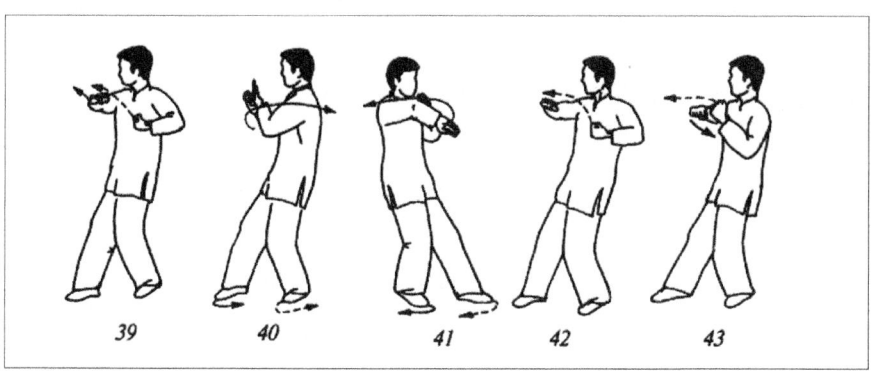

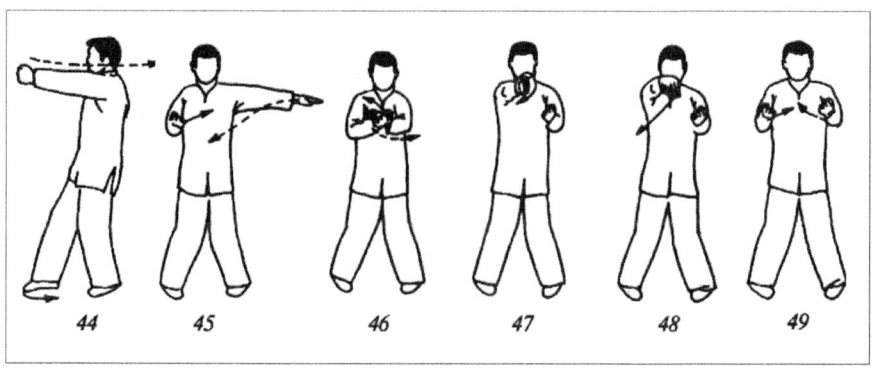

Repeat all the movements of this part of the form, with the other hand (Fig.50-79).

50 51 52 53 54 55 56

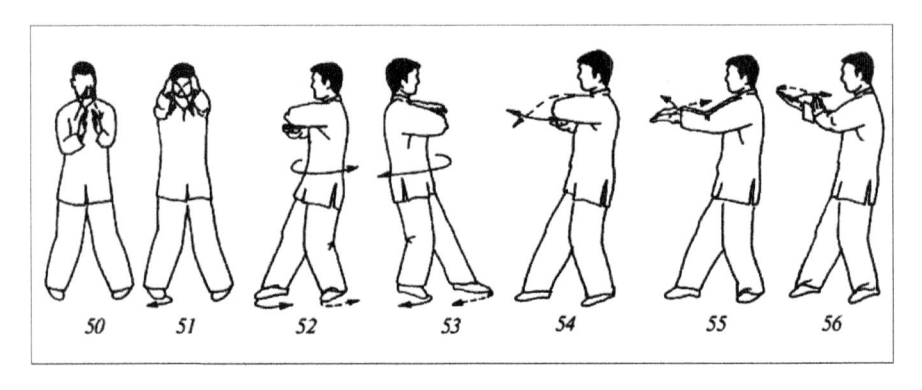

57 58 59 60 61 62

63 64 65 66 67 68

69 70 71 72 73

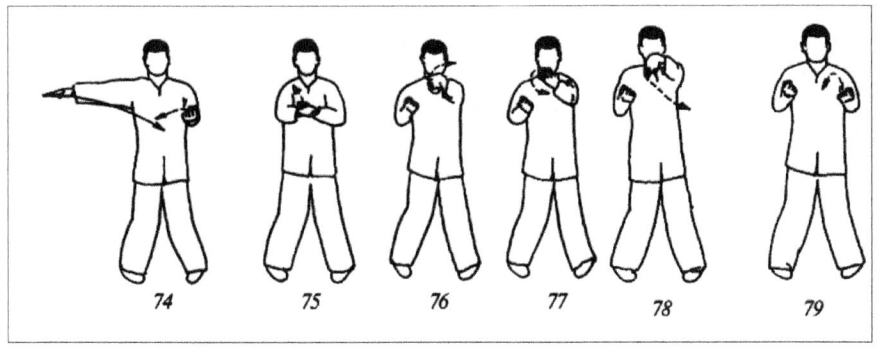

74 75 76 77 78 79

Part 5

Side kick - Bong Sau - upward punch with the fist

With the left hand make the Pak Sau to the right and complete the movement with the imitation of grab (Fig.80, 81). Move the left hand to the left to the Lan Sau position. At the same time make the side kick with the left foot to the left at the middle level (Fig.82, 83).

Lower the left leg down. With the right foot, make a small step-up forwards. At the same time, make the right Bong Sau. The left hand is near the chest in the Wu Sau position (Fig.84). Lower the elbows down and cross the arms in front of the chest (Fig.85).

Make the adjacent step forward with Bong Sau twice more, complete the combination with the upward punch with the right fist (Fig.86-89).

Turn 90 degrees to the right, and make the right Gum Sau (Fig.90).

With the fingers of the left hand make a direct punch forwards at the face level (Fig.91, 92). Rotate the left hand clockwise, then squeeze it into a fist and move to the chest (Fig.93, 94).

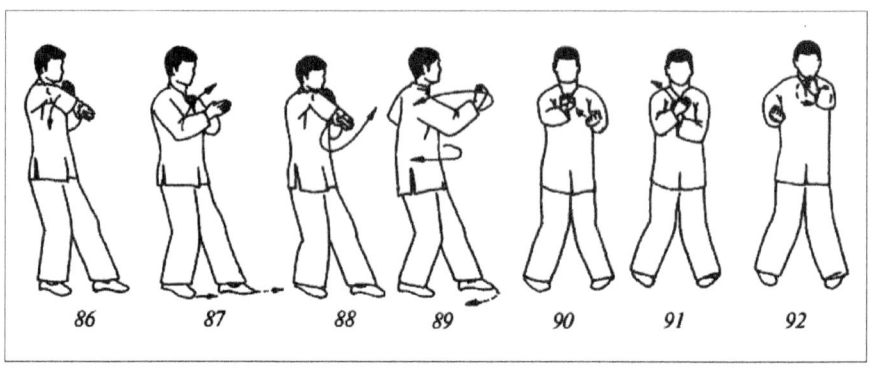

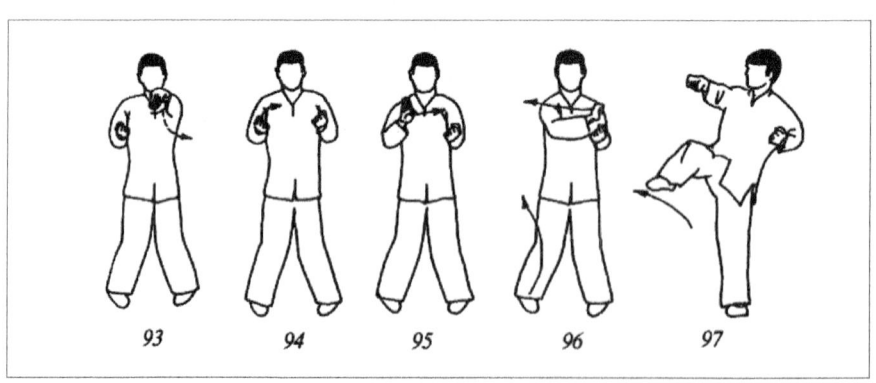

Repeat all the movements of this part of the form with the other hand (Fig.95-109).

98   99   100   101   102   103

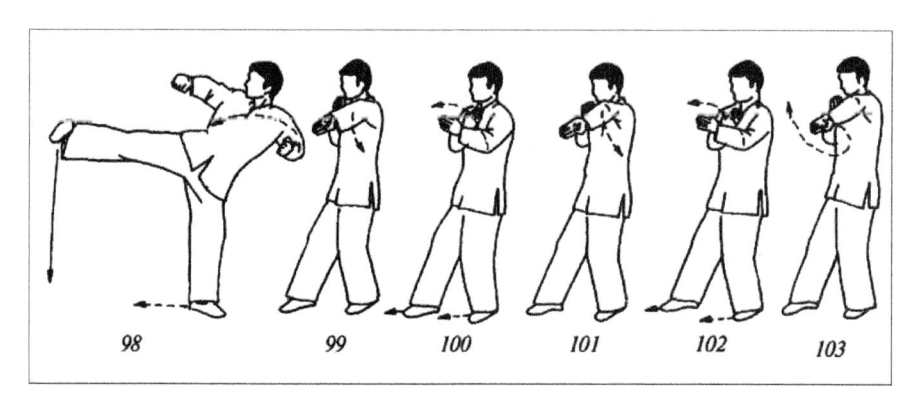

104   105   106   107   108   109

Part 6

Direct kick - lower Bong Sau – punch with the palms

Turn 90 degrees to the left (Fig.110). With the heel of the left foot put make a direct kick at the waist level (Fig.111). Lower the foot on the ground and make a step-up with the right foot. At the same time make the double Bong Sau with both hands on the lower level (Fig.112). Lower your elbows down and bring both arms to the Tan Sau position (Fig. 113). Twice more make an adjacent step forward with the same movement of the hands (Fig. 114-116). Once more make the step-up forwards. Bring both hands up and down. The palms are directed to the side, fingers - up and forward (Fig. 117). With both hands, make the Gum Sau block at the solar plexus level (Fig. 118). Place the right foot to the left foot. At the same time make a push forwards with both hands (Fig. 119, 120).

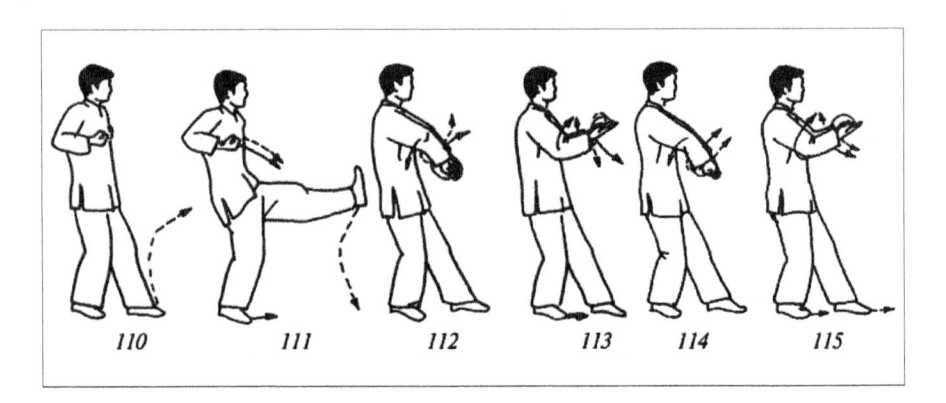

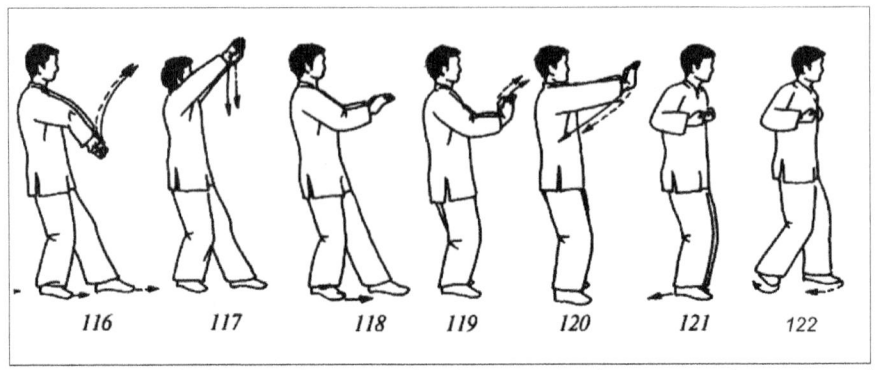

With the right foot make a step back, turn 180 degrees to the right and make all the movements of this part of the form to the other side (Fig.121-134).

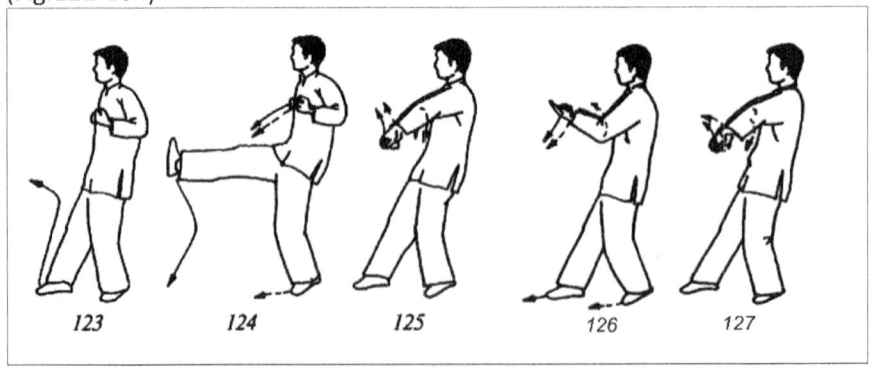

| 128 | 129 | 130 | 131 | 132 | 133 | 134 |

Part 7
Gum Sau - direct punch with the fist

Turn 90 degrees to the left. With the left foot make a kick to the left. The fingers of the left foot are directed to the left (Fig.135-137).

Lower the foot on the ground and turn to the right. At the same time with the left palm make the Gum Sau block (Fig. 138). Turn to the left and make the Gum Sau block with the right palm (Fig.139). Turn to the right and make the Gum Sau block with the left hand (Fig. 140).

Get back to the frontal stance and with the left fist make a direct punch forward (Fig. 141).

Turn to the left. With the right palm make the Gum Sau block (Fig. 142). Get back to the frontal stance and make a direct punch with the right fist forward (Fig. 143).

Turn to the right and make a block with the left palm (Fig. 144). Get back to the frontal stance and a direct punch with the left fist forward (Fig.145).

Make two more punches with the right and then with the left fists (Fig. 146, 147). Rotate the left hand at the wrist clockwise, then squeeze it into a fist and move to the chest (Fig.148-150).

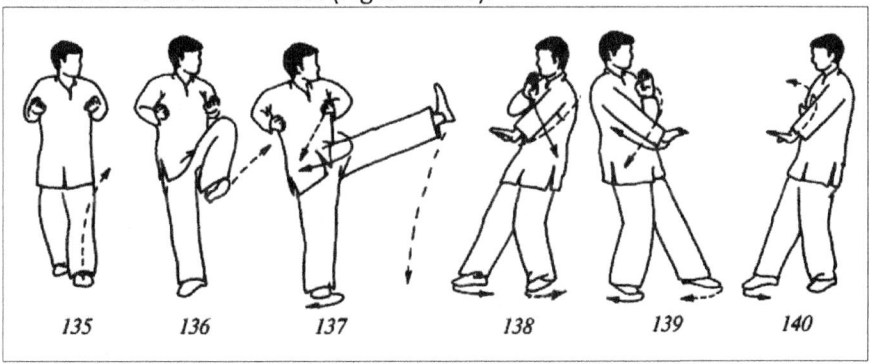

| 135 | 136 | 137 | 138 | 139 | 140 |

141 142 143 144 145 146

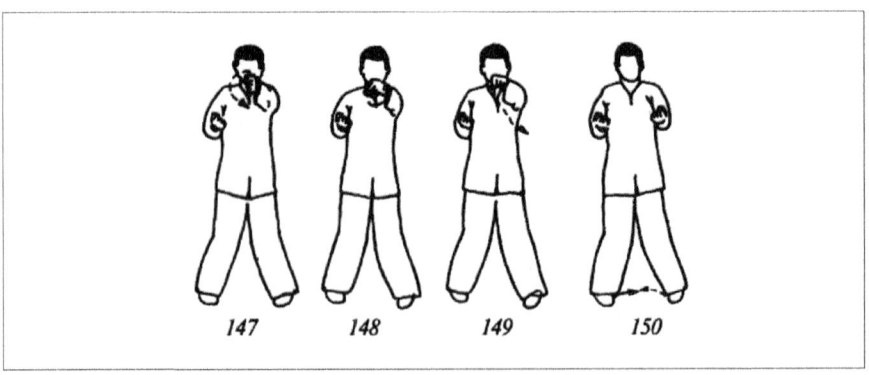

147 148 149 150

Part 8
The final form

Move the heels together, then the toes. Straighten the knees and lower the arms down at the sides (Fig. 151, 152).

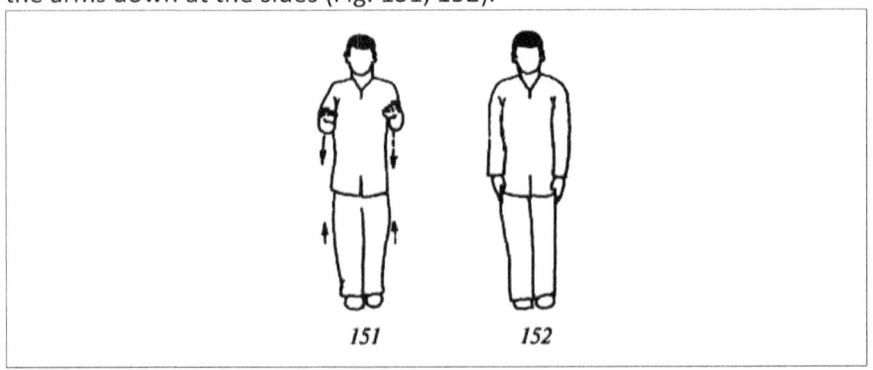

151 152

Martial combinations

Combinations, relating to this level, differ with a great variety of technical actions and are built to conduct the fight against few attackers. Widely used: the Bong Sau block, turns of the body, elbow punches and feet actions. People start studying martial combinations immediately after mastering the Chum Kiu form good enough. A summary of the movements of this form, originally proposed by the master Leung Ting is given below.

Pak Sau – elbow punch

The opponent takes a step forward with the left foot with the punch with the right fist to the torso. From the frontal stance, turn the body to the left. With the right palm make the Pak Sau block. The opponent continues the attack with the upward punch with the left fist to the torso. With the left palm block this attack, the hand takes the Lan Sau position. With the right foot take a step forward. Simultaneously, make a circle punch with the right elbow put to the jaw or neck of the opponent. Control the opponent's limb with the left hand (Fig. 153-157).

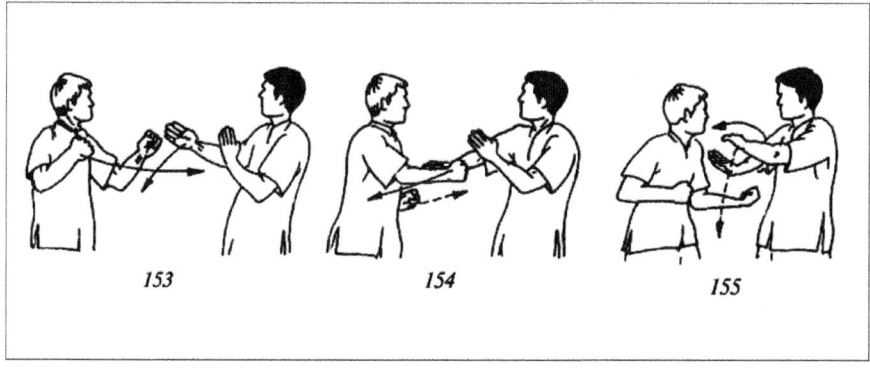

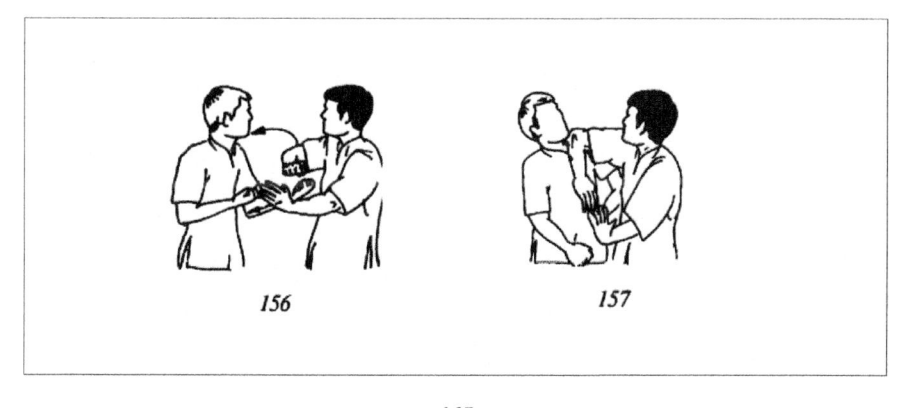

153 *154* *155*

156 *157*

Wu Sau – bending of the arm behind the back

You and your opponent are in front of each other in the frontal stances. He covers your left hand on top with the left palm. At the same time he makes a direct punch with the right fist to the head. With the right hand make the Wu Sau block, thus stopping his attack. With the right hand grab the attacking opponent's limb at the wrist. Place the left palm on his elbow. Then bend the opponent's arm behind his back (Fig. 158-163).

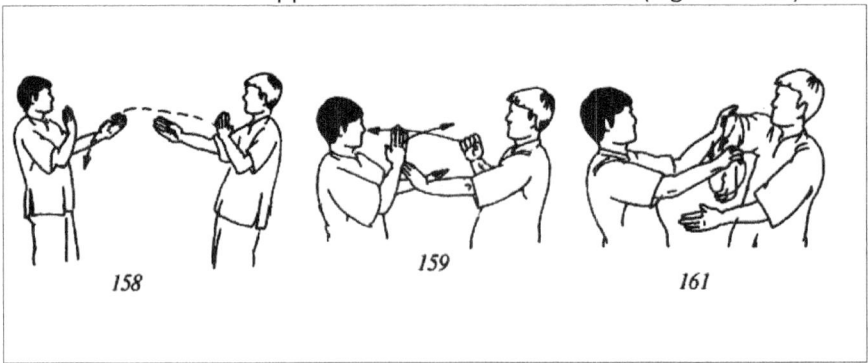

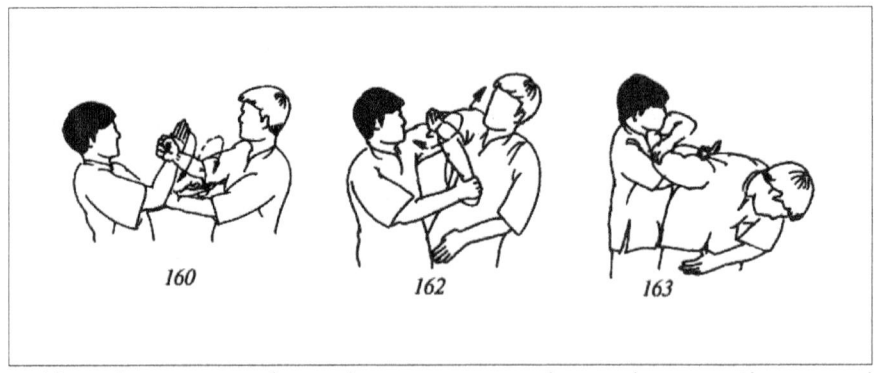

After that you can force the opponent to lower down on the ground using the frontal trip-up, or kick to his popliteal crease. Then you can make a series of direct "finishing" punches to the head.

Bong Sau - interception - direct punch with the fist

You and your opponent are in front of each other in the frontal stances. He makes a direct punch with the left fist to the head. Turning the torso to the left make the Bong Sau block with the right hand. Then with the left hand intercept his attacking limb and lower it down. Squeeze the right hand into a fist and move it along the short arcuate path to you – upwards a little, and then forwards - making a punch to the chest or head (Fig. 164-168).

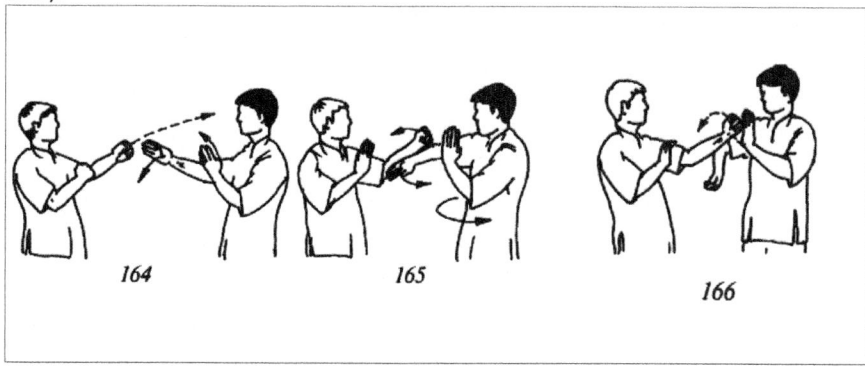

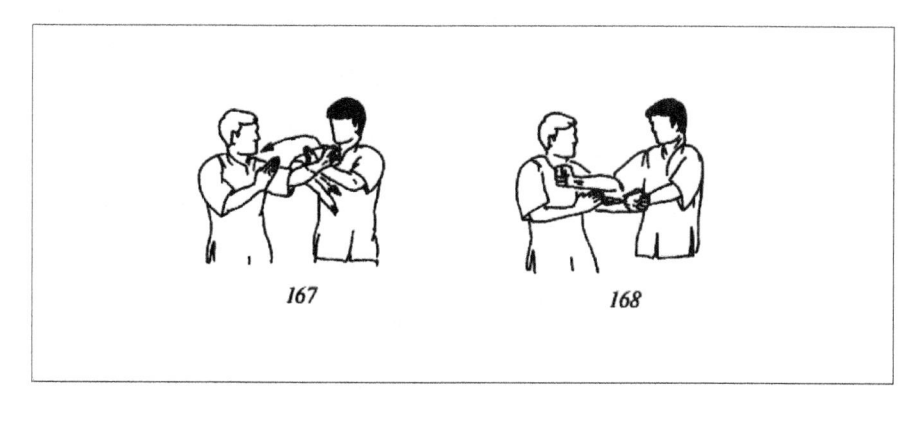

Lan Sau – punch with the fist, punch with the edge of the palm, Gum Sau – punch with the fist

Three opponents attack you from three sides: right, left and front. The opponent on the right grabs your right hand with his left hand. Move your grabbed limb to the Lan Sau position. Thus you will take his hand to the side and upwards, this will prevent the continuation of his attack. After that, make a direct punch with the left fist to the head or a poking punch with the fingers to the throat. Then turn to the left and make the preemptive punch with the edge of the left palm from you to the throat of the approaching opponent. At this time, the opponent, attacking from the front makes a direct punch with the right fist to the abdomen. Make the Gum Sau block down with the left palm. At the same time make a direct punch with the right fist to the head or with the fingers - to the throat (Fig.169-173).

169

170

171

172

173

This combination is a "template", i.e. on its basis, most of the combinations are modeled to defend against the attacks of some opponents. They vary the sequence of the opponents' attacks, their directions and options of the counteractions.

Bong Sau, interception and upward punch with the fist

The opponent takes a step with the right foot forwards and makes a direct punch to the head with the same name fist. Turn to the right and make the Bong Sau block with the left hand. With the right hand intercept the opponent's attacking hand. At the same time make an upward punch to the jaw with the left fist (Fig. 174-176). The counter punch can be made both from the "inner gates" side, and from the "outer gates" side of the opponent.

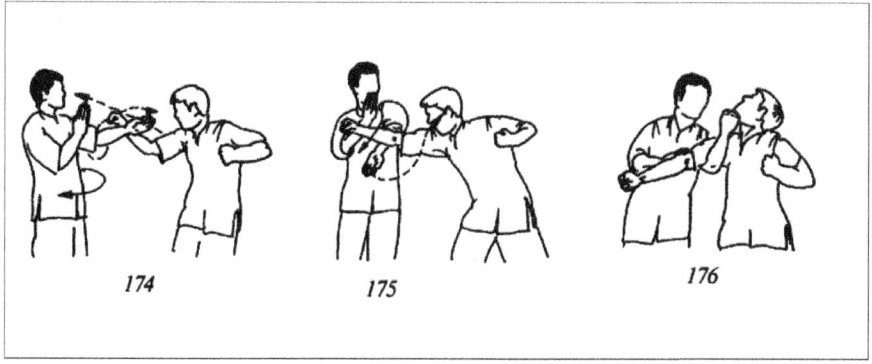

174 *175* *176*

Lan Sau - side kick

The opponent takes a step with the left foot forward. With the left hand he grabs your left hand, pulling it towards him. At the same time, he makes a direct punch to the face with the right fist. Giving the left hand the Lan Sau position (forearm is in a horizontal plane in front of the chest and taking the elbow to the left a little and up), push forward - to the left and upward a little, preventing the opponent to attack and fixing his hands in the high positions. Make a side kick to the torso or abdomen with the left foot (Fig.177-179).

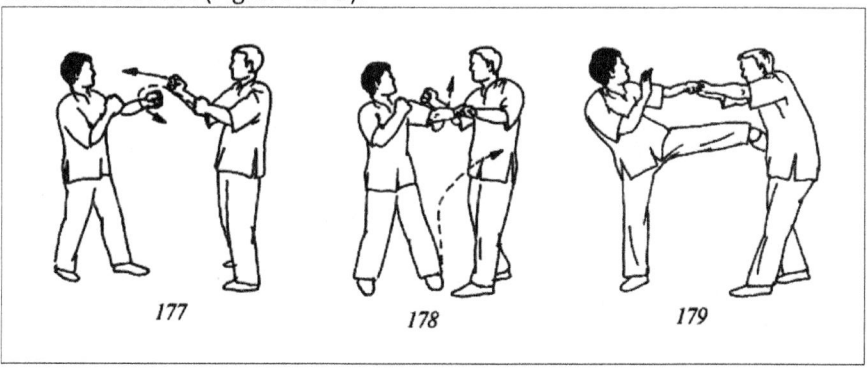

177 *178* *179*

Double Tan Sau - direct kick with the foot

The opponent is approaching you in front, intending to grab your clothing with both arms. Moving your hands forward, place them between the hands of the opponent. Expand the palms up and give them the Tan Sau form. Spread both hands to the sides, opening the body for the opponent's attack. Then make a direct kick with the foot to the abdomen or chest of the opponent (Fig.180-182).

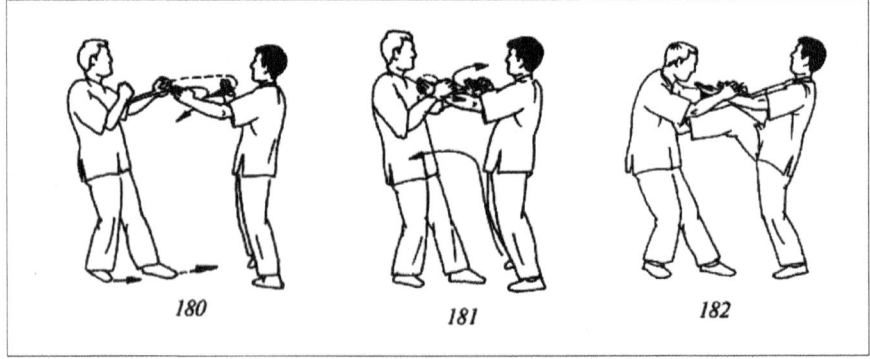

180 181 182

Bong Sau - Man Sau

The opponent takes a step with the right foot forward and at the same time makes a direct punch with the right fist to the abdomen or torso. Turn the torso to the right and make the lower Bong Sau with the left hand, diverting the attack of the opponent to the side. At the moment when the opponent will divert the attacking limb back, move your left hand in an arc up and forward, making a punch with the edge of the palm to his throat or face (Fig.183-185).

183 184 185

Man Sau

The opponent makes a downward chopping strike with a stick to the head. Bring your left arm forward toward the strike so that the weapon would "slide" along your limb, moving away to the side from you. The left hand, in the process of the straightening it at the elbow, turns outwards the palm, fingers - forward and upward. Then, on the return movement of the hand, turn the palm down and make a covering movement in order to control the movement of the stick. At the same time with the right fist make a direct punch to the face of the opponent (Fig.186-189).

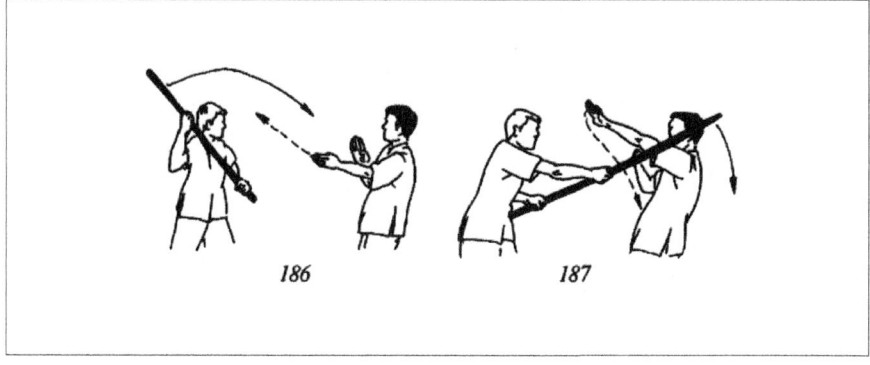

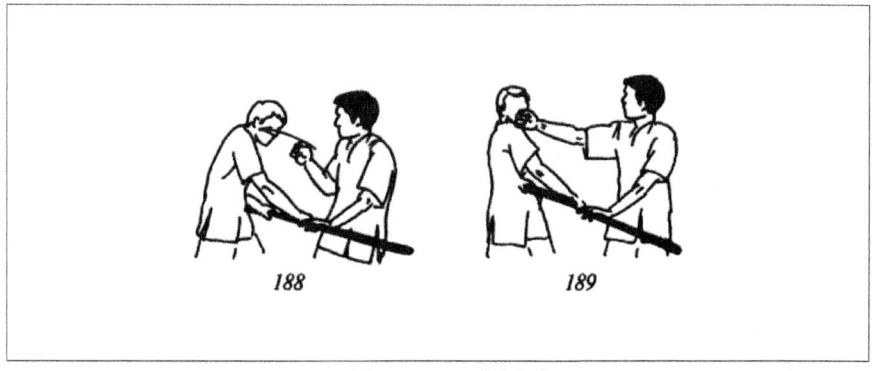

186

187

188

189

Turn and kick

The opponent approaches from behind and grabs your left shoulder with the left hand. Turn to the left. The center of the turn is the right foot. With the left hand knock the grabbing hand of the opponent and move it to the side. At the same time with the left leg make a kick to the abdomen or groin area. The toe of the kicking left foot turns to the left (Fig.190, 191).

190 *191*

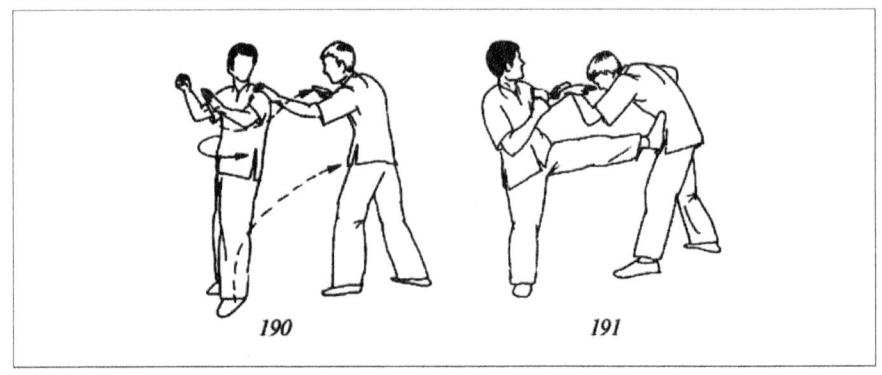

Gum Sau – punch with the fist

The opponent makes a circle kick with the right leg to your ribs on the left. Turn to the left. With the right palm make the Gum Sau block, trying to place the palm at the knee of the kicking leg. Then turning the torso to the right and taking a step with the left foot forward, make a direct punch with the left fist to the head of the opponent (Fig.192-195).

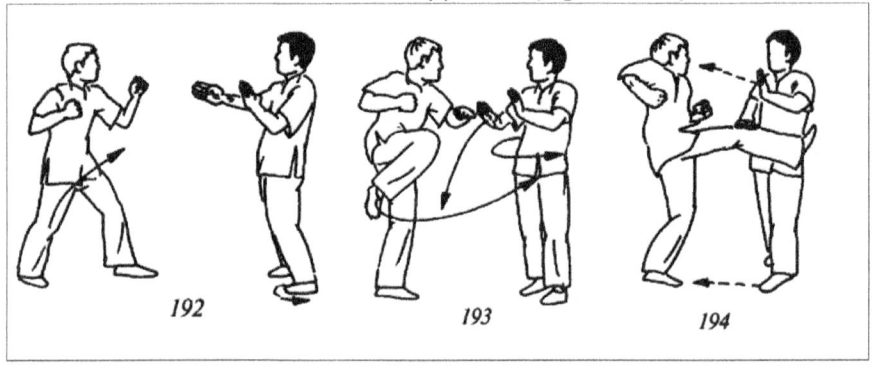

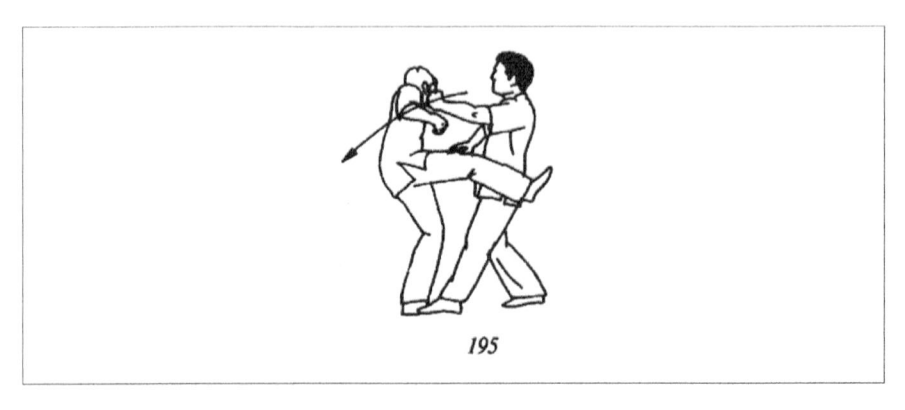

192 *193* *194*

195

Biu Jee
"Darting Fingers"

Biu Jee is the highest form in the Wing Chun Kuen technique. Even the name itself says that the main idea of Taolu is the attack with the fingers to the vital points on the human body. In addition to the fingers' attack there are widely used movements of the elbows, hands and fists. The manner of implementation is aggressive, but at the same time, is soft and flexible, reminding the dangerous movements of a snake.

Biu Jee consists of twelve parts:

1). Initial form;
2). Crossing arms;
3). Direct punch with the fist- poke with fingers;
4). Elbow punch - double poking strike with the fingers;
5). Elbow punch - lower poking strike with the fingers;
6). Elbow punch - upper poking strike with the fingers;
7). Double block;
8). Upper block;
9). Triple attack with the fingers;
10). Grabbing hands - side punch with the fist;
11). Triple bow;
12). Final form.

Part 1
Initial form

Starting position: stand straight, toes are together, arms are lowered down at the sides (Fig. 1). Squeeze the hands into fists and raise them to the chest (Fig. 2). Bend the knees. Dilute the toes outwards at 90 degrees angle. Heels remain on the place (Fig. 3). Dilute the heels to the external side. You are in the Yee Gee Kim Yuen Ma stance (Fig. 4).

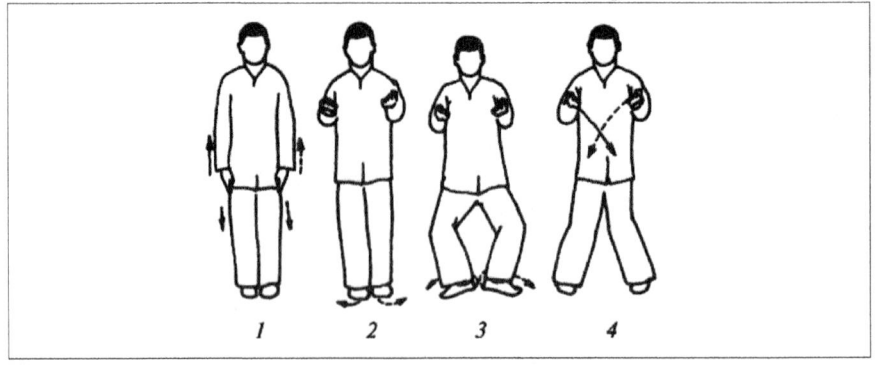

Part 2
Crossing arms

Unclench the fists and move down both hands from the chest. During the movement the forearms are crossed with each other, the left hand is over the right hand (Fig. 5). Raise up your crossed hands, fingertips are at the same level with the nose (Fig. 6). Squeeze the hands into fists and move them to the chest (Fig. 7).

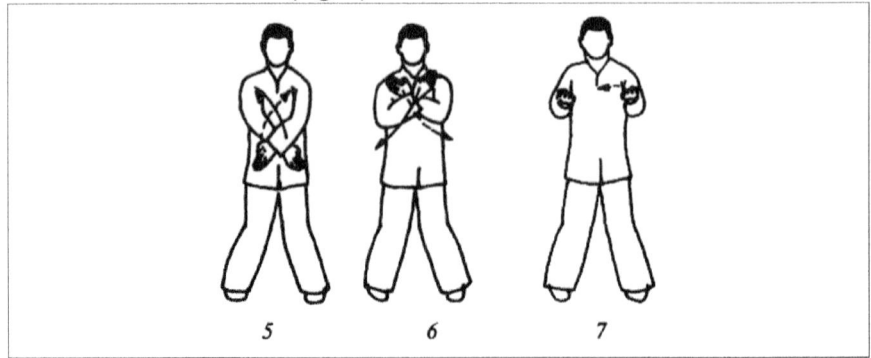

Part 3
Direct punch with the fist - poke with fingers

Move the left fist to the middle of the chest and moving it forward, make a direct punch to the face (Fig. 8, 9). Unclench the fist and expand the hand to the right. The fingers as if continue the attack with a poking movement forwards (Fig. 10). Raise the fingers up - forward (Fig. 11). Lower the fingers down (Fig. 12). Expand the palm down and make a rotation around the wrist in a clockwise direction (Fig. 13). Having made a circle, the hand takes a horizontal position again, palm down (Fig. 14). Make a movement with the fingers horizontally to the left, then to the right (Fig. 15, 16). Rotate the hand in a clockwise direction, and then it takes a vertical position, fingers are directed forward, the palm – to the right (Fig. 17, 18). Make a movement down with the fingers, then move up (Fig. 19, 20). Rotate the hand clockwise, squeeze it into a fist and move to the chest (Fig. 21 - 23).

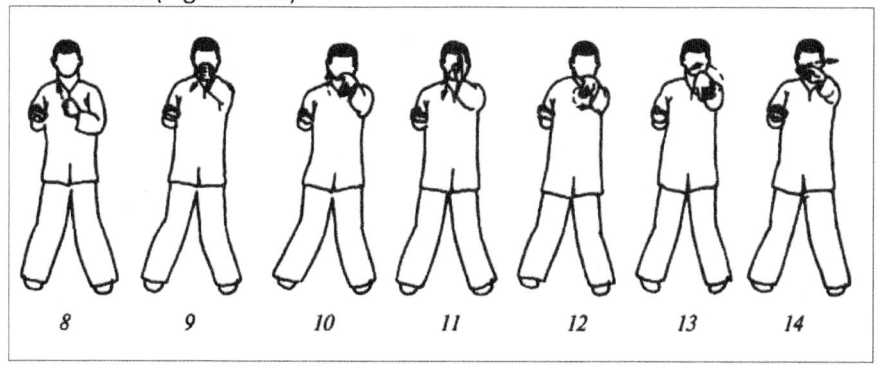

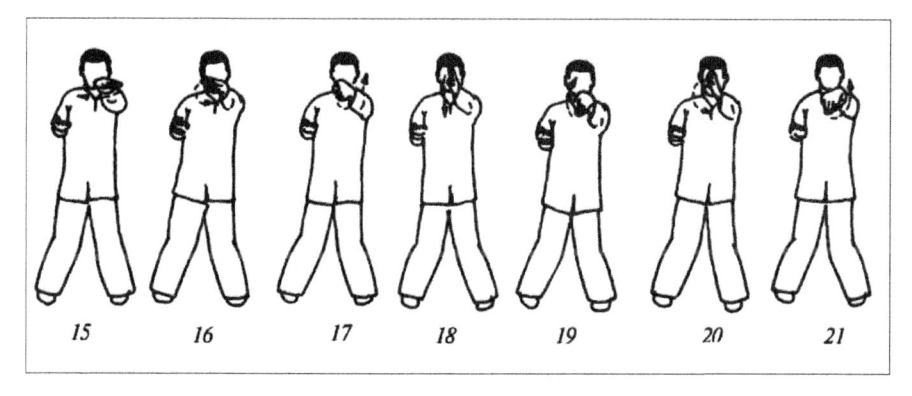

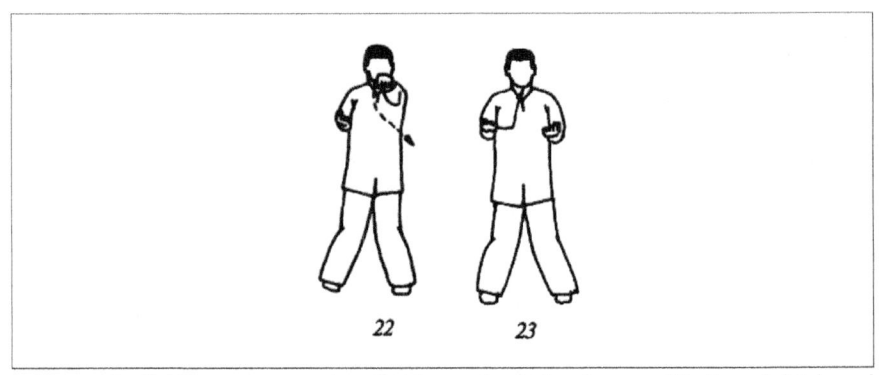

Repeat all the movements of this part of the form with the right hand (Fig. 24-38).

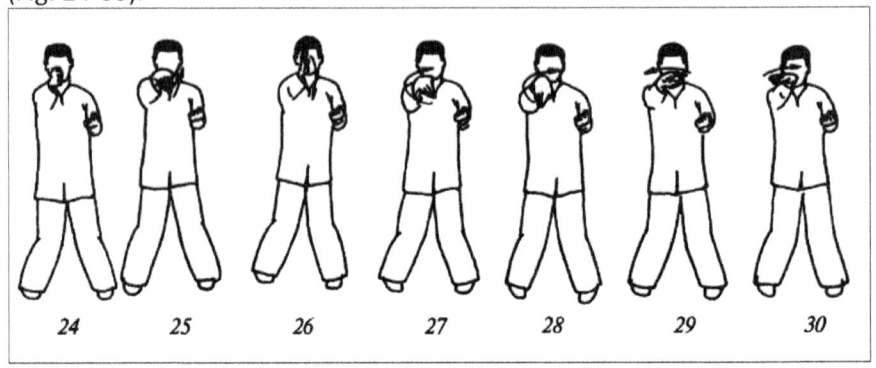

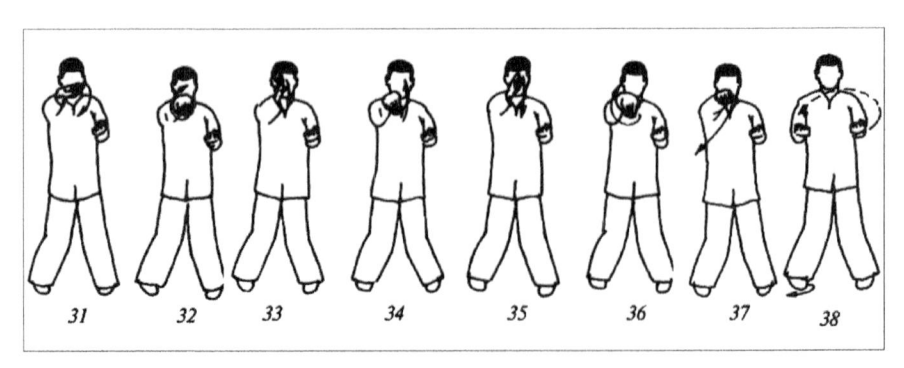

Part 4
Elbow punch - double poking strike with the fingers

Turn 90 degrees to the right. Simultaneously with the rotation, make the circle punch with the left elbow (Fig. 39). Turn 180 degrees to the left. At the same time make a circle punch with the right elbow. The left fist moves back to its starting position (Fig. 40). Turn 180 degrees to the right. At the same time make a circle punch with the left elbow (Fig. 41).

Move the right arm under the left arm. Palm is directed down, fingers - forward (Fig. 42). With the fingers of the right hand make a poking Biu Jee punch forward. The hand is in a vertical position, palm is directed down, fingers - forward (Fig. 43). Make a similar attack with the fingers of the left hand, at the same time step – up with the left foot to the right foot. During the second strike the right hand remains on place (Fig.44).

Squeeze the hands into fists and move them to the chest (Fig. 45). Turn 90 degrees to the left. With the left foot make a circular movement forward to the left and back, and then make a similar movement with the right foot and with the left foot again (Fig. 46- 52).

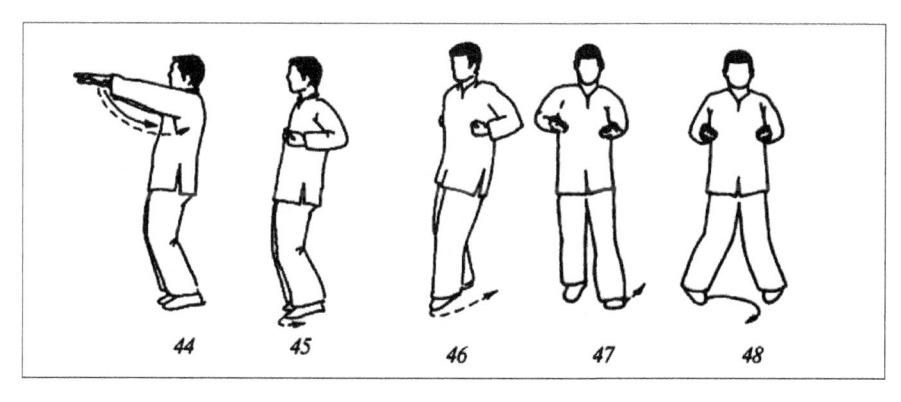

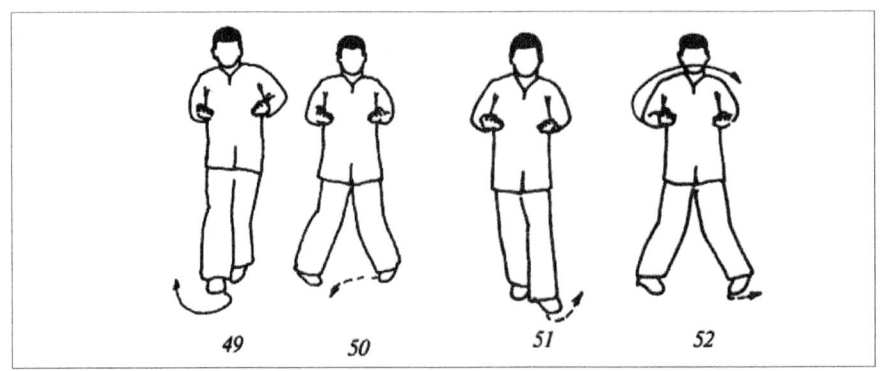

Repeat all the movements of this part of the form with the other hand (Fig. 53-65).

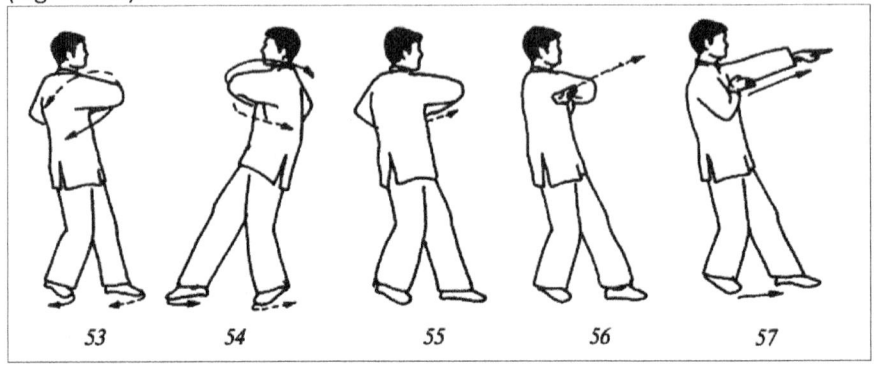

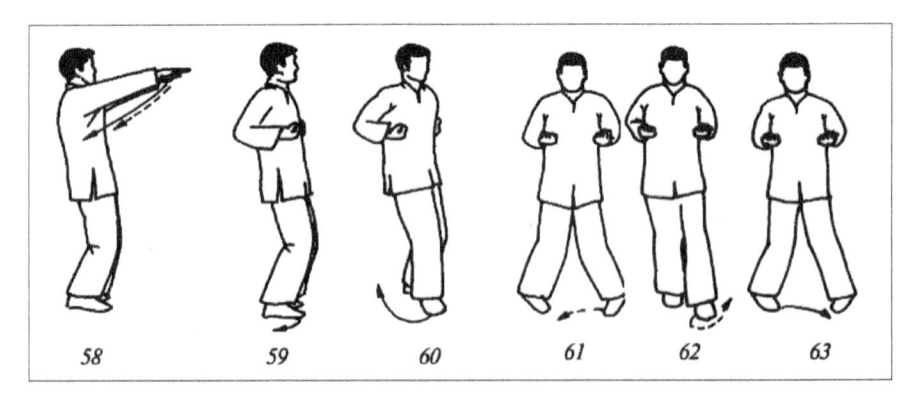

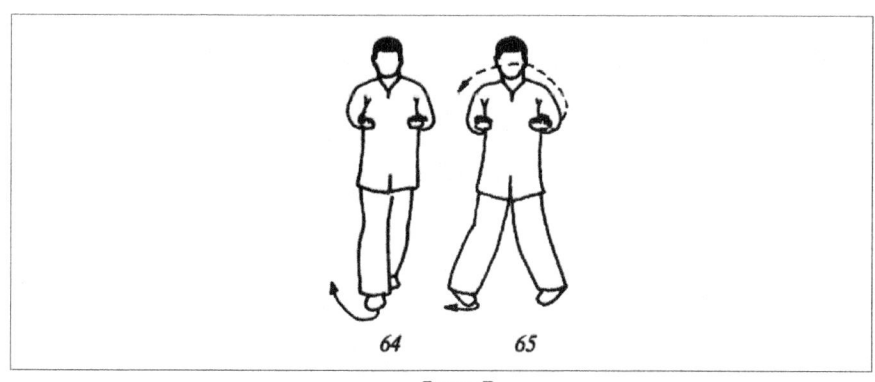

Part 5

Elbow punch - lower poking strike with the fingers

Turn the torso 90 degrees to the right. With the left elbow make a circular strike, then move the right arm under the left arm (Fig. 66, 67). With the fingers of the right hand make a poking strike at the head level, palm is directed down (Fig. 68). Squeeze the right hand into a fist and move to the starting position to the chest. At the same time with the fingers of the left hand make a poking punch at the abdomen level, palm is directed to the right (Fig. 69).

Turn 90 degrees to the left. With the left hand make the Gum Sau block. With the fingers of the right hand make a direct poking punch forward at the face level. The hand is positioned vertically, palm is directed to the left (Fig. 70, 71).

Rotate the hand counterclockwise, squeeze it into a fist and move to the chest (Fig. 72, 73).

Repeat all the movements of this part of the form with the other hand (Fig. 74 - 81).

Part 6
Elbow punch - upper poking strike with the fingers

Turn the torso 90 degrees to the right. With the left elbow make a circle punch, then move the right arm under the left arm (Fig. 82, 83). With the fingers of the right hand make a poking punch at the head level, palm is directed downwards (Fig. 84). Squeeze the right hand into a fist and move it to the starting position to the chest. At the same time with the fingers of the left hand make a poking punch at the face or throat level, palm is directed to the right (Fig. 85).

Turn 90 degrees to the left. With the left hand make the Gum Sau block. With the fingers of the right hand make a direct punch forward at the face level. The hand is positioned vertically, palm is directed to the left (Fig. 86, 87).

Rotate the hand counterclockwise, squeeze it into a fist and move it to the chest (Fig .88, 89).

Repeat all the movements of this part of the form with the other hand (Fig. 90 - 97).

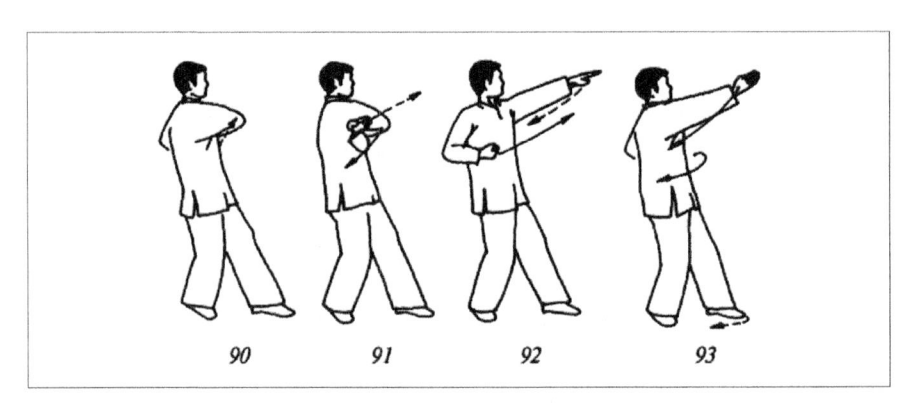

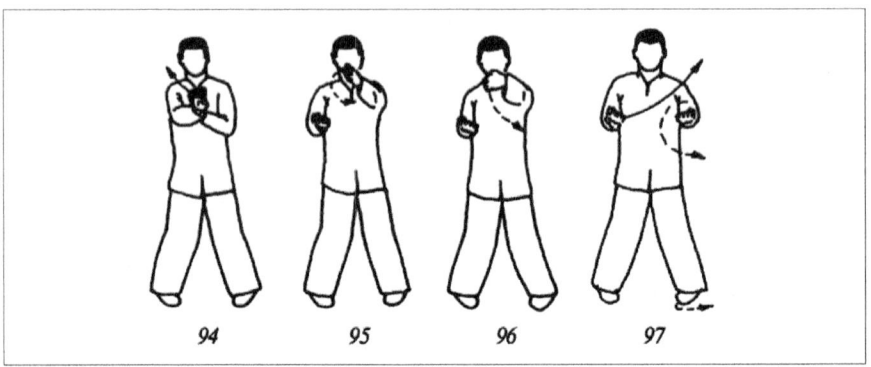

Part 7

Double Jum / Gan Sau block

Turn 90 degrees to the left. With both hands, make the double block, consisting of the Jum Sau block with right hand and Gan Sau block with left hand (Fig. 98). Turning to the right, then to the left twice, make a similar movement (Fig. 99, 100).

Turn 90 degrees to the right and make the Gum block with the left hand (Fig.101). With the fingers of the right hand make a direct punch forward at the head level. The hand is in the vertical position, palm is directed to the left (Fig. 102).

Rotate the hand counterclockwise, squeeze it into a fist and move to the chest (Fig. 103, 104).

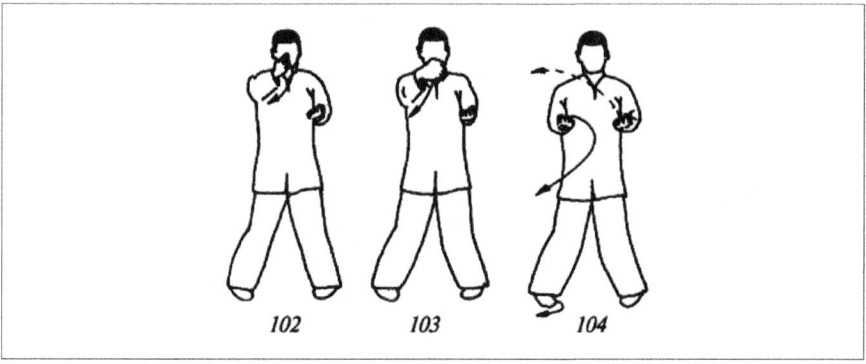

Repeat all the movements of the parts of the form with the other hand (Fig.105-111).

109   *110*   *111*

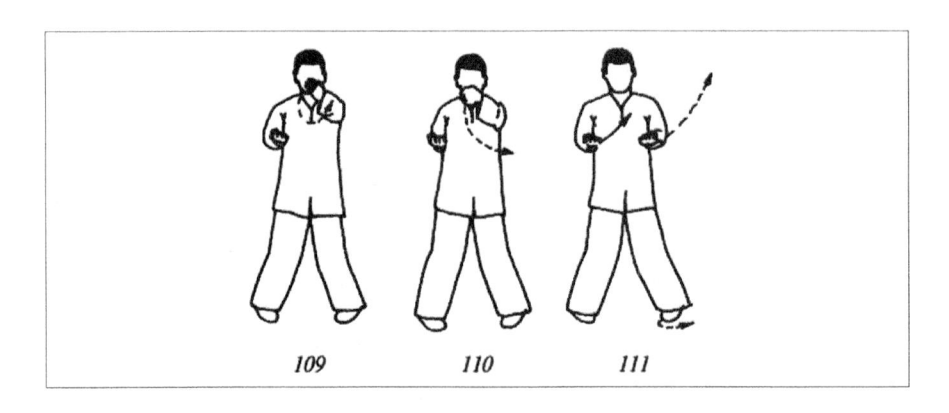

Part 8
Upper block

Turn the torso to the left and lift the straightened left arm up and to the left. Palm is directed backward, the edge of the palm upward (Fig. 112). Turn the torso to the right and make a similar movement (Fig. 113). Turn the torso to the left and make a similar movement once again (Fig. 114). Turn the body 90 degrees to the right. With the left hand make the Gum Sau block (Fig. 115).

Turn 90 degrees to the left. With the left hand make the Fook Sau movement (Fig. 116). Turn to the right to the starting position. Simultaneously, the left hand takes the Gum Sau form (Fig. 117). Make this movement twice more (Fig. 118-121).

With the fingers of the right hand make a direct poking punch forward (Fig. 122). Rotate the hand counterclockwise, squeeze it into a fist, and move it to the chest (Fig. 123, 124).

112   *113*   *114*   *115*

116 117 118 119 120

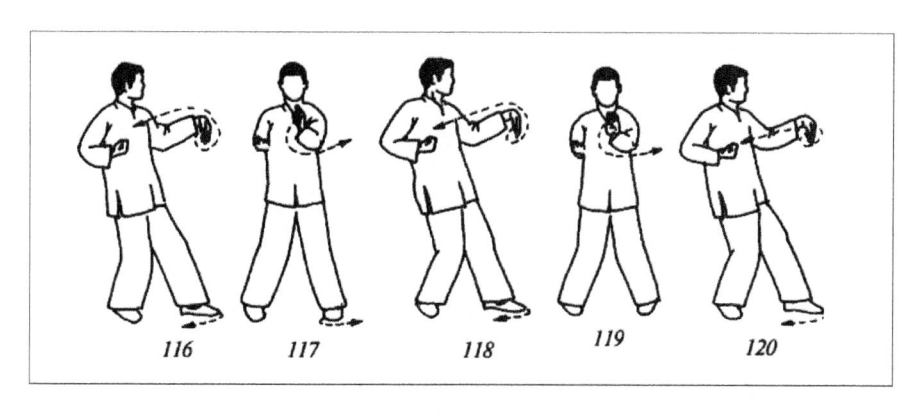

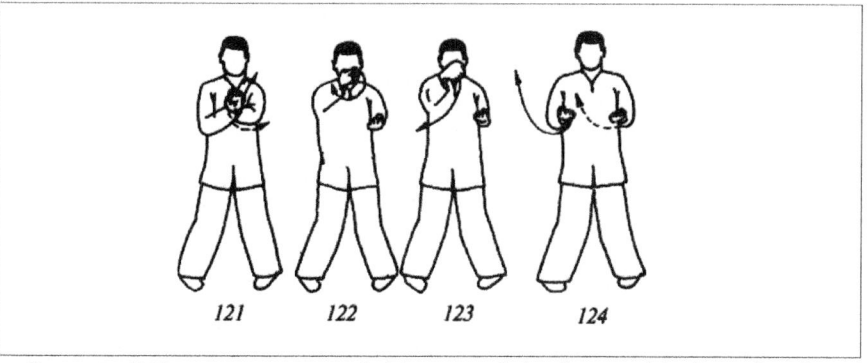

121 122 123 124

Repeat all the movements of this part of the form with the other hand (Fig. 125-137).

125 126 127 128

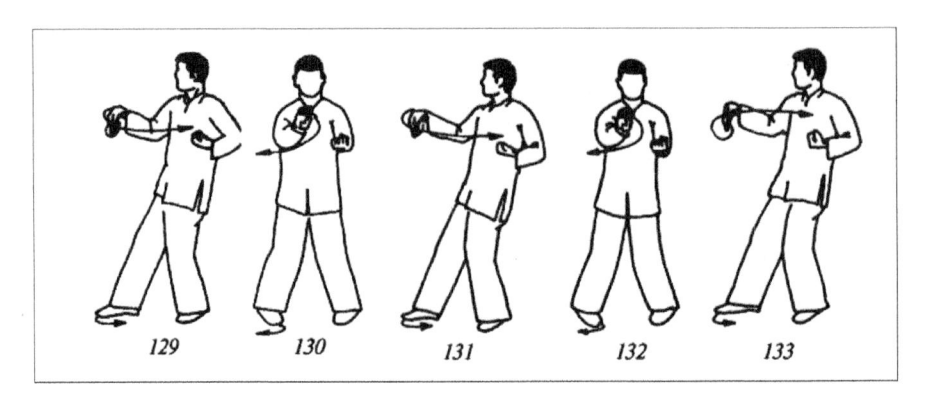

129	130	131	132	133

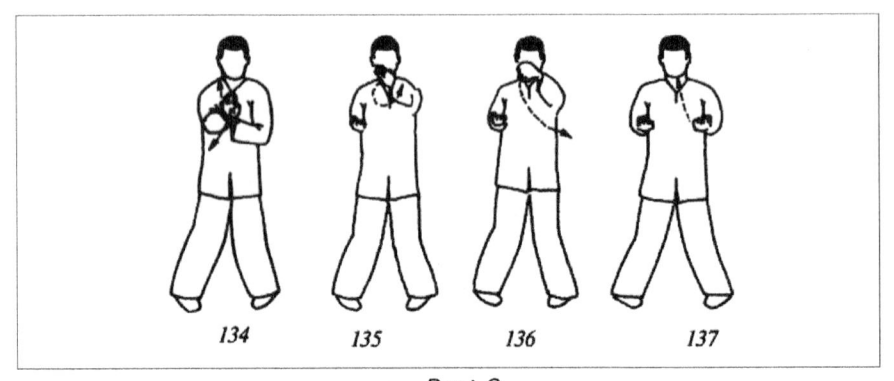

134	135	136	137

Part 9
Triple attack with fingers

With the fingers of the left hand make a direct poking punch forward at the face level (Fig. 138). Move the right hand under the left straightened arm forward (Fig. 139). With the fingers of the right hand make a direct poking punch forward at the face level. At the same time move the left hand back under the right arm (Fig. 140). With the fingers of the left hand make a direct poking punch forward at the face level. At the same time squeeze the right hand into a fist and move to the chest (Fig. 141).

Turn 90 degrees to the left. Expand the left palm up, and at the same time with the turn make a chopping punch from left to the right at the face level (Fig. 142). Turn 90 degrees to the left. Expand the left hand palm down, and at the same time with the turn make the chopping punch from you to the left (Fig. 143).

With the left hand make the Gum Sau block (Fig. 144). With the fingers of the right hand make a poking punch forward at the face level. The palm of the attacking hand is directed to the left (Fig. 145). Rotate the right hand anticlockwise, squeeze it into a fist and move to the chest (Fig.146, 147).

138   *139*   *140*   *141*   *142*

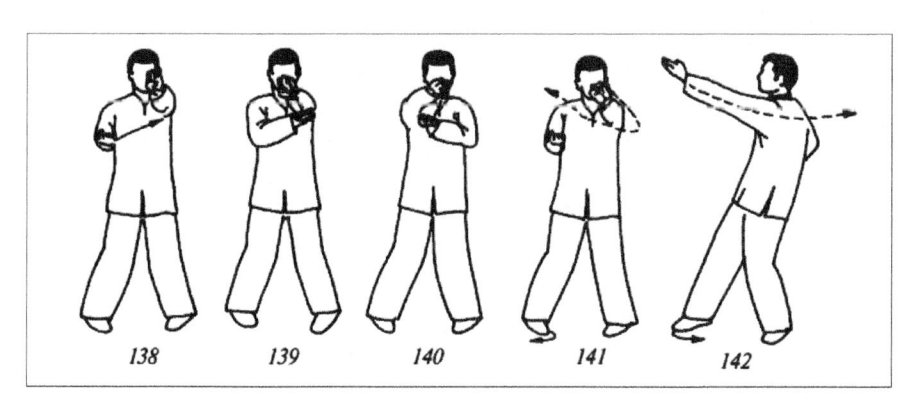

143   *144*   *145*   *146*   *147*

Repeat all the movements of this part of the form with the other hand (Fig. 148-157).

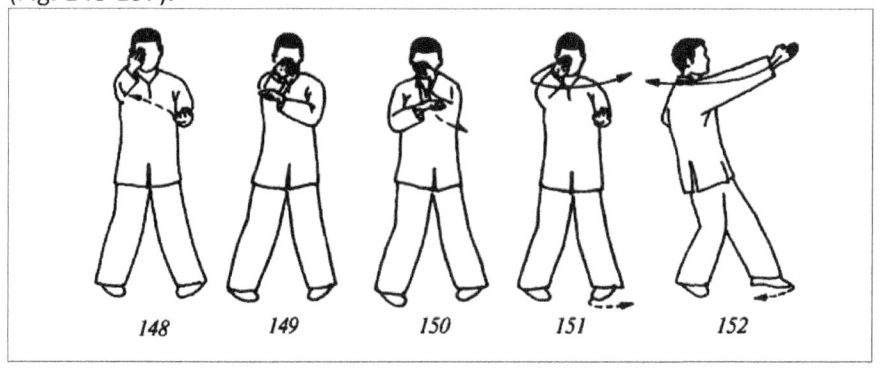

148   *149*   *150*   *151*   *152*

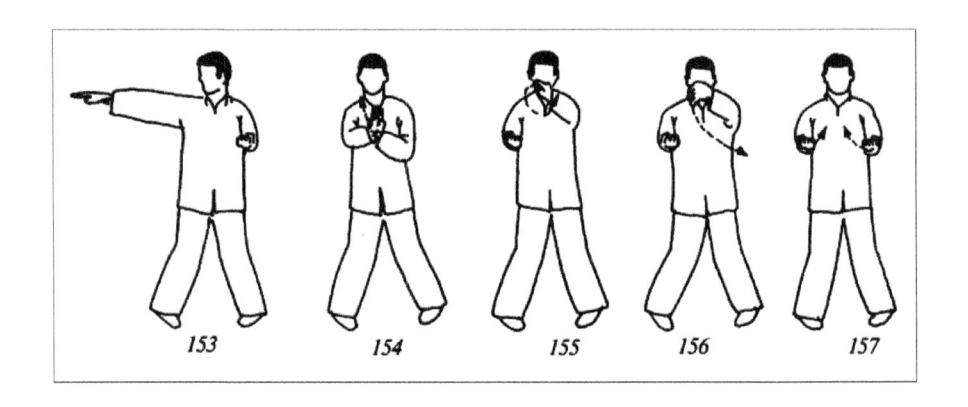

153 154 155 156 157

Part 10
Grabbing hands - side punch with the fist

Form the hands for the grab and sharply straighten them forward (Fig. 158, 159). Squeeze the hands into fists (Fig.160).

Turn 90 degrees to the left (Fig. 161). Sharply turn to the right. Move the right fist to the chest. At the same time make a side punch at the chest level with the left fist (Fig. 162). Unclench the left hand and take it back, the elbow lowers down (Fig. 163). With the fingers of the left hand make a direct poking punch forward at the face level, palm is directed upwards (Fig. 164).

Rotate the left hand clockwise, squeeze it into a fist and move to the chest (Fig.165, 166).

158 159 160 161 162 163

164 *165* *166*

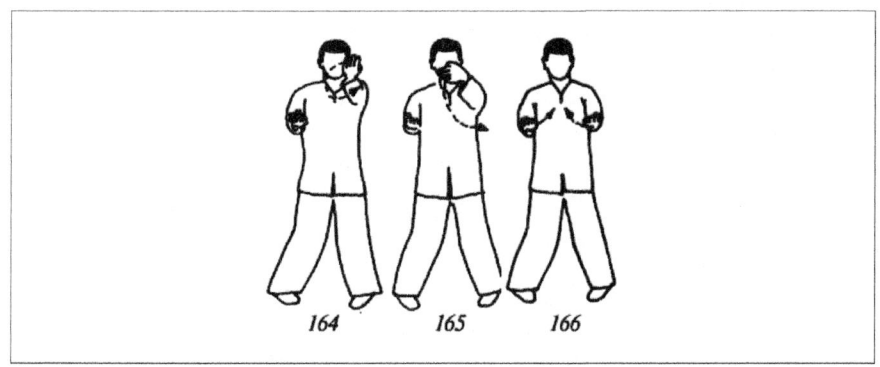

Repeat all the movements of this part of the form with the other hand (Fig.167-175).

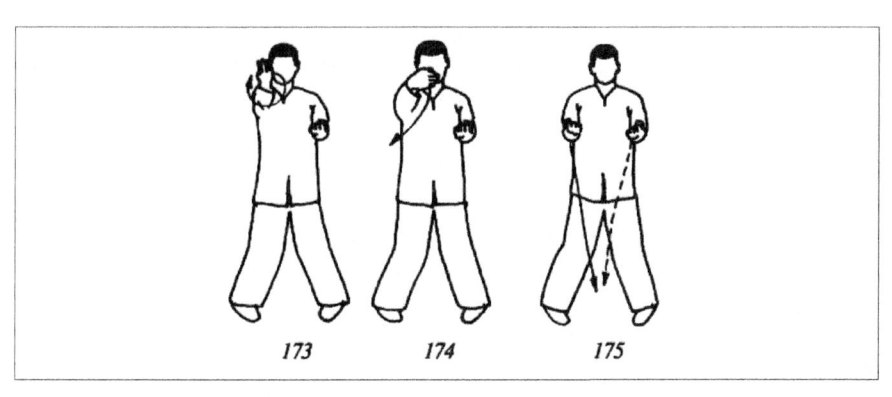

167 *168* *169* *170* *171* *172*

173 *174* *175*

Part 11
Triple bow

Bend and straighten both hands down (Fig. 176). Stand straight, moving the hands up and to the sides (Fig.177). The hands take the basic fighting Wing Chun position (Fig.178). Repeat this movement twice more (Fig.179-184).

First with the right and then with the left fists make direct punches forward at the face level (Fig.185, 186).

Rotate the left hand clockwise, squeeze it into a fist and move to the chest (Fig.187, 188).

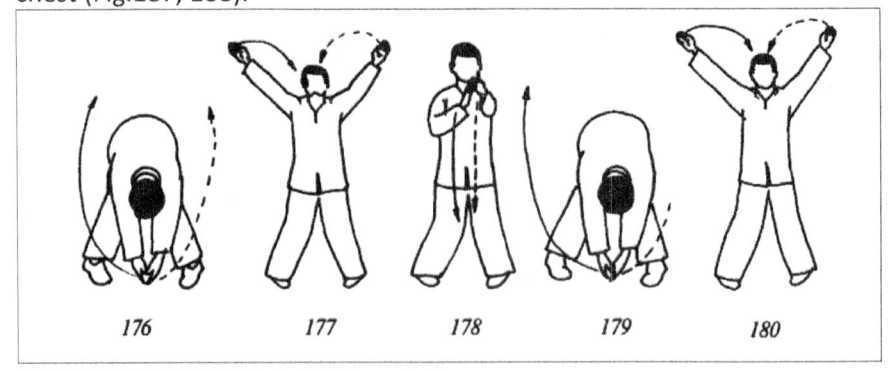

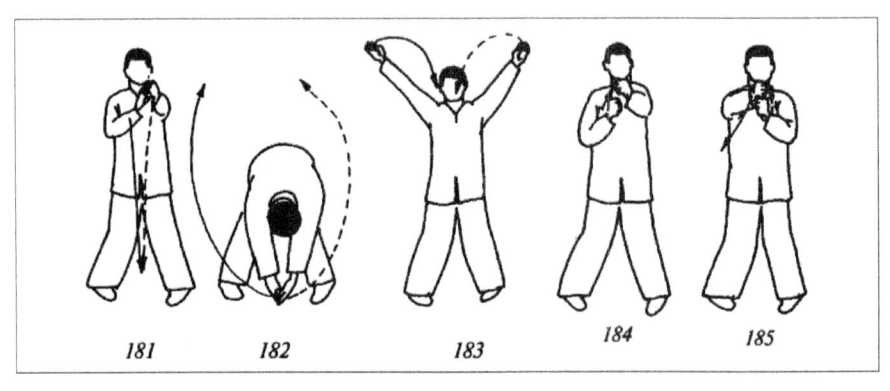

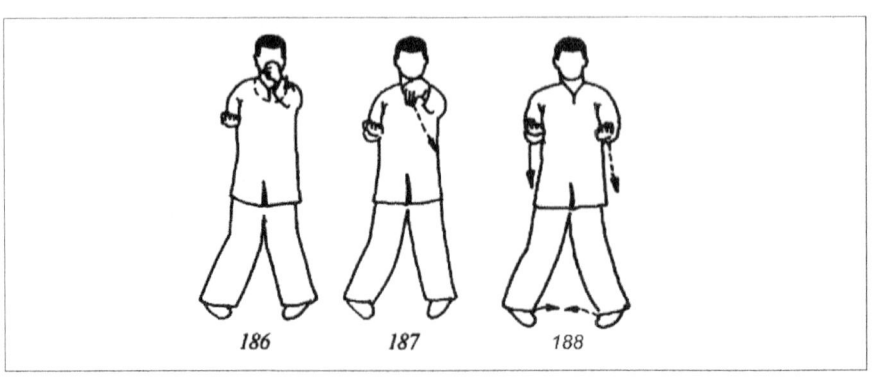

176 177 178 179 180

181 182 183 184 185

186 187 188

Part 12
Final form
Move the heels together, then the toes. Straighten your knees and lower the arms down at the sides (Fig.189).

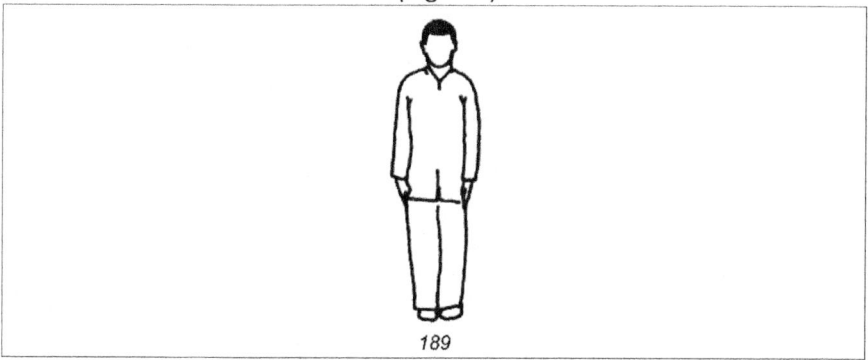

189

Martial combinations

The main weapons in the combinations of this level are fingers, hands and open palms. The ability to strike with the fingers in combat is considered the highest manifestation of skill in the Wing Chun Kuen art. To reach it, you must firmly seize all the other techniques of the school, as well as the ways of sticking to the limbs of the opponent and methods of their blockings. The movements are extremely dangerous and therefore they require a special attention and caution during the training. A summary of the decoding of movements of this form, originally proposed by the master Leung Ting is given below.

Tan Sau - Biu Jee

You and your opponent are in front of each other in the frontal stances. The opponent with his left hand touches your same name hand and takes it out - down. At the same time with his right fist he makes a short direct punch to the head. Make the Tan Sau block with the right hand and neutralize the attack of the opponent. Grab the right hand with the right hand and take it down, trying to cross it with his left hand. With the fingers of the left hand make a direct poking punch to the throat. Continuing the attack, lower the left hand down to control the hands of the opponent. At the same time with the fingers of the right hand or the edge of the palm make a punch to his neck at the left (Fig.190-196).

190 *191* *192* *193*

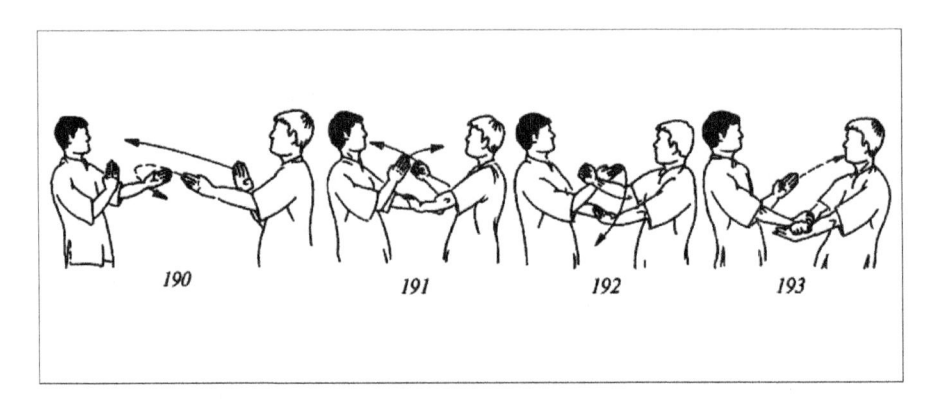

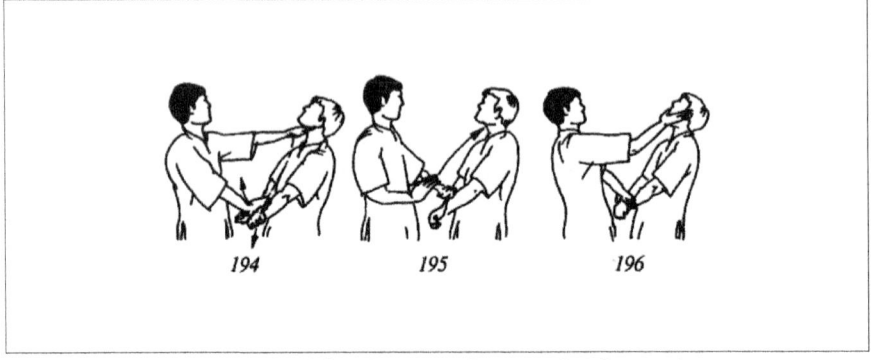

194 *195* *196*

Double block – strike with the edge of the hand

You took the frontal fighting stance, the opponent is in front of you in the left-hand stance. With the right foot he makes a circle kick to the upper part of the body. Turn the torso to the left and make the double Jum / Gan Sau block. After that, with the left foot take a step forward. Pick up with the left hand the opponent's attacking leg from below. And with the edge of the right hand, make a horizontal chopping punch to his neck. At the same time with the strike, expand your upper part of the body to the right (Fig.197-200).

197   198   199   200

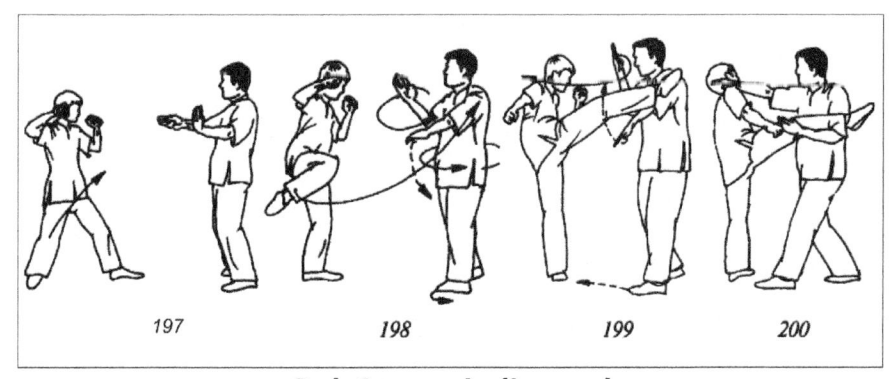

Pak Sau – circling palm

You and your opponent are in front of each other in the frontal stances. The opponent takes a step with the left foot forward. At the same time, he grabs with his right hand your right hand and pulls it down. Then he makes a short direct punch to the head with his left fist. With the left hand make the Pak Sau inside - out, neutralizing the attack. The hand of the grabbed right hand moves in an arc to the left - up – to the right until the edge of his right hand is directed upwards. Then make a pushing movement with the down. This will cause painful feeling in his wrist joint and force him to release the grab. Taking advantage of this, move the right hand into his "inner gates" and make a punch with the base of the palm to the solar plexus. At the same time with the left palm control his right shoulder. Finish the attack with a circle punch with the right elbow to the head (Fig.201-206).

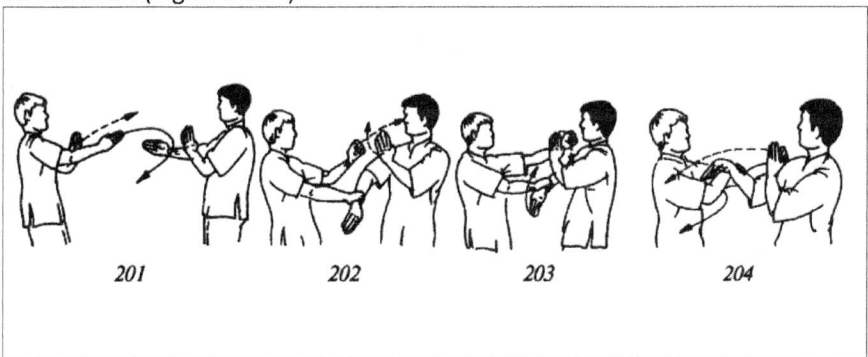

201   202   203   204

205 *206*

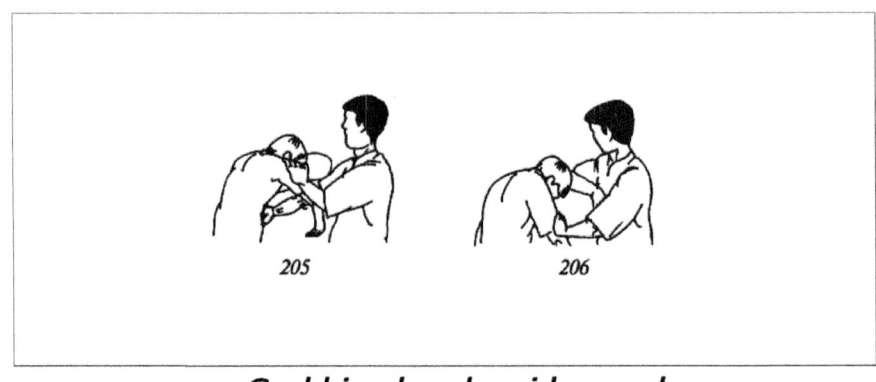

Grabbing hands - side punch
with the fist

You and your opponent are in front of each other in the frontal stances. He approaches you and makes a direct punch to the head with the right fist. Move forward your right hand toward the attack. Turn the torso to the right, simultaneously grab with both hands the attacking hand and pull back past you. The opponent will lose the balance. To return to a stable position, he will be forced to go back. Taking advantage of this fact, turn to the left and make a side punch with the right fist to the head. You can strike with your fingers to the eyes or throat. With the left hand continue to control his right arm (Fig.207-210).

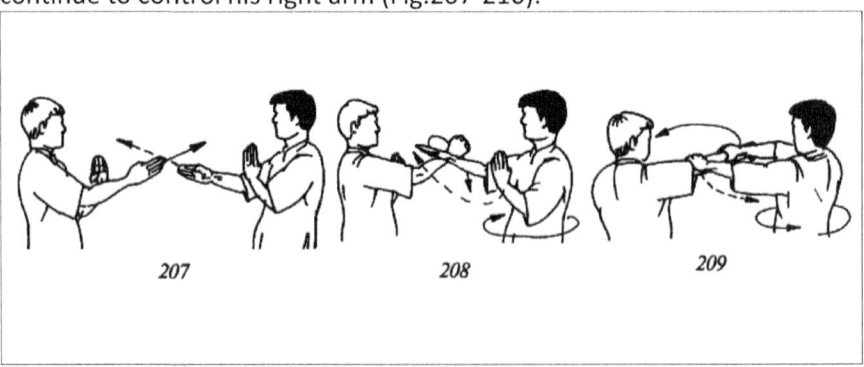

207 *208* *209*

210

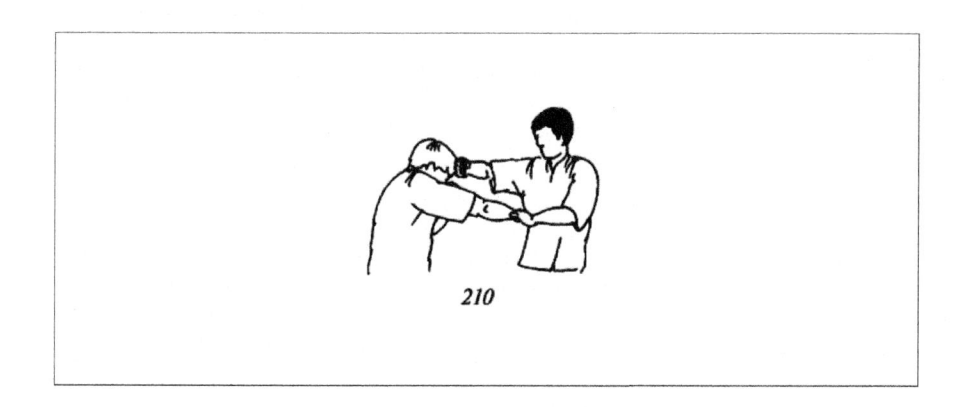

Chapter 13
Training at the wooden dummy

The last and the highest stage of study and practice of the Wing Chun Kuen technique is the training at the wooden Mook Yan Jong dummy. Exercises at the wooden dummy can solve a number of problems:
- *Train and strengthen the limbs;*
- *Contribute to the development of the ability to keep the attack at right angles;*
- *Allow to work out the traumatic techniques that cannot be trained in pair without causing harm to the partner.*

There are different complexes that are trained at the wooden dummy in various schools of China. So in Foshan schools the Mook Yan Jong Fa form consists of 140 movements in the Nguyen Te Cong direction - one hundred and eight movements, Yip Man taught the form of one hundred and sixteen techniques.

This part presents a complex of exercises at the wooden dummy, developed by the master Yip Man.

Mook Yan Jong is a cylindrical wooden pole 150 -180 cm. length, and a diameter of 25 - 30 cm. There are two "upper" hands, "lower" hand and "leg". These elements make up the "body" of the dummy, which are attached to the frame of two beams passing through holes in the top and bottom parts of the column.

The beams are fixed to two perpendicular rectangular poles, called persistent. The poles are rigidly fixed to the wall, floor or are dug into the ground (Fig. 1).

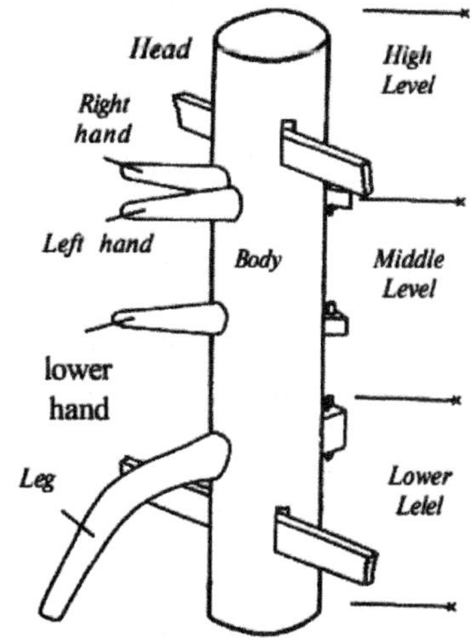
Head
Right hand
Left hand
Body
lower hand
Leg
High Level
Middle Level
Lower Lelel

1

While training at the wooden dummy, try to get smooth and continuous movements, which follow each other.

Mook Yan Jong Fa complex consists of eight parts:

Part 1 - *ten movements;*
Part 2 - *ten movements;*
Part 3 - *ten movements;*
Part 4 - *nine movements;*
Part 5 - *twenty-one movements;*
Part 6 - *fifteen movements;*
Part 7 - *fifteen movements;*
Part 8 - *twenty six movements.*

Part 1

Take the starting position: the left-handed frontal Yee Gee Kim Yuen Ma stance (Fig. 2). With the left hand grab the right hand of the dummy, turn to the left and with the right hand grab the head of the dummy (Fig. 3). With the right hand make the Bong Sau against the right hand of the dummy (Fig. 4). Step out in an arc to the foot of the dummy with the right foot. With the right hand make the Tan Sau block against the right hand of the dummy. At the same time make a punch to his right side with the left palm (Fig. 5). Bring the right foot back to the starting position. Make the double Jum / Gan Sau block (Fig. 6). Turn the torso to the right. Make a small adjacent step to the right. With the left hand make the lower Bong Sau. With the right hand - Tan Sau against the left hand of the dummy (Fig. 7). Step out in an arc to the foot of the dummy with the left foot. With the left hand make the Tan Sau block. At the same time with the right palm make a punch to the left side (Fig. 8). Bring the left foot back to the starting position. With both hands make the double Jum / Gan Sau block (Fig. 9). Make a chopping Jum Sau block to the right hand of the dummy with the inner edge of the left forearm. At the same time the right hand "covers" the right hand of the dummy (Fig. 10). With the left hand "cover" the right hand of the dummy. At the same time with the right hand circle his right hand anticlockwise and make a direct punch with the palm (Fig. 11).

Make this part of the form to the other side (Fig. 12-21).

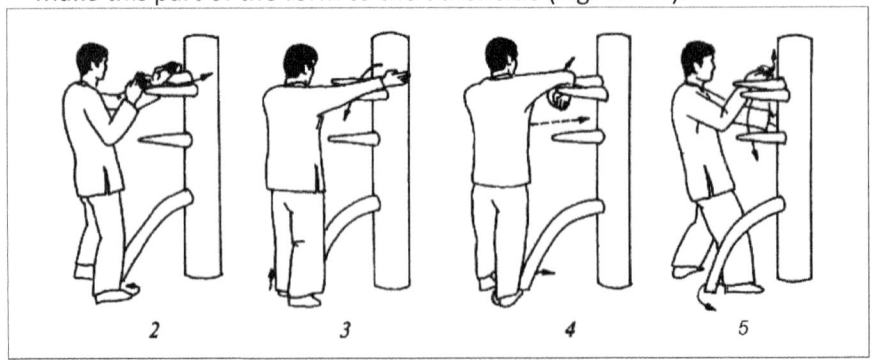

2 3 4 5

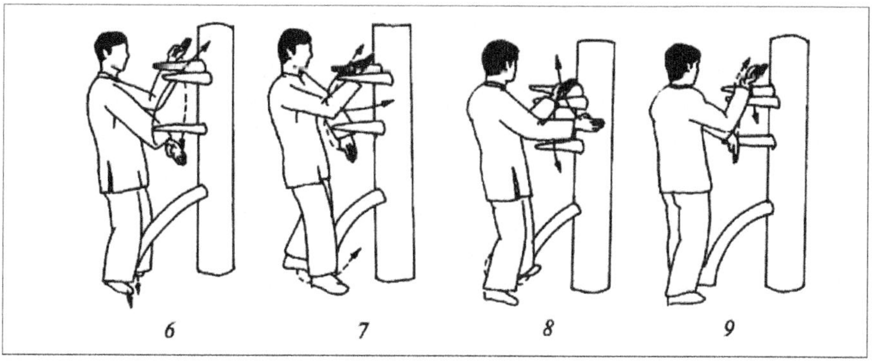
6
7
8
9

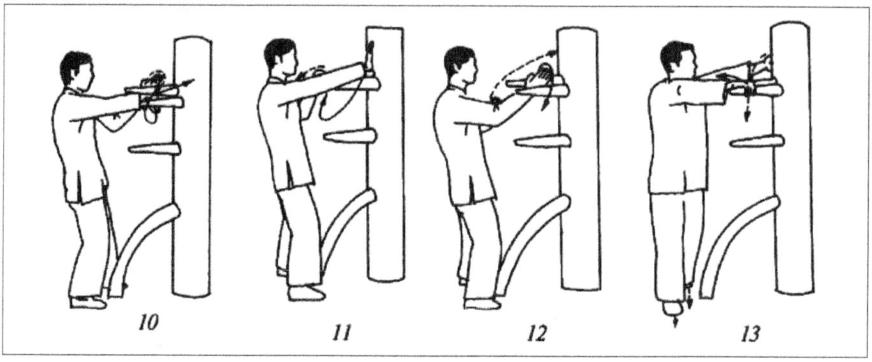
10
11
12
13

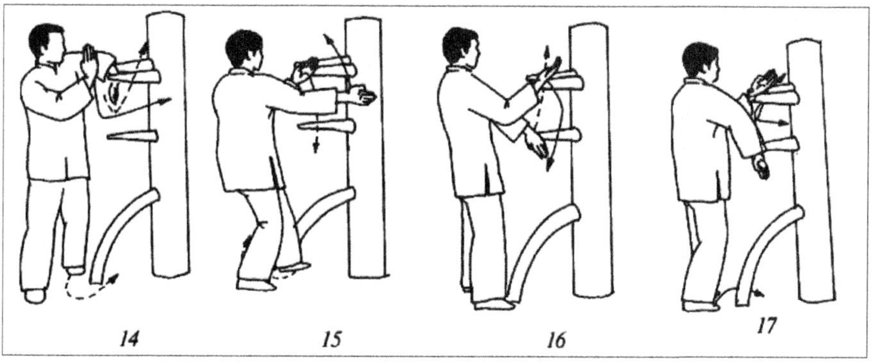
14
15
16
17

18	19	20	21	22

Part 2

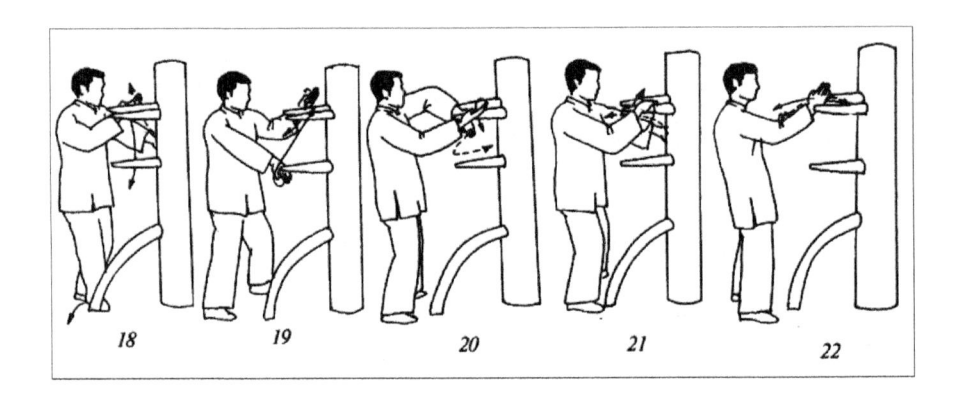

From the starting position, with the right palm make the Pak Sau from the inside out to the right hand of the dummy (Fig. 22). Make the Pak Sau with the left palm from inside out to the left hand of the dummy (Fig. 23). Make the Pak Sau with the right palm from inside out to the right hand of the dummy (Fig. 24).

Turn to the right. Make the Pak Sau from outside to inside to the right hand of the dummy with the left hand (Fig. 25). Make a chopping punch from you with the edge of the left palm (Fig. 26). Press on the right hand of the dummy with the left palm. At the same time, make a direct punch with the right fist to the bottom part of the dummy (Fig. 27).

Make the latest series of movements with the right hand (Fig. 28-30). At the same time make a push up to the hands of the dummy with both hands (Fig. 31).

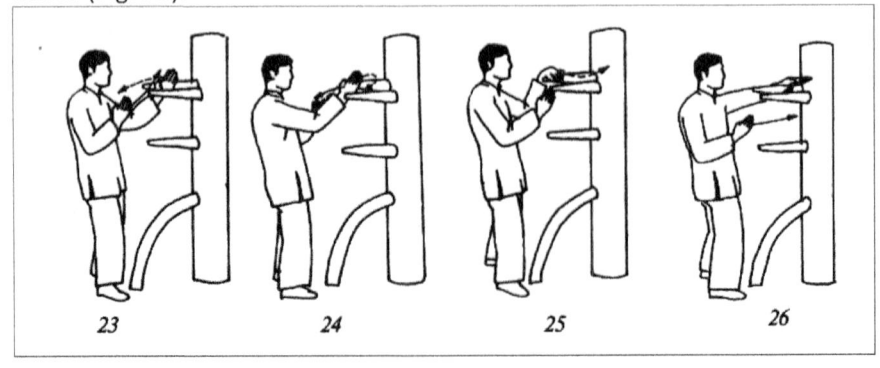

23	24	25	26

27 28 29 30 31

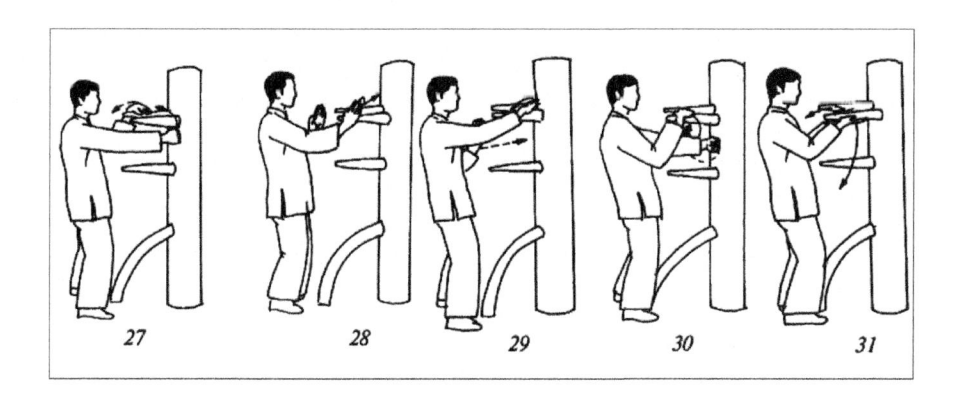

Part 3

Turn to the left. With the right hand make the lower Bong Sau (Fig. 32). With the right foot take a step forward in an arc to the right side of the foot of the dummy. At the same time with the left palm make the Pak Sau outside - in to the right hand of the dummy and a punch with the edge of the right palm under its right arm (Fig. 33). Stand back a little back left foot. Right foot put on the body side impact dummy. The right hand block simulates Bong Sau (Fig.34).

Lower the right foot down and make this series of movements in the opposite direction (Fig.35-37).

Lower the left leg down. Turn the body to the left and make the Jum / Gan Sau double-block with the arms (Fig. 38).

With the inner edge of the left forearm, make a chopping Jum Sau block to the right hand of the dummy. At the same time the right hand "covers" the right hand of the dummy (Fig. 39). With the left hand "cover" the right hand of the dummy. At the same time with the right hand circle his right hand anticlockwise and make a direct punch with the palm (Fig.40).

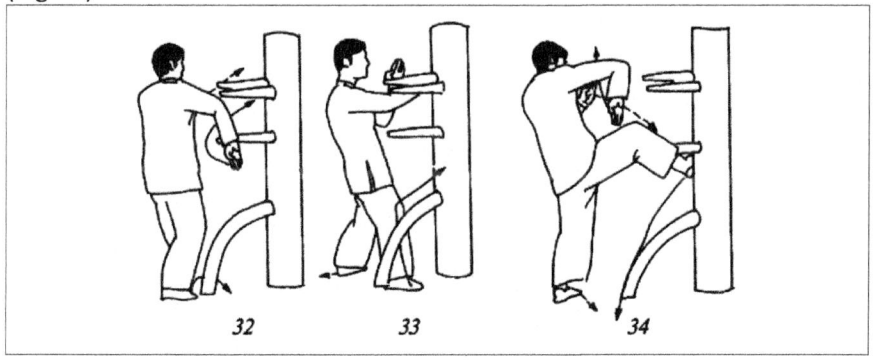

32 33 34

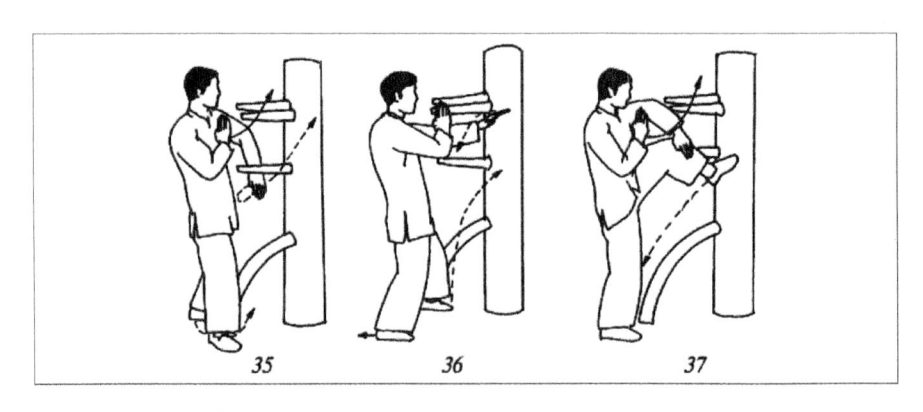

35   36   37

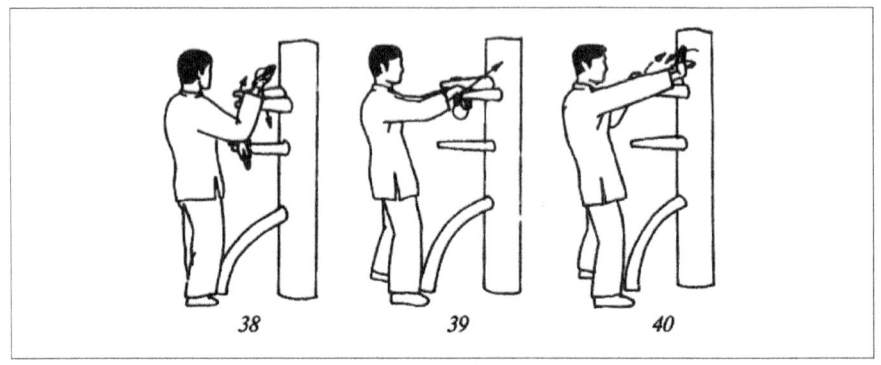

38   39   40

Part 4

With both hands make the double Jum Sau outside-in (Fig. 41). With both hands circle the hands of the dummy and make a double punch with the palms to the lower part of the body (Fig. 42, 43). With both hands, make the double Tan Sau block inside - out (Fig. 44). Straighten the arms and make punches with palms between the hands of the dummy to its upper part (Fig. 45).

With both hands make the double Jum Sau block outside - in (Fig. 46). Turn to the right. The left hand remains in the Jum Sau position. With the right hand make the Huen Sau movement and circle the left arm of the dummy (Fig. 47). Turn to the left and make a similar movement changing the roles of the hands (Fig. 48). Turn to the right and make a similar movement again (Fig. 49). Return to the starting position. With the left hand "cover" the right hand of the dummy. At the same time with the right hand circle its left hand and make a direct punch with the palm to the upper part (Fig. 50).

41 42 43 44

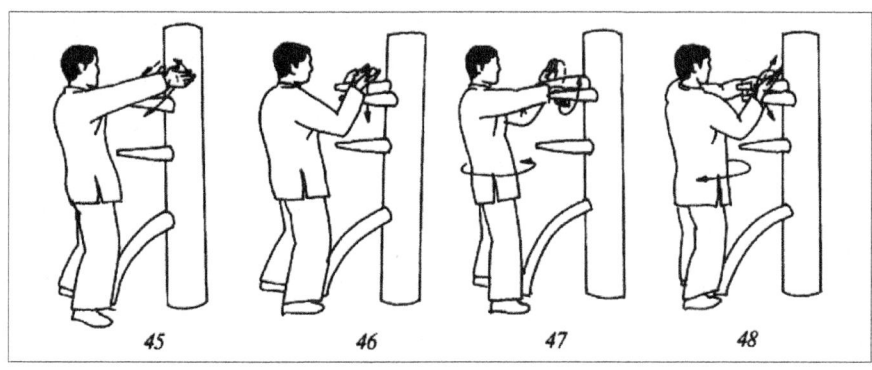

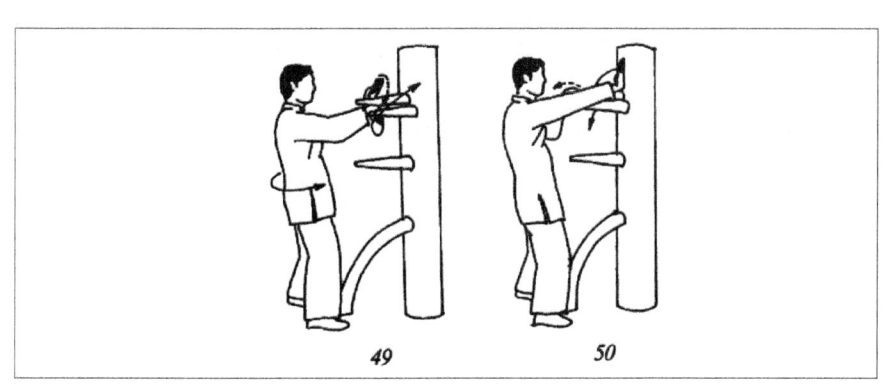

45 46 47 48

49 50

Part 5

Turn to the left. With the left foot make a small adjacent step to the left. With the right hand make the Bong Sau block from inside to the right hand of the dummy (Fig. 51). Turn to the right. Move the right hand to the Tan Sau position. With the left palm make a punch to the lower right part of the body of the dummy. At the same time with the right foot make a kick to the "knee" of the dummy (Fig. 52). Lower the foot on the ground. With both hands make the double Jum / Gan Sau block (Fig. 53). Turn to the left. With the right hand make the Jum Sau to the left hand of the dummy. With the left hand make the Huen Sau to the right hand of the dummy (Fig. 53). Turn to the right. With the left hand make the Jum Sau to the left hand of the dummy (Fig. 54). With the right hand make the Huen Sau to its left hand (Fig. 55). Turn to the left. With the right hand make the Jum Sau to the left hand of the dummy. With the left hand make the Huen Sau to its right hand (Fig. 56). Return to the starting position. With the right hand make the covering movement to the left hand of the dummy. With the left palm make a punch to the lower right part of the torso (Fig. 57).

Make this part of the form to the other side (Fig. 58-62).

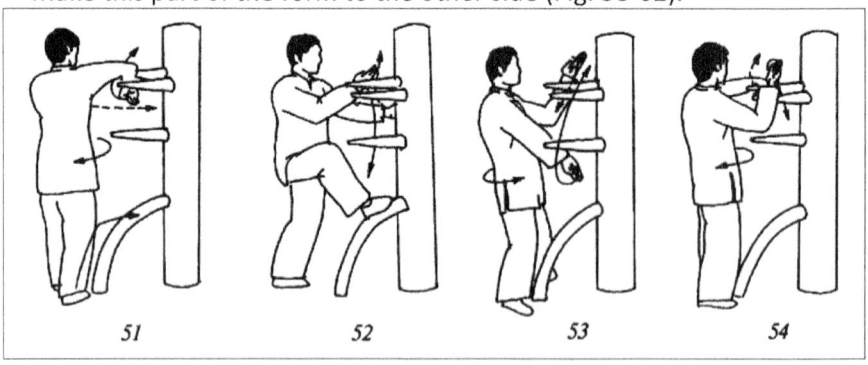

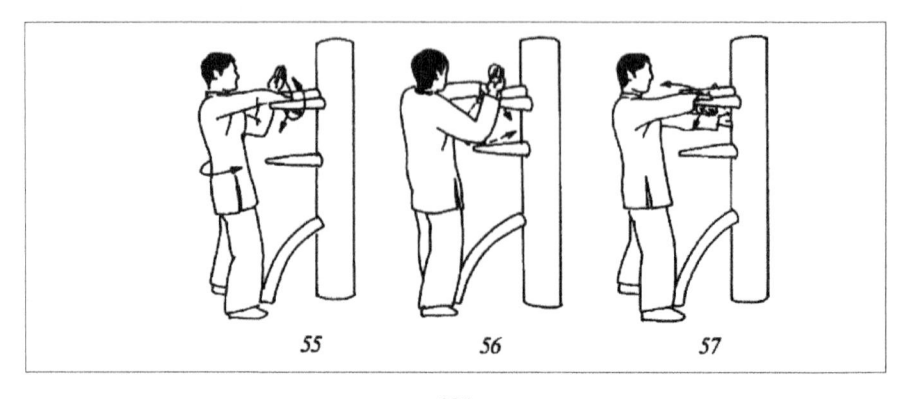

51 *52* *53* *54*

55 *56* *57*

| 58 | 59 | 60 | 61 | 62 |

Part 6

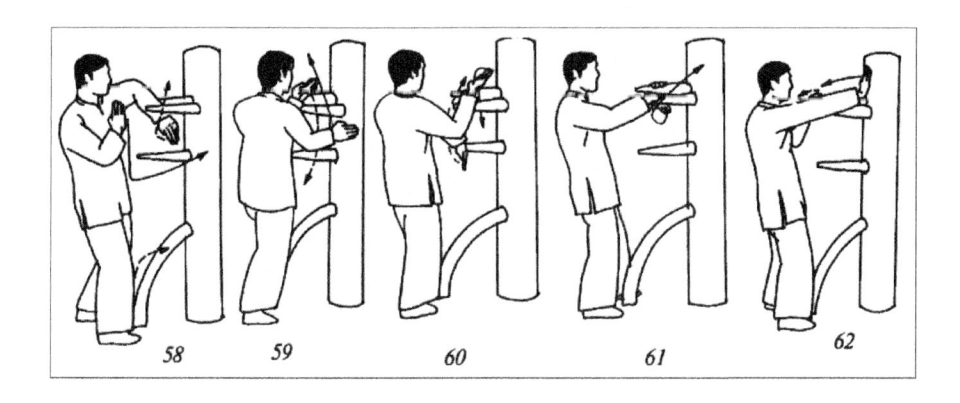

With the right hand make the Pak Sau inside - out to the right hand of the dummy (Fig. 63). Moving the right hand to the right, with the back side of the wrist press from inside - out on the left hand of the dummy (Fig. 64). With the right palm make the Pak Sau again from inside - out to the right hand of the dummy (Fig. 65). Push down on the right hand of the dummy with the right palm. With the left palm make a punch to the bottom right part of the dummy (Fig. 66). Turn the torso to the right. With the right hand make the Tan Sau inside-out to the left hand of the dummy. With the left hand make the lower Bong Sau (Fig. 67). Return to the starting position. With both palms make a direct push-punch forward. At the moment the right palm takes vertical position, fingers up, and the left - fingers down (Fig. 68). Turn to the right and make the Bong Sau with the left hand from inside to the left hand of the dummy (Fig. 69). Step out in an arc to the left leg of the dummy with the left foot. At the same time with both palms make a push-punch to the middle part of its body (Fig. 70). Return the left leg to the starting position. With both hands make the double Jum / Gan Sau block (fig. 71). With both palms make a push – punch to the body of the dummy (Fig. 72). Turn to the left and make the right Bong Sau from inside to the right hand of the dummy (Fig. 73). Step out in an arc to the right side of the leg of the dummy with the right foot. Make a push – punch to the middle part of the body of the dummy with both palms (Fig. 74).

Return the right foot to the starting position. With both hands make the double Jum / Gan Sau block (Fig. 75). Turn the torso to the left. With the right hand make the Jum Sau block. With the left hand make the Huen Sau (Fig. 76). With the right palm "cover" the left hand of the dummy. With the left hand circle his right hand and make a punch with the palm to the lower left side of its body (Fig. 77).

63 64 65 66

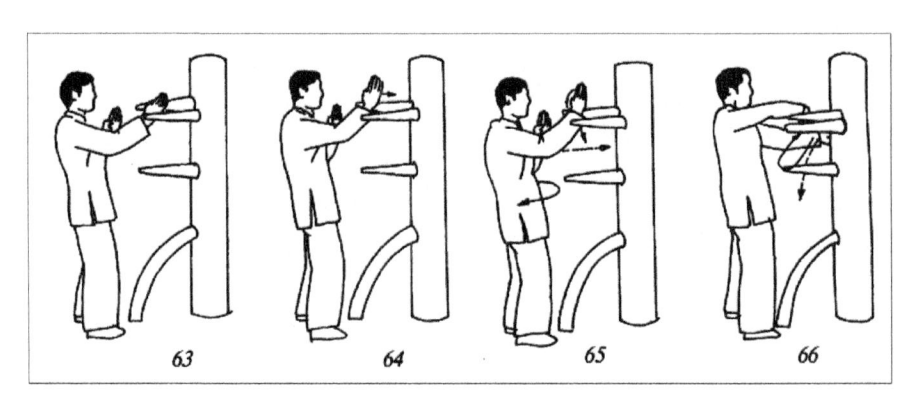

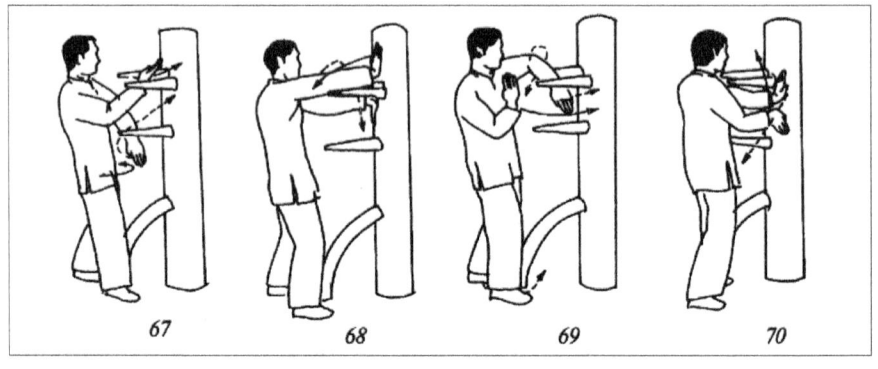

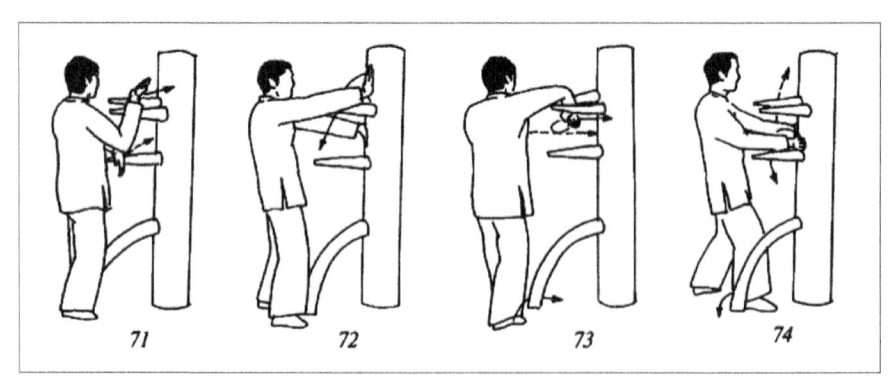

67 68 69 70

71 72 73 74

75 76 77

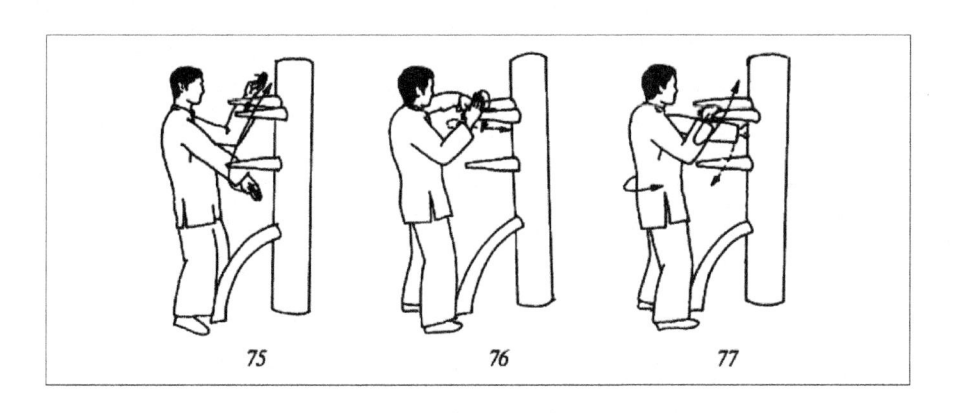

Part 7

Turn to the left. With both hands make the double Jum / Gan Sau block (Fig. 78). Turn to the right and make a similar movement in the other direction (Fig. 79). Turn to the left and take a small adjacent step with the left foot to the left. With the right hand make the Bong Sau from inside to the left hand of the dummy (Fig. 80). Turn to the right. Without breaking contact with the right hand of the dummy, move the right hand from the position Bong Sau to the position "Grabbing hand". Grab the right hand of the dummy at the outside. Simultaneously, with the edge the left palm make a chopping punch from you to the upper part of the body of the dummy (Fig. 81). Turn to the left. Push on the right hand of the dummy from outside – down with the left palm. At the same time with the right palm make a punch to the upper part of its body (Fig. 82).

Repeat this series of movements in the opposite direction (Fig. 83-85).

Turn to the left. With the right hand make the Bong Sau from inside to the right hand of the dummy (Fig. 86). Turn approximately 90 degrees to the right. With the right foot take a small step forward and take the stance of crossed legs. Then with the left foot make a kick to the right lower part of the body of the dummy. At the same time the right hand is moved in the Tan Sau position and the left palm makes a direct punch to its torso (Fig. 87).

Make this series of movements in the opposite direction (Fig. 88, 89).

Bring both legs to the starting position. Turn to the left and with both hands make the double Jum / Gan Sau block (Fig. 90). Turn to the left. With the left hand make the Jum Sau movement outside-inside to the right hand of the dummy. With the right hand "cover" his left hand and circle its hand in the Huen Sau circle (Fig. 91). With the left hand "cover" the right hand of the dummy. With the right hand, circling around the left hand of the dummy, make a direct punch with the palm to the upper part of its body (Fig.92).

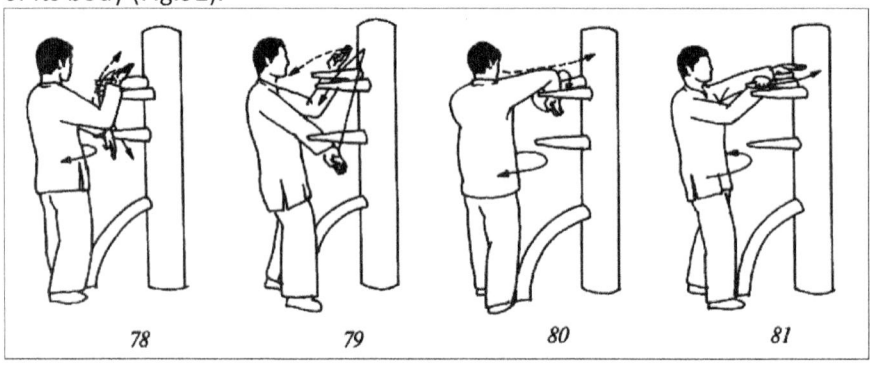

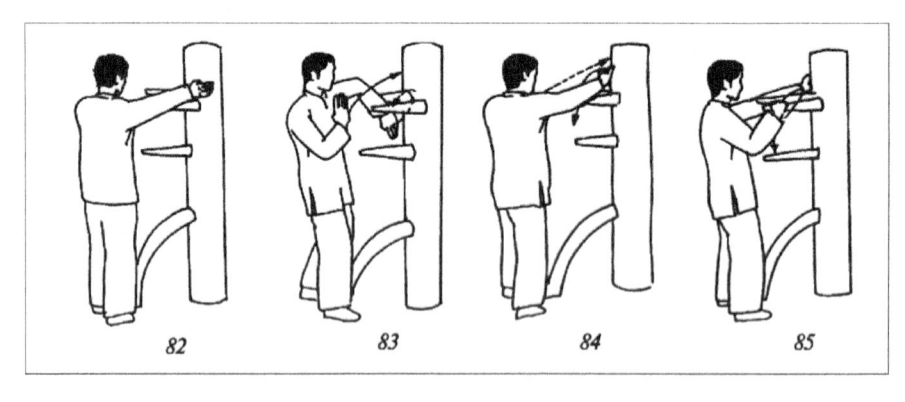

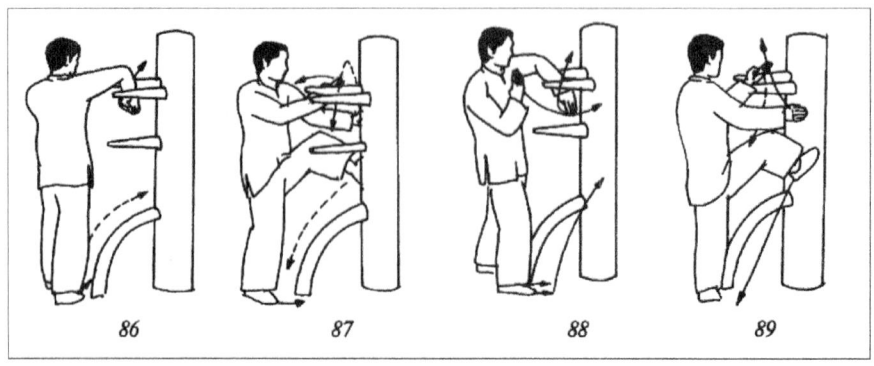

90   91

Part 8

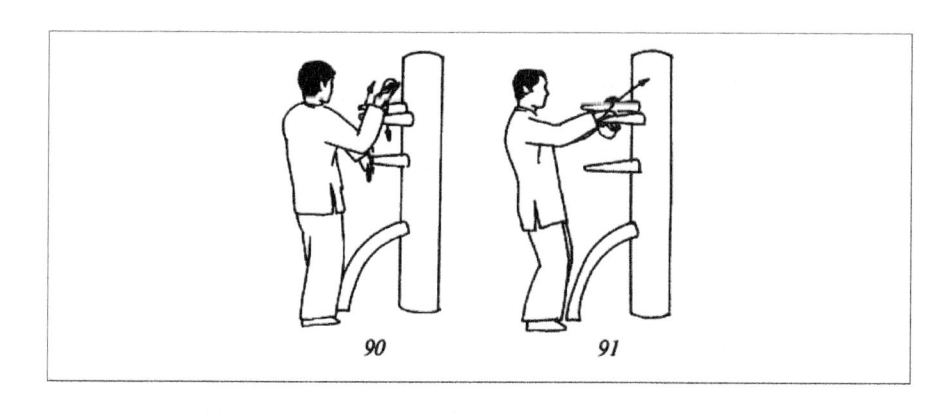

Turn to the left. With the right hand make the lower Bong Sau (Fig. 93). Turn to the right and make the lower Bong Sau with the left hand (Fig. 94). Turn to the left and make the lower Bong Sau with the right hand (Fig. 95). With the right hand make the Tan Sau from inside - out to the left hand of the dummy. At the same time with the left foot make a direct kick to the lower part of its body (Fig. 96). Immediately thereafter, lower the left leg down sharply and make the downward kick with the foot to its "knee". The right hand takes the Wu Sau position, the left - Bong Sau (Fig. 97).

Make this series of movements in the opposite direction (Fig. 98-102).

Lower the right foot on the ground and make a small adjacent step with your left foot to the left. At the same time with the right hand make the Gum Sau block (Fig. 103). With the right foot take a step forward in an arc to the right side of the leg of the dummy. With the left hand make the Pak Sau from outside-in to the right handoff the dummy. At the same time with the right palm make a punch to the lower part of the torso of the dummy (Fig. 104).

Repeat this series of movements in the opposite direction (Fig. 105, 106).

Turn to the left. With the right palm make the Gum Sau block (Fig. 107). Turn to the right. With the left hand make the Pak Sau block outside - in to the right hand of the dummy. At the same time with the right foot make a trampling kick to its knee (Fig. 108). Lower the right foot down and repeat this series of movements in the opposite direction (Fig. 109, 110).

Lower the left leg down. With the right foot make the bong Sau block from inside to the right hand of the dummy (Fig. 111). Turn to the right. Move the right hand of the position Bong Sau to the position of "Grabbing palm" and grab his right arm with both hands. At the same time with the right foot make a trampling attack to the "raise" of its foot (Fig. 112). Lower the foot on the ground and make this series of movements in the opposite direction (Fig. 113, 114).

Lower the left foot on the ground. Turn to the left and with both hands make the double Jum / Gan Sau block (Fig. 115). Turn to the left. Make the Jum Sau movement with the left hand from outside-in to the right hand of the dummy. With the right hand "cover" its left hand and circle its hand in the Huen Sau circle (Fig. 116). With the left hand "cover" the right hand of the dummy. With the right hand, circling around the left hand of the dummy, make a direct punch with the palm to its upper part of the body (Fig. 117).

Final movement

At the same time make a push from the bottom with both hands to the hands of the dummy - Tok Sau (Fig. 118).

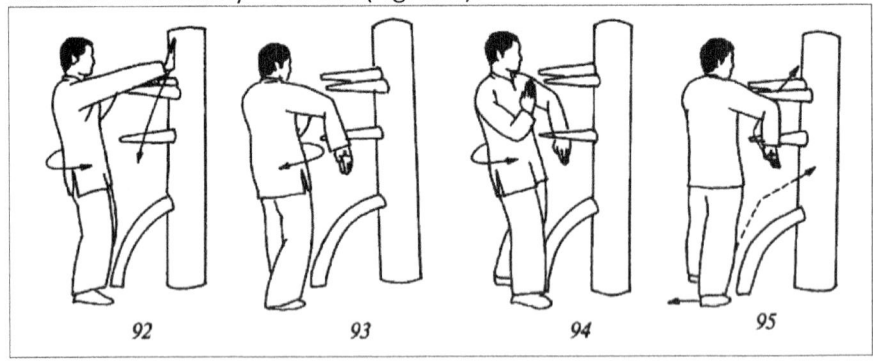

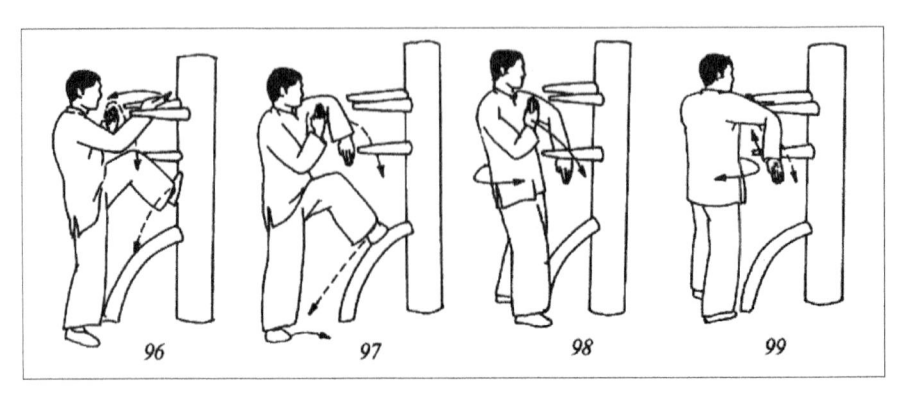

100   101   102   103

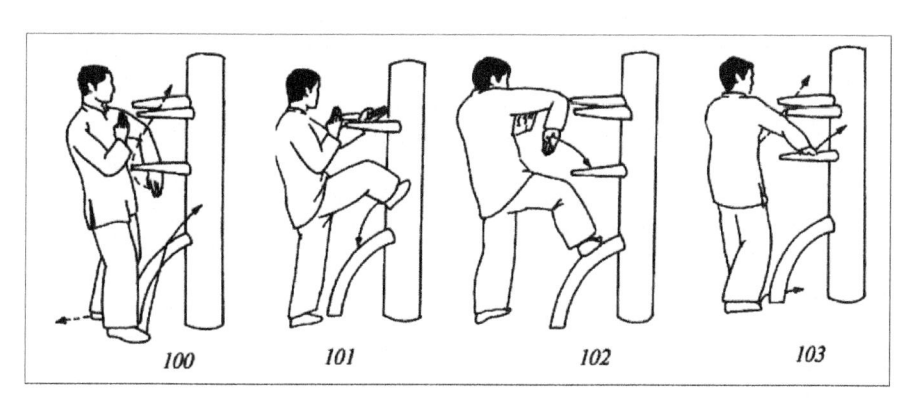

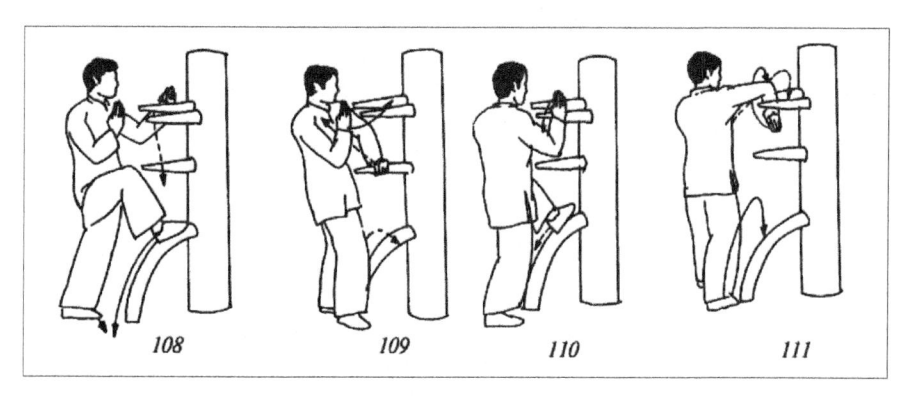

104   105   106   107

108   109   110   111

112 *113* *114* *115*

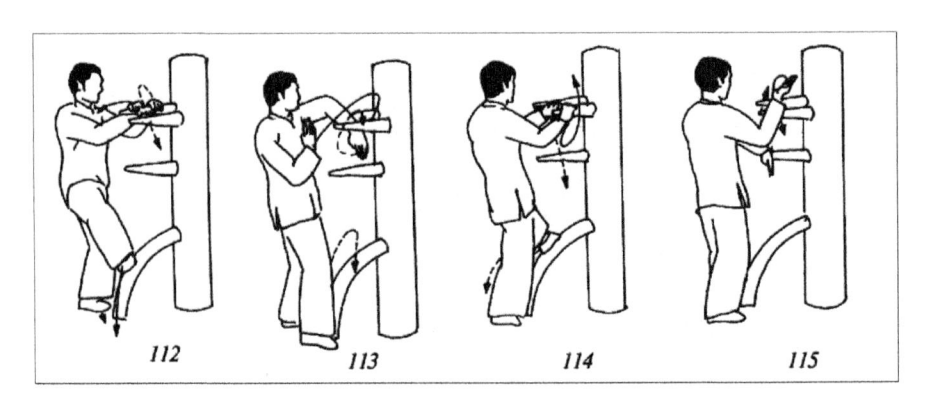

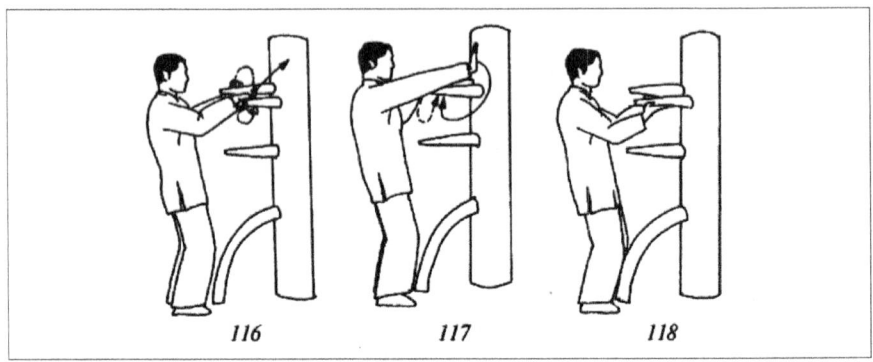

116 *117* *118*

Lower the hands. **The form is finished**.

Conclusion

Wing Chun Kuen, despite its apparent simplicity, is a vast, complex and varied style of Wushu. The whole learning process is structurally streamlined and is strictly regulated.

At the first stage the basic techniques is studied: stances, movements, strikes, blocks and throws. Then they proceed to the study of the complex of formal Siu Lim Tao exercises. Parallel they learn the basic forms of Chi Sau and Lop Sau.

At the second stage they study the Chum Kiu form, the advanced techniques of Chi Sau, Lop Sau and Fon Sau, as well as the tactics of fight against multiple attackers.

At the third stage they study the location of vital points on the human body, methods of their destruction and resuscitation. This stage corresponds to the 'Attacking fingers" technique - Biu Jee and the exercises at the wooden dummy.

At the fourth stage they learn to work with weapons and a variety of methods of the "Secret Transmission".

In this paper, the author tried to give an enhanced picture and to reveal the subtleties and nuances of the traditional Wing Chun Kuen in the transmission of Grand Master Yip Man.

In the subsequent papers there will be an attempt to acquaint the readers with the branch of the Vietnamese Wing Chun Kuen of the master Nguyen Te Cong, characterized by grace and fluidity of movements and specific "animal" forms. There is also preparing the paper – work, devoted to the description of the most interesting version of this kind of the martial arts, leading tradition from famous Chan Wah-Shun and his son Chan Yiu Min. Its special feature is the harmonious combination of techniques of traditional Wing Chun Kuen with a strong and powerful Southern Shaolin Wushu technique.

Printed in Great Britain
by Amazon